E 214 - 1 - 33901

LEARNING THEORY

LEARNING THEORY

Robert C. Bolles

University of Washington

Holt, Rinehart and Winston

New York Chicago San Francisco Atlanta
Dallas Montreal Toronto London Sydney

Library of Congress Cataloging in Publication Data

Bolles, Robert C.
Learning theory.
Bibliography: p. 220
Includes indexes.
1. Learning, Psychology of. I. Title.
LB 1051.B468   153.1'5   74-22266

ISBN: 0-03-010756-3

PREFACE

This book is intended to meet the need for a concise textbook on learning. It is intended to be short enough to be used for a one-quarter course in learning and to permit the instructor to embellish where he will without having to spend all his time covering the text. This brevity has been achieved mainly by means of exclusion. The reader will find nothing here on human learning, on the developmental aspects of learning, or on the physiology of learning. All these areas have much to contribute to our total understanding of how behavior depends upon experience, but they can scarcely be more than mentioned in the first course in learning. So the present text is limited to the treatment of animal learning. The book emphasizes the theoretical issues in learning rather than the data of learning experiments. Again, the instructor is free to cite his own favorite studies to illustrate the phenomena of learning.

The book is in two parts. The first seven chapters describe the thinking of the classical theorists, starting with Thorndike and Pavlov and ending with Skinner. In this part of the book I present the classical heritage upon which all modern developments are necessarily based. In the second part, the last three chapters, I describe some contemporary developments. Some of these developments are based upon recently discovered phenomena, whereas others are derived from new or newly activated theoretical ideas. It should be noted that I am not theoretically neutral, and in the second part of the book I actively advocate two ideas that are becoming increasingly popular. One is that a given animal's ability to learn particular things must be viewed within a broad evolutionary context. The second is that learning consists not in the acquisition of an S-R association but in the assimilation and storage of information about the environment.

I would like to thank a number of authors and publishers for permission to reproduce their work, Andrea Stockton for her art work, and several colleagues whose comments on the manuscript were most helpful. I would particularly like to thank several classes of students, from whom I learned how to organize this material, and the National Science Foundation, whose support over a number of years has made it all possible.

Seattle, Washington
November 1974   R.C.B.

CONTENTS

PART II   The Contemporary Scene

LEARNING THEORY

PART
I

THE
CLASSICAL
HERITAGE

Although a great number of people have contributed in one way or another to our current understanding of learning, there are a mere half-dozen or so who have made the big contribution of organizing their ideas into unified patterns that can be called "theories." That these individuals have had the vision and courage to undertake such syntheses, often with very inadequate data, is reason enough to give them honored places in the anals of psychology and reason enough for the student of psychology to know who they were and what they were trying to do. Today's student should also understand the classical theorists because their conflicting stands on important theoretical issues illuminate and clarify these issues. The ultimate resolution of these key theoretical issues will be, we hope, facilitated by a better understanding of how earlier theorists approached them. But perhaps the most important reason for understanding the classical heritage of our learning theorists is that the different theorists started from different basic assumptions and had different views of behavior; by understanding how the classical theorists attempted to cope with the problems as they saw them we may be better able to solve the problems as we see them.

CHAPTER
1

THORNDIKE

Edward L. Thorndike (1874–1949) was one of the first American psychologists. He was certainly the first to do learning experiments with animals. His doctoral dissertation, published in 1898, included the famous puzzle-box experiment. Thorndike's entire professional career after 1899 was spent at Teacher's College, Columbia University. There he studied animal and human learning, the educational process, and the nature of the English language. Thorndike was enormously productive; in terms of the number of books and papers published, he was the most prolific psychologist ever. But, more than being a hard worker, Thorndike was a great innovator.

3

A great physicist once said, "In science you make progress by standing on the shoulders of your predecessors." The experimental psychologist David Zeaman once observed that the same principle applies in psychology, except that "in psychology you make progress by stepping in the faces of your predecessors." Zeaman may have overstated the point somewhat, but there is some truth in his observation. Theoretical advances in psychology have tended to be made at the expense of earlier theories of how things are. Each of the major learning theorists offered his ideas largely in defiance of earlier conceptions of learning, and his ideas and theories have then in turn been overturned and replaced by the work of later theorists. This ferment in the analysis of learning still continues today, so that we may expect that our current conceptions, procedures, and hypotheses will in time be replaced by sounder ideas, more sophisticated procedures, and better theories.

The learning theorist is basically a skeptic. He looks about and observes that his culture, his tradition, and the prevailing theoretical ideas all tell him one thing. But he asks: "What if it is not like that? Suppose this or that assumption is false and something else is true." He then proceeds to examine the implications of his new assumption. For example, one assumption that has been part of Western thought for the last 2500 years is that there is a profound difference between man and beast. Man is said to have free will, and his behavior is said to be governed by his intellect and his reason. By contrast, animals are supposed to be little machines, simple automatons. They have reflexes and some instincts but no reason and no free will. This fundamental gulf between man and animal is still accepted by a large part of our culture. But a little more than a century ago Charles Darwin asked: What if it is not like that? What if there is continuity between man and the animals? What if man just has a little more of something than the animals have—if the difference is not in kind but in quantity? Man, Darwin suggested, may simply have specialized during evolution in the development of his intellect, precisely as other animals have specialized in the development of wings or in the development of a respiratory system that works under water. Darwin's theory of evolution was, of course, not widely accepted at first—indeed it was highly controversial, and many scientists could not accept the new idea but clung instead to the traditional notion of a gulf between man and beast. But with time the new idea has come to prevail, and Thorndike had a great deal to do with bringing about this acceptance.

Conceptions of Learning before Thorndike

When Thorndike came on the scene, there had already been a few men who had attempted to close the theoretical gap between man and animal. For example, Romanes (1882) had argued that animals are really quite intelligent, in some instances showing intelligence comparable to that of man. His data, however, were not systematically obtained; they consisted largely of anecdotal accounts of remarkable exploits by pets and other special animals. Such arguments were interesting but had little impact. The prevailing view was still that there is a great gulf between man and animal.

There was another very old tradition, the tradition of interpreting human learning in terms of associationism. Philosophers from the time of John Locke had argued that man learns through experience and that learning consists of the association of ideas. For example, if a man sees the color white, he is inclined to think of the color black. The reason is that black and white sensations have been associated in his experience many times before, so that his mind contains the association of the respective ideas. Thinking of white makes him think of black; seeing white makes him think of black. This kind of explanation was obviously applicable only to people. Only people, it was assumed, can have ideas, so it is only people who can profit from experience in this manner. By contrast, animals were assumed to be devoid of intelligence, incapable of associating ideas. They were assumed to be governed by reflexes, by instincts—to be, in effect, simply machines. This conception of a basic difference between man and animal was the prevailing conception at the turn of the century and is still characteristic of the layman's thinking today.

The fundamental dichotomy between man and animal embodies the distinction between intelligence and instinct, or between mind and matter, and it probably reflects a very basic predisposition of the human mind to accept as an explanation of the events that he observes either a mentalistic or a mechanistic interpretation. The behavior of man had always been interpreted in terms of events in his mind. Other kinds of physical systems were interpreted in terms of mechanical properties; the behavior of, for example, rocks, billiard balls, or cannon balls was always explained in terms of physical events. But this distinction between the mental and the mechanical is purely arbitrary and traditional. Primitive peoples characteristically believe that physical phenomena like the stars and the weather, as well as the living things around them, are animated by spirits; or they explain the behavior of natural events in terms of the moods of their gods. It is thus perfectly possible to have a philosophical system in which some kind of spiritualism or mentalism pervades all of nature. This kind of approach is not limited to primitive man. Aristotle built a magnificent philosophical system in which the behavior of all things, living and inanimate alike, was explained on the basis of spiritual principles. Even in the twentieth century Henri Bergson proposed that all living matter is characterized by a vital force, that is, by a sort of spiritual principle.

By contrast, it is also possible to explain, at least in principle, the most mentalistic of events, the mind of man itself, in terms of mechanical principles. Such an explanation was first attempted by the early atomistic philosopher Democritus. In more recent times, particularly since the end of the nineteenth century, it has become increasingly fashionable to extrapolate from the physical and biological sciences to explain the activities of the animals and even of man in mechanistic terms—in terms of the nervous system or the biochemistry of the body. Although this kind of approach has always had some appeal, by the end of the nineteenth century most psychologists were content with a dualistic philosophy; they assumed a world of the mind to explain man and his doings and a physical world to explain mechanical systems, as well as living things excluding man.

But, as psychology has developed in the twentieth century, one of its most important achievements has been the reconciliation of the inconsistencies in this dualism. What has happened is that psychology has gradually developed a third kind of explanatory system, one that is concerned primarily with the laws of behavior, without making any commitments to whether the underlying causes of behavior are mentalistic or mechanistic. Behavior has its own laws, and to a large extent these are the laws of learning. In recent times Skinner has made this point of view rather well known. But the traditional dualism has been difficult to dispel. One difficulty is that the earlier theorists were not entirely consistent; some of them were frankly mechanistic, whereas others could be accused of being mentalistic. Apparently it has been difficult even for psychologists to see that there can be other kinds of explanatory models, models that are neither mentalistic nor mechanistic but are purely psychological in character. Let us see how Thorndike first attempted to deal with this problem.

The Puzzle-Box Experiment

Thorndike's famous puzzle-box experiment was conducted as part of his doctoral dissertation research begun at Harvard University and completed at Columbia. A hungry cat was put in the box, and outside was a dish of food. In order to get out and eat the food, the cat had to work a mechanical contrivance attached to the door. In one instance, for example, a string was attached to a latch on the door, then run over some pulleys and down into the puzzle box. When first put in the box, the cat struggled and scratched, pawed and meowed as if trying to escape from the cage. Ultimately, in its scratching and pawing at things, the cat would accidentally (whatever that means) pull the string. The door would open, and the cat would walk out and eat the food. Thorndike promptly put the cat back in the box for the next trial. Again the cat gave a lot of frantic behavior, but it soon pulled the string again, escaped, and received another bite of food. Over a series of such trials, the cat became increasingly efficient in getting out of the box. The performance of several individual animals, shown in Figure 1.1, reveals that there was considerable trial by trial variability, but also that there was steady progress. We can visualize a smooth "learning curve" indicating that the expected performance of a cat on a given trial gradually improves with the number of prior trials.

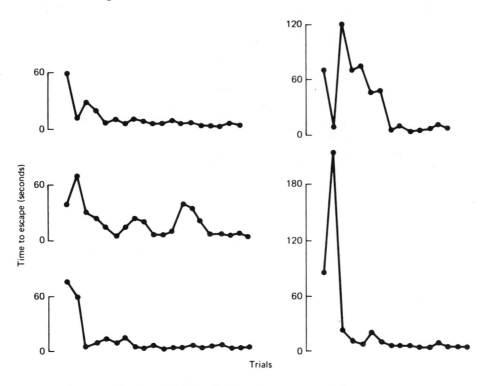

Fig. 1.1 *Trial by trial learning curves of five cats required to pull a loop of string to escape from a puzzle box. The cats were trained about 10 trials a day. (From Thorndike, 1898.)*

That is all there was to the basic experiment, but Thorndike ran a number of variations of the procedure, requiring different responses, and looking at other kinds of animals. We will have occasion to refer to some of his other research, but for the moment let us turn to Thorndike's theoretical account of the cat in the puzzle box. He asked what it is that is learned in this kind of situation. Granted that something is associated with something, precisely what psychological elements are associated to produce the improvement in behavior? He noted that there were a number of logical possibilities, according to the logic of that era. Learning in people was assumed to consist of the association of ideas. Was it possible, for example, that for the cat the idea of pulling the string became associated with the idea of the puzzle box and the food outside? Another possibility is that the idea of pulling the string became associated directly with the stimulus situation itself, so that when in the box the cat conceived the idea of pulling the string. Thorndike dismissed both these possibilities on the following grounds. He argued that, were the cat suddenly to "get the idea," the learning curve would show more or less random behavior up to the point at which the animal grasped the idea and that there would then be a sharp improvement in behavior and merely random fluctuation after that point (see Figure 1.2). We would say of human behavior that the person gets insight into the solution of the problem. He would suddenly understand the principle of the door and the latch and how to get out. But Thorndike emphasized that none of his cats showed this insight type of learning curve. In every instance the data suggested a relatively slow, gradual, and continuous improvement in performance over successive trials. Thorndike therefore reached the very important conclusion that the learning of his cats probably consisted of the automatic formation of an association between the stimulus situation and the correct response. The animal learns not a connection between ideas but rather some kind of direct connection between the stimulus and the response.

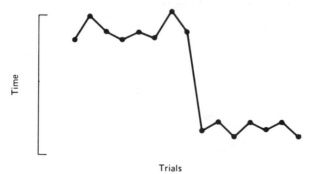

Fig. 1.2   *Trial by trial performance that might be expected from a cat in a puzzle box if the learning consisted entirely of "insight" into the correct manner of solution.*

This was a new idea. Learning in people had always been assumed to be an intellectual kind of process, involving ideas, appreciation of experience, awareness of logical relations, and so on. These mental activities were believed to be synonymous with intelligence. The other side of the dualistic picture was the reflexive or instinctive behavior patterns of animals, which were assumed to be fixed. But Thorndike was proposing to throw out this dichotomy and abolish this difference between man and animal. Here his cats were behaving intelligently, in the sense that they were learning to get out of the box; that is, they were modifying their behavior as a result of experience, but the modification was accomplished by a mechanical kind of process. It was automatic; it did not require insight or ideas. Animals had been credited for some time with fixed or reflexive S-R connections, but Thorndike was proposing that there could be *learned* S-R connections. To put it another way, Thorndike argued that his cats were displaying intelligent, even creative, behavior in learning to get out of the box, but that this learning occurred without thinking and with minimal awareness on the cats' part.

By the end of the nineteenth century, a number of writers had come to recognize a special form of S-R learning, which was said to occur in the context of well-practiced motor skills. A response that is initially voluntary becomes, with sufficient practice, automatic or habitual. The layman still uses the word "habit" in this sense. It was generally supposed that if a voluntary or conscious act were repeated often enough it would become attached directly to a stimulus, so that it would no longer require awareness. It could be said to occur habitually or instinctively.[1] In effect, Thorndike was borrowing the concept of habit and changing its meaning. Habit was to mean an unthinking response to a stimulus. Not only is a response that ultimately becomes free of consciousness a habit; so also is a learned response that has never been in consciousness.

Thorndike's Theory of Learning

Thorndike observed that two special features of his experimental procedure were necessary to guarantee learning. First, it was necessary for the cat to be hungry. If the cat had been well fed when it was put in the puzzle box, it might not have gotten out of the box in the first place and surely would not have shown any learning to get out. More likely, it would have curled up and gone to sleep. In short, Thorndike was telling us that the explanation of learning must also include some motivational principles, such as that the cat has to be hungry. Second, Thorndike told us that food is also necessary. When Thorndike developed his theory of learning in his 1911 book *Animal Intelligence*, he put the matter quite plainly: Learning occurs if and only if the response has some "effect" upon the environment. If the effect of the response is pleasant, then learning occurs. If the effect of the response is unpleasant, then the behavior is weakened rather than

---

[1] The word "instinct" was frequently used (for example, by such an authority as Wilhelm Wundt) to refer, not to innate behavior, but to behavior that occurs without awareness. Walt Disney helped to keep this usage alive. He gave us such constructions as "Jojo knew instinctively that the boy was on the other side of the hill." What this means is only that Jojo went to the boy, who was on the other side of the hill, and that he did so without having to think about it.

strengthened. For example, if the cat is punished when it gets out of the box, it will quit getting out. But if the hungry cat is fed, then learning occurs, as Thorndike reported. This principle is Thorndike's famous *law of effect*. In his own words:

> Of several responses made to the same situation, those which are accompanied or closely followed by satisfaction to the animal will, other things being equal, be more firmly connected with the situation, so that, when it recurs, they will be more likely to recur; those which are accompanied or closely followed by discomfort to the animal will, other things being equal, have their connections with that situation weakened, so that, when it recurs, they will be less likely to occur. The greater the satisfaction or discomfort, the greater the strengthening or weakening of the bond. (Thorndike, 1911, p. 244)

The law of effect maintains that learning consists of the strengthening of a connection between a stimulus situation and a response and that this connection will be strengthened (or, as we would say, reinforced) if the response has the effect of producing satisfaction to the animal, or weakened if the response has the effect of producing discomfort or an annoying state of affairs.[2]

A lot of earlier writers had believed in and had advocated the principle of hedonism—not the epicurean idea that pleasure is good but the psychological principle that people choose to do what is pleasant. Indeed this hedonistic principle had been an important part of British associationist philosophy, starting with Thomas Hobbes and Locke and running through to Herbert Spencer. Thorndike's law of effect provides an explanation of why people appear to be hedonistic: It is not that a man chooses pleasure, as the mentalistic tradition had maintained, but that men make those responses that in the past have produced pleasure because previous pleasures have strengthened, that is, reinforced, those particular responses. Prior learning produces just that behavior that is likely to maximize pleasure. Thus, although the principle of hedonism offered a serviceable description of behavior, Thorndike's law of effect appeared to be more basic. Actually Thorndike rarely used the words "pleasure" and "pain." He chose instead to substitute the behaviorally defined words "satisfiers" and "annoyers." A satisfier was defined as a state of affairs "which the animal does nothing to

---

[2] The idea that satisfaction or dissatisfaction, or pleasure and pain, could produce stronger or weaker connections in the nervous system was anticipated by Herbert Spencer (1880). Although Thorndike was probably familiar with Spencer's writings, it would not be fair to say that Thorndike stole the idea of reinforcement from him. Thorndike's law of effect was highly original in two important respects: It was an assertion about behavior rather than a speculation about events in the nervous system, and it was generated by and in turn generated a great deal of experimental research, whereas Spencer was not interested in data.

avoid, often doing such things as attain and preserve it," and an annoyer was defined as a state of affairs that the animal commonly avoids and abandons (Thorndike, 1911, p. 245). Thus we can see that for Thorndike the ultimate explanation of behavior lay in the orderliness of behavior itself, not in what he took to be mentalistic concepts like pleasure and pain.

Although Thorndike was relatively careful to strip the mentalistic concepts, or at least mentalistic explanations, from his behaviorism, he was not as careful to keep out neurological concepts. Indeed, he seems to have been unable to resist the temptation to reduce the law of effect and his other behavioral principles to physiological events. He spoke about neurons firing and being connected, he spoke about traces of stimuli, and he incorporated most of the hypothetical neurological machinery that was fashionable in his time. Perhaps at that time such speculations lent an air of legitimacy or a scientific aura to a theorist's work. Today, largely under the influence of Skinner and other modern behaviorists, we are much more sophisticated about separating our behavioral laws from both mentalistic and neurological speculation. But it is no discredit to Thorndike that he was not able to be a pure behaviorist, much as he might have liked to be. The incredible thing was that he was able to be a behaviorist at all, to make any kind of systematic contribution to this third realm, when the conventional realms of mentalism and mechanism were so firmly established and were, in fact, the only explanatory realms available at the time.

Implications of the Theory

In the attempt to minimize still further the mentalistic thinking that prevailed at the beginning of the twentieth century, Thorndike undertook a number of experiments to show that even with human subjects learning is an automatic process that builds a direct connection between a stimulus and a response with minimal awareness. A human subject can provide two kinds of data: improved performance over trials and a statement about what he is aware of. Thorndike's purpose was to demonstrate the former in the absence of the latter.

In one typical experiment, subjects were instructed to learn a number concept. A series of numbers was presented, each one on a card; some numbers were said to be positive instances of a number concept and some not. At first the subjects performed at a chance level, but over a number of trials the concept appeared to be learned; the group as a whole came to perform at about 90 percent accuracy; that is, they could characterize 90 percent of the stimulus numbers according to whether they were or were not illustrations of the concept. Thus the problem had clearly been solved. At this point Thorndike asked his subjects to verbalize what the number concept was. What was the concept that everyone appeared to have learned? The subjects reported a marvelous variety of hypotheses: If the last number was odd and was wrong then the next one is right; if the sum of the digits is even, then it is right; if any digit is repeated then the number is right; and so on. There was, in fact, no numerical concept; all numbers came from a collection of random numbers. However there was a small smudge in one corner of some cards, a fingerprint type of smudge. If the smudge was there then that number was correct, and if there was no smudge it was not. Apparently Thorndike's subjects were responding on the basis of the smudge because the group as a whole had learned the concept. All subjects in this particular experiment denied having seen the smudge or having responded on the basis of it. Most of them claimed that they had figured out the numerical concept, but clearly all their number-playing games were rationalizations, or after-the-fact fabrications. Thorndike concluded that human subjects can learn to respond consistently on the basis of a particular stimulus yet be quite unaware of what stimulus they are responding to. It follows, he said, that reinforcement has an automatic effect. It must stamp in the appropriate S-R connections as if it were a mechanical device, one in which the intellect and awareness of the subjects need not play any part. Thorndike reported a vast number of similar experiments.

More recently, there has been renewed interest in the question of learning without awareness. A famous experiment conducted in the Skinnerian tradition was reported by Greenspoon (1955); it was originally done in the context of a classroom demonstration. A subject was brought to the front of the room and interviewed. During the first several minutes, members of the class were instructed to record the operant rate of a certain kind of verbal behavior, specifically, using plural nouns. After the base line was determined, the experimenter started reinforcing plural nouns. Behavior was controlled in Greenspoon's experiment simply by giving social approval, nodding, smiling, saying "mhmm, that's right," and so on. After just a few minutes on this reinforcement schedule, the subject showed a sharp increase in the use of the reinforced verbal forms. Once this high rate of responding had been established, it was extinguished by removing reinforcement. At the conclusion of the experiment, the subject was asked if he had been aware of being manipulated—did he know that his behavior was being changed? Greenspoon claimed that his subjects reported having been quite unaware.

Both Thorndike's original experiments and the more recent verbal-conditioning experiments of Greenspoon and others have been subject to considerable criticism. It has been said that, of course, people know what they are doing; they are aware of the contingencies in the situation, but they are reluctant to admit that they know. In Thorndike's experiment, for example, subjects may have noticed the smudge, but to rely on it or to admit relying on it would have seemed tantamount to cheating; they therefore invented the impossible numerical hypotheses to cover up. Similar criticisms have been directed at Greenspoon's study. It appears that when properly interviewed subjects can report more awareness of what has been happening than was apparent when Greenspoon interviewed his subjects. Recent reviews of this literature (e.g., Saltz, 1971) indicate that the question is still unresolved.

Thorndike discovered another phenomenon, which he believed showed the automatic nature of learning. He called it the "spread of effect." In a typical Thorndikean experiment, he would read slowly a long list of perhaps 100 or 200 words. The words might be household items like table, chair, door, window, and so on. The subject was instructed that for each item there was a number from one to ten, which he was supposed to guess. Typically Thorndike would give no feedback for most of the items, but for an occasional item he would say "yes, that's right" (positive reinforcement). At some point in the experiment the word "table" might be read, the subject might say "six," and Thorndike would give no feedback. The next item might be "chair," the subject might say "four," and Thorndike would say "right," and so on through the list. Then, typically, after going through the list once, Thorndike would give a retention test, which consisted of going through the list a second time to see to what extent the subject would give the same or different responses to the items. Thus, the experiment consisted of determining the probability that subjects would repeat the responses made to particular items. It is obviously an impossibly difficult learning task. The list is given only once; it is long, confusing, and boring; and the subject receives feedback for only a few of his responses. But, in spite of these handicaps, some evidence of learning is found. The repetition rate for responses that had been reinforced (by Thorndike saying "right") might be 20 percent. Thorndike concluded (erroneously, as we shall see shortly) that, if there were no learning, the repetition rate would have been 10 percent, for there were ten possible number responses. So a repetition rate of 20 percent looks like learning; there appears to be evidence for the law of effect. There is not very much learning because of the difficulty of the task, but there is some, and it is usually statistically reliable.

Thorndike discovered that there is an increased repetition rate not only for the correct response—that is, for the one that has been reinforced—but also for the immediately neighboring responses. The kind of results obtained are illustrated in Figure 1.3. Thorndike argued that the response-strengthening powers of reinforcement, the satisfying effect of hearing "right," can be seen only on the specific S-R connection to which it is applied but also on other neighboring S-R connections, both those before and after the reinforced one. The basic phenomenon is still somewhat controversial. Some analysts, like Hilgard & Bower (1974), contend that the spread of effect, which they describe as the last stronghold for a Thorn-

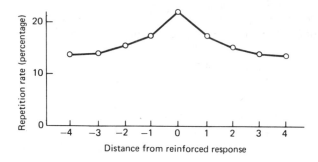

Fig. 1.3 *Conceptualization of the spread-of-effect phenomenon. The repetition rate is not only higher for the reinforced response but for the responses in a series immediately before and after the reinforced response. Thorndike predicted a symmetrical gradient but the results of experiments are often asymmetrical.*

dikean interpretation of human learning, does not really exist. But other theorists, like Postman (1962), take a more optimistic view. Postman claims that much of Thorndike's theory is still viable and that the spread-of-effect phenomenon has managed to survive a great amount of criticism at both the theoretical and methodological levels.

There were certain methodological problems in much of Thorndike's original experiments. One of the things that marred his research was that he rarely used appropriate control groups. It turns out that if human subjects are asked simply to guess numbers and given no feedback at all the repetition rate is not 10 percent, as Thorndike supposed, but more like 15 percent. It seems that people do not guess numbers randomly; they tend to avoid repetition, to use series of numbers in fixed patterns, and so on, which makes the prediction of numbers generated by people appreciably easier than the prediction of numbers generated by a truly random sequence. The proper base line for assessing the spread of effect is thus closer to 15 percent than to 10 percent, so the effect is not as pronounced or as dramatic as Thorndike believed. It is not clear if the effect exists at all once the appropriate controls are used to assess it (see Figure 1.3).

In the last analysis, it is probably immaterial whether or not there really is a spread-of-effect phenomenon. We seem to have come to the point in the analysis of human learning where many other kinds of mechanisms seem more interesting, more important, and much more fertile experimentally. So Thorndike's real contribution to the analysis of human learning is not that he was right (or wrong) about learning occurring without awareness but simply that he seriously raised the possibility. Learning in human subjects did not *necessarily* require awareness, and Thorndike inspired other psychologists to think about this possibility and to engage in research to prove him either right or wrong.

Punishment

All of Thorndike's early statements of the law of effect included both a positive law of reinforcement and a negative law of punishment. This symmetry reflected the age-old custom of using both reward and punishment to control behavior and the perhaps equally ancient belief in the pleasure-pain principle. Therefore the readers of Thorndike's 1932 book must have been startled to discover that although he retained the law of reinforcement, he repudiated the law of punishment. The law of effect was no longer symmetrical; it was said to work only one way, in the positive direction. Thorndike said that his experiments had forced him to abandon the law of punishment. These experiments were essentially like those used to demonstrate the spread of effect. The chief difference was that, whereas some of the subjects' responses were given the feedback "right" (reinforcement), others were given "no" or "that's wrong" (punishment). Thorndike found that, whereas positive reinforcement had the expected effect of increasing the repetition rate to approximately 20 percent, "no" had the paradoxical effect of also increasing the repetition rate to approximately 15 or 16 percent. There was clearly no weakening of the "punished" response. Even though it now seems doubtful that "no" produces much response strengthening, because we now know that the base-line repetition rate is higher than 10 percent, the data do support Thorndike's argument that there is no weakening of the response. In a carefully controlled study with a large number of subjects, Stone (1953) found that telling the subject "wrong" can in fact increase the repetition rate slightly. Thorndike proposed again on the basis of relatively little experimental evidence, that when punishment is effective in weakening behavior, which it surely is in some situations, its effect is not direct and automatic, as with a positive effect, but is indirect, much more specialized, and apparently dependent upon what the punishment in question makes the subject do. We shall have more to say about this remarkable conjecture in Chapter 4.

Motivation

Thorndike's primary law of learning was the law of effect. He always attached the greatest importance to it and defended it most earnestly. But, at the same time, Thorndike had some secondary laws of learning. One, which he called the *law of exercise*, stated that sometimes merely making a particular response in a given situation will strengthen the connection between them. If an S-R sequence is repeated often enough, the connection may become strengthened. But he emphasized that such repetition is a particularly inefficient way to produce learning, and in his later writings he minimized it altogether. He produced a number of experimental results that seemed to show that exercise by itself rarely produces learning. When learning occurs through repetition, typically we can find some satisfying effect that is being produced, either intentionally or not. So ultimately the secondary law of exercise faded out of Thorndike's own thinking about learning.

But there was another secondary law to which he attached much more importance. It was really a motivational principle. It is not clear what we should call it because Thorndike himself gave it different names from time to time, but let us call it the *law of readiness*. The basic concept is that a particular state of affairs will prove to be satisfying only to the extent that the subject is ready for it. A simple example is that food is a satisfier (a reinforcer) only when the animal is hungry. A sex object is a satisfier only when certain hormonal and developmental requirements have been met. The same principle applies to the aversive case. A certain state of affairs may be an annoyer just because of the momentary state of the organism. On the other hand, it is clear that there are events, like electric shock, that are nearly always annoyers. The animal is nearly always ready to find shock annoying. In human applications the situation is more complex. We often do not know what a particular individual may be ready for at a given moment. Is it praise, power, recognition, or success that will satisfy him? Human motivation depends upon characteristics of the individual, as well as on his immediate circumstances. But, in any event, we must know the person's state of readiness before we can know whether we can reinforce him in a particular way.

There is yet another complication, which Thorndike illustrated with the example of a person who reaches for a piece of candy. In reaching for the candy, a wholly different kind of act is put into readiness: eating the candy. The individual reaches for the candy; picks it up, which is satisfying; puts it in his mouth, which is satisfying; and eats it, which is also satisfying. We thus have a sequence of actions in which the effect of each response in turn puts the organism into a state of readiness for the effect of the next response. This is presumably how chains of behavior are built up, so that ultimately the individual can reach for the candy, put it in his mouth, and eat it all more or less as one act. Thorndike recognized, quite properly, that there is an enormous latitude in the kinds of reaction sequences humans can learn. And, by the same token, there has to be great latitude in the kinds of readiness that people can have and in the states of affairs that can be satisfying.

The concept of readiness can also be applied to intellectual tasks. For example, if a subject is presented with a pair of numbers, as in Figure 1.4, and instructed that they represent an arithmetic problem, he may respond "13," "42," or even "minus 1." Now, if the response "13" is reinforced, the subject will rapidly acquire the short-term readiness, or "set," to add such numbers. Thus, we see that readiness itself can be learned in certain instances. Thorndike believed that a large part of human performance involves such learned readiness.

$$\begin{array}{r} 6 \\ 7 \\ \hline \end{array}$$

Fig. 1.4 *A stimulus pattern that leads to different responses depending upon the subject's readiness or "set" to respond in a particular way.*

There is an obvious contrast between Thorndike's learning principles and his motivational principles. The learning system was empirically sound, it remained relatively unchanged for twenty-five years, and it was extremely productive experimentally. On the other hand, the motivational system was generally untestable, it underwent continual alteration, and it was experimentally sterile. In some situations, like the readiness interpretation of the arithmetic problem, the applications are so vague and the determination of behavior so uncertain that this approach never has attracted much attention.

It is doubtful that Thorndike himself was ever satisfied with the law of readiness—because he kept modifying it. For example, in 1911 he spoke of the "susceptibility" of an S-R connection, of how likely it is to be strengthened by its effect. In 1913, in his book *Educational Psychology*, susceptibility was transmuted into the law of readiness. In the attempt not to imbue readiness with mentalistic properties, Thorndike went too far in the other direction and attempted to speculate about its neurology. He said that when a nerve is ready to conduct—when its threshold is low—there will be a state of readiness. If a neuron is actually called upon to conduct when in this state, its conduction will be satisfying. He noted that the readiness of some neurons is highly modifiable, whereas the readiness of others is not. Thus, the nerves that conduct noxious stimuli are never in a state of readiness. Viewed in these terms, motivation can be seen as the particular pattern of readiness that exists in the nervous system at a particular moment. By the time that he published his 1935 book Thorndike had attempted to expand the readiness concept (though at that point he called it the "okay reaction") in an attempt to deal more adequately with the apparent spontaneity and richness of human behavior.

Thorndike's Impact and Contribution

Although Thorndike's thinking had an enormous long-term impact, it was not very influential at first. Apparently most psychologists did not take him too seriously. We shall see in the next few chapters that his view of learning, particularly his hypothesis that learning depends upon the "effect" of the response, was almost banished from psychology. It was not until the 1930s that Thorndike, with the help of a number of other psychologists, was finally able to sell the idea that learning depends upon the occurrence of particular events, which today we call reinforcers. It may be difficult for today's psychology student to conceive of a time when learning was not attributed to reinforcement, but that is the way it was for thirty years or so after Thorndike first proposed the idea. During the 1930s, when Thorndike became extremely active in the study of human learning, he also became the dominant figure in learning theory. In our later chapters on Hull and Skinner we shall see how many of their ideas flowed directly from Thorndike.

Let us summarize Thorndike's basic contributions. Perhaps his foremost accomplishment was to break down the mentalistic-mechanistic, intelligence-instinct, or man-animal dualism that had such a hold upon psychological thought at the turn of the century. He accomplished this feat primarily by emphasizing that behavior is something different from the mechanisms of the nervous system. The basic unit used for describing behavior was no longer to be an idea or a nerve cell; rather, it was to be the S-R connection. It would be many years, however, before psychologists were ready to accept this type of approach to the study of behavior. Many of Thorndike's early critics, evidently confusing what he called effect (the consequence of the response) with affect (pleasure and pain), rejected the law of effect out of hand because of its subjectivity or aura of mentalism. (It is curious that no one dismissed his neurological speculations on the grounds of their being unrealistic.)

Thorndike also proposed that *all* learning involves the formation of new S-R connections. This proposal again was a radical departure from established thinking. In animals S-R connections were supposed to be fixed, reflexive. Learning in man was supposed to involve the association of ideas. Thorndike gave us a new alternative: Learning involves association, but it is S and R elements that are connected. This basic assumption was to play a tremendously important role in the subsequent development of learning theory. Indeed, it is really the S-R hypothesis that made possible all the developments that we are to consider in this book.

Thorndike also gave us the concept of reinforcement, the idea that learning occurs when a response produces a particular kind of event, like a satisfying state of affairs. Before Thorndike, learning in man had been presumed to consist simply of the gathering of experience.

Finally, of course, we are indebted to Thorndike for initiating laboratory studies of animal learning. Earlier workers had made systematic observations of animals and had noted the occurrence of learning, but Thorndike was the first to study the subject systematically using standardized apparatus and standardized procedures. It should also be emphasized that Thorndike introduced a variety of experimental techniques for studying human learning and verbal behavior. He was one of the great innovators.

References for Further Reading

Thorndike's own voluminous writings make generally poor reading and cannot be recommended. An important and fortunate exception is his dissertation (Thorndike, 1898). Written when he was twenty-three years old, it is spirited and even arrogant. It has been reprinted in the book *Animal Intelligence* (Thorndike, 1911), which contains a wealth of interesting observations in addition to the original puzzle-box studies and includes one of the first statements of the law of effect.

An invaluable source on biographical information about many of the older psychologists is the series *History of Psychology in Autobiography*, originally edited and published by Murchison. Thorndike's own contribution to the series is very short and very uninformative (Thorndike, 1936). Joncich (1968), however, has written a long and loving biography that tells us much about the man, his work, and his academic world.

Postman has written two critical but generally sympathetic reviews of Thorndike's work, focused mainly on the historical ramifications of the law of effect (Postman, 1947, 1962). One of the toughest questions raised by Thorndike, and one dearest to his heart, was whether learning can occur without awareness. This question, which is still with us, has been reviewed by Dulany (1968) and Saltz (1971); they are generally unsympathetic to Thorndike's position.

CHAPTER
2

PAVLOV

Ivan P. Pavlov (1849–1936) is Russia's most famous scientist. He first won enormous fame and distinction for his research on the physiology of the digestive system. This research was characterized not only by a variety of ingenious procedures but also by Pavlov's utter dedication to his work. Just before the turn of the century, at the same time Thorndike was putting cats in puzzle boxes, Pavlov encountered a methodological problem that was ultimately to prove more important and more interesting than his physiological research. He had discovered conditioning. From then on all his energies and all the resources of his laboratory in Leningrad were devoted to conditioning. Pavlov was above all else a dedicated scientist. One story told of him is that, because of his distinction, he was offered an increased food allowance during the hard times of the Revolution but that he refused it until extra food was made available for his dogs.

Let us begin Pavlov's story where he began it, with his research on the digestive system of the dog. He originally discovered that, when food is placed in the dog's stomach, the stomach walls secrete a variety of juices that facilitate digestion. A series of studies showed that the amount secreted and the duration of secretion are functions of the kind and amount of food put in the stomach. To simplify the measurement of what is going on inside the dog, Pavlov developed an ingenious surgical technique for externalizing a portion of the stomach. A slice of stomach tissue was cut loose and brought out and attached to a hole made in the side of the body. Pavlov's skill as a surgeon was demonstrated by the fact that he was able to accomplish this surgery without disrupting the blood supply or the nervous connections to the stomach. The final preparation, shown in Figure 2.1, was a dog that had, in effect, two stomachs. Most of the original stomach still served its primary function, but connected anatomically to it was a small externalized stomach, or "Pavlovian pouch," the interior of which could be observed while the animal was digesting its meal. It was found that the secretions of the artificial stomach corresponded quite precisely with the secretions and other activities of the original stomach. It was through this kind of preparation that Pavlov worked out the details of digestion, including the neural re-flexes involved. He discovered, for example, that more is secreted and that secretion is more persistent with meat than with other kinds of food. So, if one has an ulcer and worries about stomach acid, he should not eat meat. Pavlov's research on the digestive system won for him one of the first Nobel prizes (1904) in medicine.

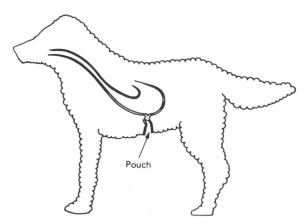

Pouch

Fig. 2.1   The Pavlovian pouch is a portion of nor-mally functioning stomach wall that has been ex-ternalized surgically.

The basic conclusion that Pavlov reached from this research was that there is an innate physiological reflex controlling the amount of gastric secretion in a very precise manner as a function of the amount and kind of food in the stomach. The same conclusion applies to salivary secretions. The kind and amount of saliva produced by the dog are very precisely graded to the kind and amount of substance put into the dog's mouth. For example, food in the mouth produces a thick, chemically active saliva, which starts the digestion process, whereas a drop of acid in the mouth produces copious watery saliva, which serves to dilute the acid.

But then Pavlov encountered a complication. He discovered that, if the esophagus was cut and externalized on the neck so that food that was chewed and swallowed would not pass into the stomach but would simply spill out of the animal's neck, the gastric secretion was still almost as great as in the normal animal when the food passed on to the stomach. He had to conclude that the stimulus for producing the reflexive secretion could consist not only of food in the stomach, the appropriate stimulus, but also of food in the mouth, an anticipatory or signaling stimulus. Then Pavlov found that all that is necessary to produce stomach secretion is to present the dish from which the animal ordinarily eats. Even sight of the attendant who ordinarily fed the animal would elicit secretion! The situation here was quite different from that involving the physiological reflex. Pavlov saw that there must be two kinds of reflexes. There are the physiological reflexes, which are invariable and are shown by all animals of a given species; they are an intrinsic part of the innate organization of the nervous system. But then there are the other reflexes, which Pavlov sometimes called "psychic reflexes," and at other times called "conditioned reflexes"; they occur only in a given individual animal as a result of its particular experience. All dogs produce gastric secretions when food is placed in their stomachs, but only a dog that has had certain regular experiences will produce gastric secretions, or salivation, when it sees its food dish.

Conceptual Background

Pavlov's conception of learning was set against the same background as Thorndike's. Learning in men was commonly interpreted as the acquisition of ideas, perceptions, logical relations, and so on, all of which are very mentalistic and not very scientific, Pavlov said. The behavior of animals was interpreted as reflexive and automatic and as having a completely determining physiological basis. But the discovery of "psychic," or conditioned, reflexes presented a dilemma. The new behavior is obviously dependent upon learning, but as a physiological scientist Pavlov could not interpret it in the same terms as learning in man. The new behavior had to be simply a new reflex. It had to be based upon physiological brain mechanisms like other reflexes rather than upon mental events. In other words, Pavlov expanded the concept of the reflex to include not only unlearned and genetically determined responses but also learned reactions.

For Pavlov, all behavior of the dog is reflexive. He asked, What is the difference between a reflex and other kinds of behavior? We all know what a reflex is. If we pinch a dog's foot, he raises it. If we touch him in the eye, he blinks it. These responses are clearly reflexes. They always occur; they are invariable and are presumably due to fixed neural pathways. But how do such behaviors differ from the behavior commonly called instinctive? Consider a chicken pecking at food. Pavlov argued that in this instance, too, there is a definite stimulus, the sight of food, and an almost invariant response. Perhaps pecking is not entirely invariant, but it is certainly quite specific and characteristic of the species. How, then, can we distinguish between the eye-blinking reflex, which is obviously a reflex, and the pecking behavior of the chicken, which is called instinctive? Perhaps reflexes are very simple, typically involving single S-R elements, whereas instincts may involve complex integrations of behavior over time. But Pavlov argued that this distinction, too, is invalid. Consider, for example, the "righting reflex." If we throw a cat up in the air, it lands on its feet. Although the photographic methods of Pavlov's time were hardly adequate to the task, he had evidently analyzed the righting reflex, and he reported that the cat runs through a fixed program of strategies. It pulls in its head and feet, which reduces the moment of inertia and produces twisting, then puts out one set of feet so as to twist the body around; it maintains this posture until it is right side up, extends its feet and head to slow the rotation, and there it is. Each part of the total pattern is a simple S-R element, so that the cat needs only to make this reaction until that happens—and then that reaction until something else happens. It is an integrated series of S-R events, and, because each part of the series is clearly a reflex, the entire performance must be classed as a reflex. How, then, Pavlov asked, is that behavior different from what is called an instinct? Similarly, a bird building a nest is displaying behavior that is clearly instinctive; but is not fetching a particular kind of twig and folding it into the nest in a particular manner a very specific, that is, reflexive, act? Is not the nest building simply a series of such reflexive acts?

Instinctive behavior is sometimes said to be motivated. The animal has to be hungry, to be sexually aroused, or to have nest-building hormones before these instinctive kinds of behavior occur. But Pavlov pointed out that the same argument applies to the simpler reflexes also. The sleeping cat has no righting reflexes. The frightened cat or the hungry cat has a variety of behaviors that unquestionably includes reflexes that are all facilitated by its motivational state. So once again, Pavlov concluded, there seems to be no basis for distinguishing between reflexes and what has commonly been thought of as nonreflexive behavior.

Pavlov designated other kinds of behavior reflexes, which illustrate how far the ordinary meaning of "reflex" can be expanded. He describes a dog that was conditioning very poorly. This dog resisted confinement, was inattentive to stimuli, and was a difficult subject in all respects. When the dog was turned loose outside the laboratory, it became a normal, happy dog, but it reacted poorly to the confinement of the experimental situation. Here then, Pavlov said, we have the "freedom reflex." Pavlov discussed a "self-defense reflex," which consists of a large number of different kinds of behavior—threatening, growling, biting, running away, and the like—each of which serves in different contexts to defend the animal. All of them taken together were said to constitute the self-defense reflex. One other reflex should be mentioned. Pavlov observed that, whenever the dog is presented with a novel stimulus, one that elicits no marked reflex of any other kind, there is still a reflexive reaction, the investigatory reflex. The dog will turn its head, or it will perk up its ears, or look at or attend to the new stimulus. The "what is it?" or investigatory reflex is, in effect, the original reflex to all novel stimuli. The investigatory reflex typically disappears after the stimulus has been presented a few times. This fading of the investigatory reflex, a phenomenon originally noted and described by Pavlov, is still called "habituation."

Pavlov's argument has been given here in some detail because it is perhaps the most explicit and most convincing statement of a very popular but usually unarticulated point of view. At one level, Pavlov's argument can be interpreted simply as a justification for his continued use of the word "reflex" to describe all behavior, whether it be innate or learned. At another level, Pavlov was revealing a conceptual bias. In order to be scientific, that is, in order to approach the problem of behavior and brain function as a physiologist, he felt obliged to think of all behavior as strictly determined by particular events, in much the same way that reflexive behavior is. Therefore he called all behavior "reflexive." At still another level of analysis, we can say that, for Pavlov, all responses are to be explained on the basis of eliciting stimuli. Whether a stimulus is connected innately to a response (an unconditioned reflex) or acquires the ability to elicit a response (a conditioned reflex), all responses have to be caused by stimuli.

The Classical Conditioning Experiment

We may now describe the typical Pavlovian experiment. Although a great variety of responses are classically conditionable, Pavlov restricted his own research to the salivary reaction, and the present discussion will be restricted in the same way. We start with the physiological reflex: Food in the mouth produces salivation. This reaction is invariant, unfailing. We therefore refer to food in the mouth as the *unconditioned stimulus* or US, and the reflexive salivation as the unconditioned response or UR.[1] During conditioning a stimulus such as a tone, which is originally neutral (some writers say "indifferent") in the sense that it elicits only an investigatory reflex, is paired with the US. After a number of such pairings, the stimulus is presented alone, without the US. If it elicits salivation it is called a conditioned stimulus, or CS, and the elicited salivation is called a conditioned response, or CR.

This new reflex is supposed to arise simply as a result of pairing the CS with the US. Food in the mouth typically precedes salivation, rather than following it, as it would have to if food were to reinforce salivation. The "effect" of the response is of no theoretical significance. If we designate the biologically important stimulus (food) as S*, then we can compare the experimental procedures of Pavlov and Thorndike by means of the following schemes.

Classical Conditioning   Reinforcement Learning

$$\text{paired}\begin{cases} S^*\text{-}R \\ \\ S \end{cases} \qquad\qquad S\text{-}R\text{-}S^*$$

In both cases the response R is assumed to become associated with or connected to the stimulus S, but the procedure for creating this association and the learning process assumed to produce it are quite different. There may be some confusion here because the US is sometimes called a reinforcer, since it does strengthen the CR in some sense. But the procedures are clearly different even when the language is confusing. There is a second point of difference between Pavlov and Thorndike. Thorndike had resolved the mentalism-mechanism question by considering behavior a third way of approaching the question, but Pavlov took the more conservative approach of explaining everything by means of mechanism. For Pavlov, there simply was no such thing as mind. Everything depended on machinery, and the behavior of the animal (or of man) must necessarily reflect corresponding events in the nervous system. As a physiologist Pavlov was concerned with the nervous system, and specifically with the cerebral cortex, not with any lawfulness that he might find in behavior.

As Pavlov came to conduct increasingly complex and sophisticated experiments with his dogs, he became increasingly careful about controlling the

---

[1] "Unconditional" is the accurate translation from the Russian because it conveys Pavlov's meaning that the response depends upon nothing other than the stimulus. But, unfortunately, when the early translations into English were made it came out "unconditioned," and this word now implies that the response is unlearned.

experimental situation. He said that it is impossible to condition a dog out in the street because there is too much distraction. Instead of giving the CR, the animal will give investigatory responses to the multitude of new stimuli that appear haphazardly. If we want to know anything of the properties of a particular response, we have to be careful that there are no distracting stimuli. Even the presence of the experimenter can be detrimental because the experimenter is likely to be reacted to as a social stimulus. In Pavlov's later experiments, the dog was conditioned in a sound-proof room and supported in a kind of sling, so that it could not move about. The experimenter isolated himself in another room, where he operated the experiment by remote control and observed the animal through a system of mirrors. Thus the essence of the Pavlovian experiment is that the entire situation is controlled by the experimenter. If some stimulus is to affect the animal's behavior, it can be only because the experimenter scheduled it to occur at a particular time.

The philosophy of this tightly controlled procedure contrasts sharply with that of Thorndike's puzzle-box procedure, for example. The latter would be called an operant experiment today. The subject controls most of the events that go on in the experimental situation, whereas the experimenter simply enforces the contingency between the response and the reinforcement. In what we now call a "free operant experiment" the experimenter must wait for the response to occur, whereas in a conditioning experiment he makes it occur by presenting the US. Thus the Pavlovian and Thorndikean (or Skinnerian) experiments differ not only in terms of the critical contingencies arranged by the experimenter but also in the extent to which the situation isolates and controls the occurrence of events in the environment.

Parameters of Conditioning Experiments

Pavlov and his colleagues discovered a great many of the phenomena of conditioning. Indeed, most of what is now known about salivary conditioning came from his laboratory. Recent developments in this country have consisted largely in extending Pavlov's basic methods to the study of other kinds of responses. He evidently believed that once the laws of salivary conditioning were found they would be applicable to any other response, hence it made little difference what response he studied. We now know that this belief is fallacious. Some responses are much more conditionable than others, and many of the rules applying to one CR have little generality to another. But these problems are all recently discovered, and very difficult, so in the present discussion we shall follow Pavlov and consider mainly salivary conditioning.

Once this decision has been made, there is a rather limited variety of eliciting stimuli or USs that can be used because the US must invariably and innately produce the UR. Food is one such stimulus. Pavlov typically used a powdered food, but his earlier research on the digestive system suggests that both the amount and the quality of secretion are functions of the kind of food used for the US. The precise specification of the US can thus be an important matter. We shall see later that these considerations become quite important when aversive stimuli like electric shock are used in the study of defensive reflexes. Pavlov also produced salivation as a UR with a noxious substance like weak acid. But in general we have to conclude that the choice of a particular UR severely limits the class of stimuli that can serve as a US, because the US has to be a strong stimulus, one that will consistently and unconditionally elicit the UR.

Pavlov found that, in contrast to the specificity of the US, there is a great range of stimuli that can serve as a CS. Virtually any kind of stimulus can be used to signal the oncoming US: a light, a noise, a piece of paper, presentation of a particular object or person, even the lapse of time. Thus, if food is given to a dog at a fixed temporal interval, say every ten minutes, the dog will eventually begin salivating about every ten minutes in the absence of any external CS. Pavlov used what may seem to us rather bizarre stimuli, like the ticking of a metronome and the sound of bubbling water. Perhaps equipment for producing these particular stimuli was easily available then; today we usually use electronically controlled tones and fields of light.

It has been discovered that, within rather wide limits, the more intense the CS, the more rapidly conditioning will proceed and the larger the CR tends to be. At one extreme, if the CS is too weak (too near the threshold of detection), there may be no conditioning. Clearly, the animal has to detect the CS; any stimulus that ensures that the animal will give a clear investigatory response is likely to facilitate conditioning. At the other extreme, if the CS is too intense, so that it evokes some type of pain or fear reaction, rather than the investigatory reflex, then it no longer serves to produce conditioning, or at least not the conditioning that we were looking for. Instead of salivation, we obtain a defensive reaction.

It is sometimes said that the CS must be originally neutral, that is, must itself evoke no particular response. This criterion is obviously too stringent. First of all, there may not be any really neutral stimuli. Any stimulus that is detectable at all is likely to invoke at least an investigatory reflex. Indeed, there is reason to think that, in the absence of such a response, conditioning will not occur. It is not even true that the CS must be emotionally neutral, in the sense that it evokes no appetitive or defensive behavior. It is only necessary that the CS be weaker or more nearly neutral than the US itself. If a sufficiently intense US is used, then the experimenter has considerable latitude in how far from neutral the CS may be. One striking illustration of this plasticity of the CS is the finding reported by Spragg (1940) that a hypodermic syringe, which initially evoked considerable defensive behavior, became, after a time, a very positive stimulus. The animals would go hunting for it after it had been used a number of times to give morphine injections. Pavlov had previously reported that a mild electric shock can be used as a CS to produce salivation.

Because stronger CSs are generally more effective than weaker ones, it is not surprising to discover that the onset of a stimulus, like a light or a noise, is a more effective CS than stimulus termination. Light or noise is better than darkness or silence.

Because the experimenter controls all the events occurring in the Pavlovian situation, it is possible to manipulate systematically the time interval between the CS and the US in ways that are not possible in an operant experiment. It is often reported that an interval of about one half-second produces the greatest amount of conditioning. If the time interval is shorter than a half-second, and particularly if the interval is negative so that the CS follows the US, a dramatic failure of conditioning is typically found (see Figure 2.2). On the other hand, for intervals longer than a half-second the rate of conditioning decreases more modestly, so that it is possible to get conditioning even with fairly long CS-US intervals, provided that a sufficient number of trials are run. It should be emphasized that these data and these conclusions are idealized. Although there is considerable evidence for a half-second optimum (see, for example, Kimble, 1961), most of this evidence comes from eye-blink studies, and the evidence from studies of other kinds of responses suggests that there may be very different optimum inter-

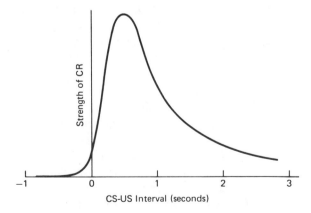

Fig. 2.2 *How the strength of conditioning is supposed to depend upon the interstimulus interval. Note the hypothetical failure of conditioning under "backward" conditions, that is, when the US precedes the CS.*

vals for different responses. For example, VanDercar and Schneiderman (1967) conditioned rabbits with different intervals while simultaneously measuring eye blink (of the nictitating membrane) and heart rate. At .25 second they found good eye-blink but no heart-rate conditioning; at 6.75 seconds they found just the opposite pattern. We may think of conditioning as occurring under both conditions but being manifest only in one or the other response system.

Pavlov distinguished between two kinds of procedures that he called, and which we still call, the "delay" and the "trace" procedures. In the delay procedure, the CS comes on and stays on until the US occurs. Usually the two stimuli overlap in time. The procedure is called delay because the onset of the US is delayed following the onset of the CS. In the trace procedure there is a momentary CS, and then at some fixed interval later the US comes on alone. Thus the CS and US do not overlap and are never actually paired. These relationships are shown in Figure 2.3. The name trace is given to this latter procedure because presumably the effective stimulus—the brain activity that really matters—is not the sensory input itself but some lingering trace of it. Perhaps because the trace is never as potent as the original stimulus, the trace procedure is not as effective as a delay procedure in producing conditioning with the same interstimulus interval.

There is a methodological consideration that arises in conditioning ex-

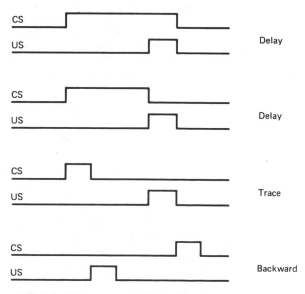

Fig. 2.3   The temporal relationships between CS and US that define two types of delay conditioning, trace conditioning, and backward conditioning procedures.

periments with different interstimulus intervals. Imagine an experiment in which there are two groups, one with an interstimulus interval of 0.3 second and the other with the CS and US separated by 3.0 seconds. In both cases we should expect to find a substantial amount of conditioning, provided that other parameters of the situation are appropriate. But the animals trained with the long interstimulus interval have ten times the amount of time available in which to respond to the CS before the US comes on. And we have ten times the amount of time in which to measure their salivation before the US, food in the mouth, produces a large UR that will obscure any CR. This is a serious methodological problem; if we are to assess the relative strength of conditioning in the two groups, we are obliged to use some test procedure that will give the two groups an equal opportunity for the CR to occur. There are three ways to do so. One is to avoid using the short interstimulus interval, so that all animals have ample opportunity to respond during conditioning. The second procedure, which was favored by Pavlov, is to omit the US on some trials and to record the amount of salivation occurring in some interval of time, like three seconds, that is the same for all animals. The first procedure is a little awkward because it limits the kinds of experiments that can be run. There is the additional problem that, even if the CR does occur, it may be very difficult to distinguish from the UR because the two merge into each other. The second procedure is a little awkward because it intermixes training trials in which the CS and US are paired with a number of test trials in which the CS occurs alone. Extinction (see next section) is likely to occur during the test trials. A third technique is simply to discontinue pairing CS and US and to measure the strength of the CR during a series of extinction trials. But again we are limited in the kinds of experiments that we can do.

Some Conditioning Phenomena

Pavlov discovered extinction, named it, and was the first to study it extensively. The extinction procedure is defined as presenting the CS alone without pairing it with the US. We should distinguish carefully between extinction as a procedure, as something the experimenter does, and extinction as something that happens to behavior: a weakening as a result of the procedure. The same word is properly used in both ways (but it is not proper to say that the animals "extinguished" or the animals "were extinguished"). Pavlov observed (see Figure 2.4) that the CR may extinguish rapidly. He noted further that, when the spacing of the test trials was increased, the response extinguished somewhat more slowly than is shown in Figure 2.4.

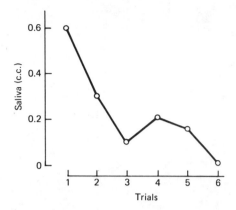

Fig. 2.4   Extinction of conditioned salivation. The CS was the visual presentation of food for 1 minute at 2-minute intervals, and the response measure was the amount of saliva secreted during CS presentation. Unfortunately, we cannot tell from Pavlov's report how often the response had been previously extinguished and reconditioned. (From Pavlov, 1927.)

Nonetheless, it is apparent that the salivary reflex is extinguished surprisingly rapidly, more rapidly than we customarily think of operant behaviors weakening when reinforcement is withheld. We may expect that different responses will be extinguished at different rates.

There are several other phenomena that Pavlov discovered, studied, and gave names to which are still used in the analysis of learning. One of these phenomena is *generalization*. Consider a situation in which the CS is a tone of 440 hertz (cycles per second), and let us suppose that sufficient pairings have been given so that this CS elicits a strong CR. At this point let us suppose that we test the subject with a different tone. If the new test tone is fairly similar to the original CS, say 500 hertz, it will typically elicit some measurable CR. It will not be as strong as that obtained with the original 440-hertz tone, but it will still have some strength. If we continue testing with tones of 600, 700, and 800 hertz, we should find a progressive decline in the strength of the response. Representative data from just such an experiment, reported by Siegel et al. (1968) are shown in Figure 2.5. Generally, the more similar the test stimulus is to the original training stimulus, the greater the response strength. Or, put the other way around, the more distant the test stimulus is, the greater the decrement will be. Perhaps such results are not surprising. If so, it is because we take generalization so much for granted. Generalization is actually an extremely important phenomenon. If it were not for generalization, learning as we know it would never be

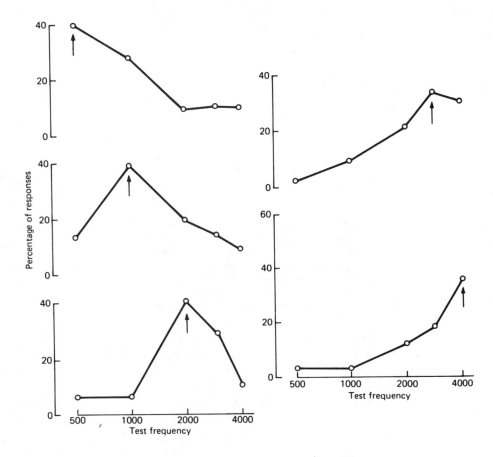

*Fig. 2.5 Probability of a conditioned eyelid re-
sponse in rabbits when tested with tones of different
frequencies. The US was an electric shock to the
cheek. The arrow indicates the frequency at which
each group was conditioned. (From Siegel et al.,
Generalization gradients obtained from individual
subjects following classical conditioning.* Journal of
Experimental Psychology, *1968, 78, 171–174. Copyright 1968 by the American Psychological Association. Reprinted by permission.)*

apparent in behavior. Consider the fact that in any learning situation any
given trial presents an enormous number of different stimulus conditions.
The animal's mood, its posture, the way it is oriented to perceive its environment—all these factors are likely to vary in a more or less random
manner from trial to trial. Even in a Pavlovian experiment, in which ex-

traneous stimulation and inadvertent variation among stimulus conditions are minimized, there still has to be some variation in the total pattern of stimulation from one trial to the next. It may make some difference whether the animal is inhaling or exhaling at the moment the CS comes on. But the important factor is not that the stimulus situation is slightly different from trial to trial but that it is largely similar from trial to trial, so that the learning that occurs on one trial can be manifest on the subsequent trial.

Although we tend to think of generalization as occurring along some easily defined dimension of a stimulus, like the frequency of a tone or the intensity of a light, much of the time in everyday experience generalization occurs from one stimulus context to another in the absence of any clearly defined stimulus dimensions. Consider, for example, the problem of learning to recognize and react in more or less the same way to a class of stimulus objects. A class of objects, like all dogs, includes stimulus patterns that differ in color, size, shape, configuration, shagginess, pattern of movement, and probably a host of other even less well-defined stimulus dimensions, but ultimately we come to respond to any of this diverse class of objects as a dog. Consider further that other dogs also recognize this class as such. Although another dog's response to this class may be different from that of people and although the dog presumably generalizes on different dimensions from those that people use, the dog also arrives at the same functionally equivalent class of dog objects.

In one sense, the opposite of generalization is discrimination. In generalization the animal responds in the same way to two similar stimuli; in discrimination the animal responds differently to two similar stimuli. Consider a procedure in which a CS+, say a tone of 400 hertz, is presented on half the trials and is always paired with food, whereas a CS−, say a tone of 500 hertz, is presented on the other half of the trials and is never followed by food. Under these conditions the CR begins to occur to both the CS+ and the CS−. But, with continued training, the response to CS− gradually drops out. Ultimately the animal continues to respond just to CS+ and does not respond to CS−. It should be apparent that, just as generalization is necessary for learning to be manifest in behavior, so there must be discrimination if an animal is to respond intelligently to the world about it. Just as we classify all dogs as dogs, we also discriminate between large and small dogs, between black ones and brown ones, between males and females, and so on. We might suppose that the intelligence of an organism could be measured by the number of different discriminations that it can make among a set of similar stimulus objects. The cartoon in Figure 2.6 shows an instance in which an individual is generalizing when ultimately, we trust, he will learn the appropriate discrimination between two classes of stimuli that are different in important ways.

Fig. 2.6

Inhibition

Pavlov argued that conditioning could involve either an active excitatory process, by which a stimulus excites a particular response, or an inhibitory process, by which a stimulus actively inhibits a response that would otherwise occur. So, just as a CS+ may cause a response to occur, a different stimulus, a CS−, may prevent its occurrence. The simplest case is one that Pavlov described as *external inhibition*. It can be thought of roughly as distraction. Suppose we have a well-established CR: salivation consistently elicited by a tone. Suppose further that, on a test trial when the tone CS is presented, a new distracting stimulus is also presented (it makes little difference whether the new stimulus is presented immediately before or during the regular CS). What we are likely to find is that the occurrence of an investigatory reflex to the novel stimulus blocks or inhibits the CR: There is no salivation. But this disruption is only temporary. If the novel stimulus is presented on a series of trials, the CR will return to its full strength, perhaps within a half-dozen trials. This habituation to, or familiarization with, the novel stimulus can be accomplished either after conditioning, as in this example, or before the original CS-US pairings. If habituation to the novel stimulus is obtained by presenting it alone on a series of trials before conditioning is begun, then when it is introduced later, after conditioning, it will have little or no inhibitory effect on the CR. Pavlov's explanation was that the distracting stimulus no longer initiates an investigatory reflex, so this behavior cannot compete with or inhibit the CR.

A quite different kind of inhibition is what Pavlov labelled *internal inhibition*. He discovered that, if extinction is carried just to the point where the CR no longer occurs and the animal is then given a period of twenty-four hours to rest, the CR will show spontaneous recovery when tested again. The extinction experience does not permanently weaken the CR. Pavlov argued that the phenomenon of spontaneous recovery proves that the waning of the CR in extinction does not represent a "dying" of the reflex or any real weakening of the learned S-R connection. It shows, on the contrary, that the response is there with at least considerable strength and that it is actively blocked by some kind of inhibitory process. It is this hypothetical inhibition that Pavlov called internal inhibition.[2]

It should be noted that, if a second extinction is begun some time after the first, extinction proceeds more quickly than it did the first time. The second spontaneous recovery is also less complete. If a series of successive extinctions are run, the amount of spontaneous recovery will continue to decline and successive extinctions will continue to go more rapidly—until finally a point is reached at which the CR is permanently extinguished.

Consider again the discrimination procedure described previously. A CS+ is consistently paired with the US, and a CS− is consistently not paired with the US. As Figure 2.7 shows, responding to CS− can be expected to drop out. But now there is the question whether the loss of responding to CS− represents a fading away or decaying of that particular reflex or whether the reflex is still there and is being inhibited in some way. The critical test is to present a novel stimulus, one that would be expected to produce external inhibition. If such a novel stimulus is presented at the same time as the CS+, it produces, as we have already noted, a marked loss of the CR on that trial (see the left-hand part of Figure 2.7). But if the distracting stimulus is presented on a trial when the CS− is presented, we find a recovery of the CR essentially to full strength (the right-hand part of Figure 2.7). Pavlov called this phenomenon *disinhibition*, and he argued that it must be due to the distracting stimulus producing interference with an active inhibitory process. This procedure for producing inhibition, that is, for associating CS+ with the US and a different stimulus, CS−, with the absence of the US, is called the *differential conditioning* procedure.

---

[2] Note that the kind of inhibitory mechanism theoretically involved in internal inhibition is quite different from that hypothesized to underlie external inhibition. Actually, both designations are somewhat inappropriate. An animal may be distracted by sudden internal stimuli as much as by external ones. Pavlov cites the instance of a dog's needing to urinate. Here an internal stimulus suppresses the CR through external inhibition. The mechanism here is simply distraction or the elicitation of competing behavior. The mechanism underlying internal inhibition, however, must be a specific tendency not to make the previously conditioned response.

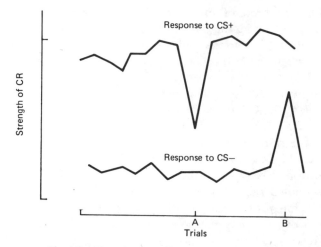

Fig. 2.7   *Hypothetical effects of a distracting stimulus. Discriminated conditioning has already been carried out so the subject is giving a strong CR to the positive stimulus and a weak CR to the negative stimulus. External inhibition is shown on trial A when a novel stimulus is presented with CS+, and disinhibition on trial B when a novel stimulus is presented with CS−.*

There is a similar procedure, which Pavlov called *conditioned inhibition*; it produces essentially the same results. It consists of pairing CS+ with the US on positive trials and presenting the CS+ together with a CS− but without the US on negative trials. With this procedure the animal will come to respond to the CS+ when it occurs alone but not when it is accompanied by the CS−. The pattern CS+ plus CS− thus serves to inhibit the CR. The same degree of inhibition is found when the CS− is presented alone, and it is also possible to demonstrate the disinhibition effect.

Wyrwicka (1972) has pointed out that there is another, comparable procedure that is also effective. The CS− is given alone on negative trials and the CS− together with the CS+ on positive trials. Wyrwicka reports that this procedure also leads to the establishment of differential control of the CR. This procedure is used implicitly in many experiments. Whenever an experiment is conducted in a particular experimental context, for example, a particular physical arrangement of the laboratory, then that context constitutes this kind of CS+. Thus we might use a flashing light to signal food and produce salivation in a Pavlovian experiment—but when the dog is removed from the harness and the other trappings of the experimental situation, the light by itself produces no salivation. Wyrwicka's procedure, the conditioned-inhibition procedure, and the differential-inhibition procedure may all be presumed to be quite comparable. In each case there is one stimulus or pattern of stimuli that elicits the CR and there is another stimulus or pattern of stimuli that inhibits it. Presumably the same kind of inhibitory mechanism is at work in each case.

A somewhat different inhibitory mechanism is suggested by the phenomenon that Pavlov called *delay of inhibition*. Let us suppose that we endeavor to establish a conditioned salivary response in a dog using a very long CS-US interval, perhaps one minute. We know from earlier discussion that such conditioning will occur slowly. But if we use an animal that has previously been conditioned (which Pavlov tended to do) and if we are patient, we can elicit conditioned salivation. Perhaps after 100 training trials a modest CR will occur shortly after CS onset—long before the food US is delivered. But if we continue training the animal another 100 or 200 trials, the CR may change: Although it may continue to gain in amplitude, it may also occur later in the CS-US interval. Ultimately the animal "waits" until just before US presentation before it salivates. That this delayed response to the CS is due to some form of inhibition is shown by the fact that if we do a distraction experiment early in the CS, the animal will salivate promptly. We have thus, once again, the disinhibition demonstration to argue that there is some active inhibition of the response early in the CS.

There are two sets of phenomena that we must mention before concluding our discussion of Pavlovian conditioning. One is interesting in that it shows a failure of conditioning where we might have expected it. And the other is a phenomenon in which conditioning seems to occur even though the experiment is arranged to make it impossible. Consider first the failure of conditioning. Suppose we have two stimuli that have been found in previous experiments to be perfectly adequate as CSs, for example, a bright light and a weak tone. We pair both with food a number of times until the combination regularly elicits the CR. Then we run a series of test trials using either the light or the tone. Typically the bright light produces the CR but the weaker tone elicits nothing. It appears that the rapid formation of a connection between the light and the food blocks or "overshadows" any connection that might have become established between the tone and food. This overshadowing phenomenon was extensively studied by Pavlov but attracted little attention in this country until quite recently (Kamin, 1969).

The second phenomenon is typically found in defensive, rather than appetitive, conditioning situations. It was discovered by Grether in 1938 (Pavlov missed it somehow). Grether first tested his animals with a bell; it elicited little reaction. Then his animals were frightened several times by a brilliant flash of light (the US). The bell was not presented on these occasions; the bell and the light were never paired. But then, when the bell was presented alone on a test trial, it produced a strong fright reaction. Grether called this phenomenon *pseudoconditioning*, and the name has stuck. It is applied in any situation in which an animal responds to a stimulus in the same manner as to the US, even though the stimulus has not been paired with the US. It is presumed to arise from heightened excitability or the arousal of a general motivational state like fear in the experimental situation, which is then triggered or augmented by any novel stimulus.[3]

The Theory of Conditioning

There can be little doubt that learning occurs in a Pavlovian experiment. The question is how this learning is best conceptualized. To keep the proper historical perspective, we shall stress Pavlov's own interpretation and shall mention only briefly some of the alternative views that have been formulated. In a later chapter some contemporary interpretations will be discussed.

It should be emphasized that Pavlov's primary concern was not to establish a theory of learning but rather to develop techniques for studying the brain. He was particularly concerned with the cerebral hemispheres. He assumed, as did most scientists early in this century, that learning is the special province of the cortex. He also assumed that learning can occur only in an animal as high as a carnivore if the cortex is intact, and his research led him to formulate a rather specialized theory of the role of the cortex in learning. The basic idea is that, when the US stimulates the cortex, it produces maximum activation at some definite point; but, because it is a strong stimulus, there is a field of neural activity radiating from this point. Similarly, the CS activates maximally a somewhat different location on the cortex, and it produces an area of activity somewhat smaller than that produced by the US. If these two fields overlap, Pavlov assumed, the sensory fields stimulated by the two stimuli should become integrated in a common field. Specifically, a neural path should develop between the two loci points. The two stimuli should become functionally equivalent, but because the

---

[3] A similar type of phenomenon, perhaps arising from the same kind of general excitability, is called *sensitization*. If we use a stimulus that initially produces some mild defensive behavior or any particularly directed behavior other than the orienting reaction, we may find that this reaction is greatly augmented simply by our giving the animal a series of USs alone. In effect, an animal may become frightened by a stimulus because it has been shocked, in spite of the fact that the stimulus is never paired with the shock so that it is not a CS in the technical sense. In recent years a good deal of methodological sophistication has gone into the question of how to control for sensitization and pseudoconditioning effects, and some discussion has centered around the question of what these effects may reveal about learning that occurs in a Pavlovian situation.

US is the stronger of the two, producing an invariable response, the basic modification must be in the activity elicited by the CS. The CS produces the same response originally elicited by the US. Pavlov eventually elaborated his theory of the brain in considerable detail and developed it to explain many of the basic facts of conditioning. For example, generalization was explained as the production by similar stimuli of similar and partially over-lapping fields of activity. As another example, the importance of temporal factors in conditioning was explained in terms of how fast brain activity spread from the point of maximum stimulation and how fast the area of activity contracted afterward.

Few psychologists today take Pavlov's brain theory very seriously. The brain theory is mentioned at all only to emphasize two facts. One is that, in Pavlov's thinking, learning consisted not so much in the construction of a new S-R connection as in the learned equivalence of stimuli. The second point is that, for Pavlov, learning arose from the altered relation of neurons in the brain, especially in the sensory areas. Because Pavlov was not a psychologist and not particularly concerned with psychological theory, he did not speak very informatively about the psychological aspects of condi-tioning. He described these aspects of conditioning in a number of different ways, using a number of different analogies. For example, he conceived of the CS as a signal; the CS signals the US. He sometimes spoke of the CS-CR connection as a "signalized reflex." At times Pavlov spoke of the CS-CR reflex itself as learned, whereas at other times he referred to the signal value of the CS or the learned equivalence of the CS and US. If the CS comes to acquire some of the properties of the US, including the elicitation of saliva-tion, then it may be that the CS signals the US, not that a new S-R con-nection as such has been learned.

Although Pavlov was not very specific about the psychological nature of conditioning, subsequent writers have been quite specific about what they thought it involves. One of the most common interpretations is that con-ditioning consists of learning by stimulus substitution. A response that is originally evoked only by the US comes, through stimulus pairing, to be evoked by the CS. The CS literally substitutes for the US in producing the same response. Although this view of classical conditioning is simple and attractive, it is not consistent with the facts as they are now known. In one of the first successful conditioning studies reported in this country, Upton (1929) conditioned a fear reaction to auditory tones. His ultimate purpose was to do generalization studies in which tones of different intensities and frequencies would be presented to determine how high and how gentle a tone different animals can hear. (This technique still remains one of the most powerful tools for studying the sensory abilities of animals.) In carry-ing out these studies Upton found that whereas the UR to shock was accelerated heart rate and respiration, the CR (the response to the tone) was a decrease in heart rate and an interruption in breathing. Such anomalies have become common in subsequent years. The CR is simply different from the UR in many instances. The difference appears to depend upon a number of factors, such as the intensity of the shock, the interstimulus interval, and especially what kind of animal is being conditioned (see Chapter 8). But, in spite of evidence to the contrary, many psychologists have assumed that the CR is merely a small edition of the UR that occurs because the CS has come to substitute for the US in eliciting it. We shall see in the next chapter that Watson had his own interpretation of how learning occurs in the conditioning situation. In Chapter 8 we shall see that alternative interpretations of classical conditioning are still being proposed.

In contrast with this unsettled question of what learning in classical conditioning consists of, there has never been much question (until recently) about the procedure that produces it. Conditioning is said to occur when appropriate stimuli, a CS and a US, are paired. The pairing of the stimuli is the all-important ingredient of the Pavlovian procedure. Indeed, we have seen that, if the CS comes to elicit the CR without benefit of pairing with the US, we call the result not conditioning but pseudoconditioning instead.

Most of this chapter has been devoted to the phenomena of conditioning and the various procedures, most of them discovered by Pavlov himself, for studying these phenomena. One reason for this emphasis is that many of these phenomena are basic to any analysis of learned behavior yet have been often distorted and reinterpreted in terms of later theorists' own convictions. A second reason for emphasizing the procedures for conditioning, rather than the hypothetical process of conditioning, is that Pavlov's own theory of conditioning was really extremely simple. Putting aside his special theory of brain functioning, the general theory of conditioning can be summarized as follows:

1. Conditioning is a hypothetical process by which a response comes to be elicited by a CS that does not elicit it initially.

2. Conditioning occurs when the CS is consistently paired with a US that does elicit the response.

3. All learning in man and beast is due to conditioning.[4]

---

[4] The student may object here on the grounds that we no longer recognize conditioning as the universal basis of learning. This objection would surely be valid if it were applied to a contemporary definition of conditioning, but the historical importance of conditioning is due to the fact that for a long time it *was* widely regarded as the universal basis for learning. It was so regarded by Pavlov. Similarly, to the first statement it might be objected that we now conceive of conditioning as a set of procedures, rather than as a process. But, again, conditioning was historically important largely because for a long time it was regarded as a special kind of learning process.

Pavlov's Contributions and Impact

In his own country Pavlov attracted a vast number of other scientists to work in his laboratory. Some were young men and students, but others were older, well-established scientists who dedicated themselves to his work. We may hope that these selfless men received the recognition due their efforts in Russia; in this country they are hardly more than colorful names adorning the pages of Pavlov's *Conditioned Reflexes*. We merely note in passing that much of Pavlov's prodigious research output was made possible by a corps of investigators who learned from him, to be sure, but who also contributed greatly to his systematic program.

Although there were some early brief descriptions of Pavlov's techniques (Pavlov 1906; Yerkes & Margulis, 1909), they conveyed little of the methodological sophistication or the theoretical underpinnings that characterized Pavlov's later work. A full account of his work and his colleagues' work did not appear in English until 1927. But by that time the general conception of conditioning had already gained tremendous popularity. The elegance and objectivity of conditioning procedures were advocated by Watson in a series of publications starting in 1916, by Smith and Guthrie in 1921, and by a number of other contemporary writers.

It is remarkable that this acceptance of conditioning as a procedure and as a theoretical model was so widespread before there were any experimental reports of classical conditioning in this country and before anything was really known about it. There were a few scattered reports of successful conditioning from Watson's laboratory in 1916 and 1920 and by Mateer (1918) and Cason (1922), but there were more reports of failures, methodological problems, and conceptual difficulties with conditioning.[5] In spite of these problems, conditioning was accepted as both a theoretical framework and a practical technique for solving a variety of applied problems. Thus 1924 saw the publication of a book by Allport on social psychology and another by Burnham on abnormal psychology. There was apparently no limit to the power or applicability of conditioning. But, as we will see in the next chapter, part of the success of the conditioning concept resulted from rather gross distortions of the theory, principles, and procedures that Pavlov was developing.

[5] The first conditioning experiment in this country was really done by Twitmyer. His doctoral dissertation (University of Pennsylvania, 1902) was a study of the knee-jerk reflex. He found his subjects giving the response to the ready signal before the hammer struck. This research attracted little attention and was abandoned; Twitmyer had been a little too far ahead of his time.

In assessing the impact Pavlov had upon the learning theorists who followed him, we have to distinguish clearly among three kinds of contribution he sought to make. His first concern was to develop a theory of the brain. Unfortunately, his model of the brain was never very influential, and with time it has become less so. Even so, a few capable workers in the field of conditioning (like Wyrwicka, 1972) who share Pavlov's concern with neural mechanisms are still able to accept and defend some of his brain-model principles.

As a theory of learning, that is, a theory about how behavior is modified through experience, classical conditioning has fared considerably better. We have seen that many of Pavlov's assumptions about what learning consists of, and the kinds of mechanisms that produce it, were very widely accepted even before his work was well known in this country. Then, even as the universality of conditioning came into question—as the domain of conditioning shrank—there was a healthy growth of interest and activity connected with the phenomena of conditioning. Today there appears to be a resurgence of interest in classical conditioning, not as distorted by early American writers but as originally discussed by Pavlov. For example, his treatment of inhibition is now being followed up after having been ignored for many years. In short, classical conditioning has survived remarkably well as a theory of learning in the seventy years since Pavlov began to develop it.

At a third level of analysis are the procedures, the phenomena, and the language of learning and conditioning. In this sphere Pavlov's contribution has been immeasurably great. Much of the terminology that we use to describe learning experiments is his. Phenomena such as extinction, generalization, discrimination, and inhibition were discovered by him. Many of his procedures have become part of the hard core of animal experimentation.

At a more abstract level, Pavlov thought that all learning, whether of elicited responses in animals or of highly conceptual behavior in humans, was due to the mechanisms of classical conditioning. This has been an immensely provocative and constructive idea. We now believe it to be wrong, but it is nonetheless one of man's great ideas. And it stirred both its detractors and its defenders to find out much more about learning.

References for Further Reading

There are no adequate secondary sources on Pavlovian conditioning, and the old primary sources are in Russian journals that are difficult to obtain. The student can do no better than to read the word of the scientist himself (Pavlov, 1927), in which he will find little data but much learned discussion of the phenomena of conditioning. This book, Pavlov's only systematic presentation, is necessary reading for any serious study of conditioning. A number of Pavlov's theoretical papers have been translated by Gantt (Pavlov, 1928, 1941), who also provides a businesslike biography of Pavlov. Cuny (1966) gives a more personal view of the man. The classic account of the early conditioning experiments in this country is Hilgard and Marquis (1940). For good reviews of more recent work on selected topics in conditioning see Prokasy (1965) and Black and Prokasy (1972).

CHAPTER
3

WATSON

John B. Watson (1878–1958) was unquestionably one of the most colorful personalities in the history of psychology. As a young man he enjoyed a meteoric rise to fame. Although he was a few years younger than Thorndike and much younger than Pavlov, his fame outshone theirs in the early years of the century. Unfortunately, his career as a psychologist came to an end in 1920, at a time when Thorndike was yet to begin working in earnest on human learning and Pavlov's major work was still to be translated into English. Although Watson did not invent behaviorism, he became widely known as its chief spokesman and protagonist. It was Watson who demanded that American psychologists become behaviorists, and—because he made his demand at just the right time—they did.

Watson received his degree from The University of Chicago in 1903, which was at that time strongly under the influence of John Dewey and strongly committed to what was called functionalism. Functionalism was a strange blend of evolutionary theory and the traditional belief in the importance of the mind. The mind was said to be the device that man had evolved for solving his unique problems. Thus Watson was brought up in the prevalent tradition: Mechanism explains the behavior of animals, and the mind explains the behavior of man. According to Jensen (1962), Watson adhered to this dualistic position in his early years, and his conversion to a strict mechanistic position was due to the influence of Jennings, who was at Johns Hopkins University when Watson went there. Jennings' classic work on the behavior of lower organisms (Jennings, 1906) had emphasized the physiological basis of the behavior of lower animals, but it also emphasized the universality of learning as an adaptive mechanism.

On the other hand, even though Watson may have originally been a dualist, much of his early research had a strong mechanistic flavor. In 1903 he published a large study correlating the learning ability of rats with the myelinization of their nervous systems. In any case, Watson very quickly established for himself the reputation of being a thoroughgoing mechanist. In a widely used textbook (Watson, 1914) he said that the study of the mind is the province of philosophy; it is the realm of speculation and endless word games. The mind has no place in psychology. A science of psychology must be based on objective phenomena, and the ultimate explanation of behavior must be found in the nervous system.

Historical Background

There was, of course, nothing new in Watson's mechanistic philosophy, nor was there anything very new in the idea that psychologists should concern themselves primarily with behavior. This proposition was clear, though implicit, in much of the animal research published early in the century. The basic behaviorist doctrine had even been stated explicitly by a few writers (for example, Meyer, 1911). There was also a conspicuous failure of the older traditionalists to analyze consciousness effectively. Sigmund Freud, too, had begun to convince us that we often do not know why we do the things we do. Further failures of the traditional method of introspective analysis were reported by psychologists at the University of Würzburg. In short, the traditional distinction between animals as machines and men as rational beings was about to topple, and Watson was there at the right time to help push it over.

Other very basic problems were confronting the psychological theorist in the early years of the twentieth century. There was the Darwinian conception of continuity between animals and man. This idea of continuity had been supported by Thorndike's discovery of intelligent but unthinking behavior in animals, for example. The reconciliation of these discoveries with the traditional view of man, as well as with the traditional dichotomy between instinct and intelligence, produced an extensive critical literature. There were a number of books with titles such as *Instinct and Intelligence* (Morgan, 1912) and *The Evolution of Animal Intelligence* (Holmes, 1911). It was also widely believed that modern techniques would soon disclose how the brain works. It was therefore necessary for the psychological theorist to formulate principles that would aid in the search for knowledge of the brain. We have already noted that both Thorndike and Pavlov were quick to infer what goes on in the brain during learning. At a minimum, it was thought necessary to make psychological principles consistent with the ways in which the brain was supposed to function. It was this set of contradictory and mutually inconsistent assumptions that Watson's behavioristic theory of learning was designed to untangle. This conceptual reorganization was accomplished, first, by throwing the mind right out of psychology and, second, by emphasizing the old concept of habit. Habit was no longer considered simply a special variety of learning but was to serve as a model for all learning. For Watson there was no problem about where instinct left off and intelligence began, nor was there a problem about where awareness began to emerge in the evolution of the animal kingdom. The philosopher might ponder such unanswerable questions, but psychology was destined to be a science, which could be accomplished only, Watson said, by observing behavior and by relating behavior to the nervous system.

Watson's solution to the problems confronting psychology was first presented in a series of lectures given at Columbia University in 1912. It was presented briefly in a paper in *Psychological Review* in 1913 and then discussed at greater length in a book published in 1914. This book, *Behavior: An Introduction to Comparative Psychology*, achieved three things. First, it showed how plausible it was to discard all the familiar mental paraphernalia from psychology. Some of this clearing out was accomplished just by means of translation; for example, feelings and emotions became merely stimuli arising within the body. Some of it was accomplished by the writing of promissory notes on the future development of physiological psychology. Thus thoughts, images, and the other contents of awareness were attributed to kinesthetic feedback from muscles in the body. When a human subject reports a thought, supposedly the stimulus to which he is really responding is the feedback from muscles in the throat. The subject is making covert or implicit speech responses and interpreting the feedback from these responses as mental contents. The second achievement of Watson's *Comparative Psychology* was a survey of the variety of methods that had been developed for the study of learning in animals. Anything we might want to know about the animal's sensory equipment, its motor capabilities, or its ability to associate sensory and motor events might be investigated scientifically by means of various kinds of apparatus and learning procedures. The third part of this important book was the presentation of the learning theory itself. Let us look at it.

The Theory of Learning

Watson's theory was simple enough. He proposed that when a stimulus and response occur at the same time the connection between them is strengthened. How strong the connection becomes depends primarily upon how frequently the stimulus and response occur together.

This theory was like Thorndike's theory in one respect: its claim that learning consists of strengthening S-R connections. But there was a critical difference in the presumed learning mechanism; for Watson there was no law of effect, there was no reinforcement (which Thorndike had emphasized), and there was a very important law of frequency, or exercise (which Thorndike had minimized). Watson's psychological principles of learning are readily translatable into his conception of the nervous system. The stimulus produces activity in a certain part of the brain, and the response is produced by activity in another part of the brain; when these two areas are simultaneously activated, by whatever means, the neural pathways between them become strengthened. Two points should be noted in Watson's neurological model. One is that there was nothing new in the concept that repeated activation of a neural circuit strengthens it in the sense of making it easier to activate in the future. We have already found this hypothesis stated by both Thorndike and Pavlov, and the basic idea had been formulated by psychologists and philosophers at least as far back as Herbert Spencer (1855). Probably everyone believed that was how the brain worked. The second aspect of Watson's theory was a little more creative. He emphasized that learning does not produce (or result from) new connections in the brain. All neural connections have to be already laid down as part of the animal's original genetic constitution. Learning can only lower the threshold of an old connection or make functional one that has been latent. It is interesting to note that today, sixty years later, we are little wiser about how the brain actually changes structurally as a consequence of learning or whether it changes at all.

Watson's theory was primarily a protest against Thorndike's theory, and he was not above criticizing Thorndike at every opportunity. He said that Thorndike's law of effect was mentalistic, nothing but an updated version of the old hedonistic principle. In an attempt to refute Thorndike experimentally, Watson (1917) trained rats to dig through sand to get into a goal box. Once in the goal box, they were required to wait for the delivery of food. According to Thorndike's theory (said Watson), because sitting and waiting are the last responses to occur, they, rather than the earlier response of digging which got the animal into the goal box, should be reinforced by the delivery of food. But the digging response was in fact learned, which was taken by Watson as disproving the law of effect. We now know, of course, that there are a variety of other possible mechanisms that can operate here. For example, digging in the sand may be intrinsically reinforcing, or the goal box may become a secondary reinforcer. There are many ways out for the contemporary reinforcement theorist, but at the time it looked as if the strength of learning depended not upon the effect of the response but upon the simple frequency with which it occurred.

Watson's law of frequency can be illustrated by means of the following example. Let us suppose we have a very simple situation in which an animal can make just two possible responses, one (R+) correct and the other (R−) incorrect. Let us suppose for the sake of simplicity that R+ and R− are of approximately equal strength initially. What happens over a series of learning trials is that R− gradually drops out and R+ becomes the much more likely response. This happens, Watson tells us, because, whereas R− may occur on half the trials, R+ must occur on every trial. R+ becomes stronger than R− because it occurs twice as often. Then, as R+ begins to acquire the advantage of frequency, it acquires also the added advantage of greater associative strength to raise its frequency even higher.

Watson also discussed a secondary law of *recency*: The most recent response is strengthened more by its frequent occurrence than is an earlier response. But the law of frequency was Watson's chief explanatory weapon. He argued that it would operate to produce learning most effectively in a situation in which the correct response alters the situation. It would operate in the puzzle box and in many maze situations in which, if R+ occurs, R− no longer can occur. It is not so true in a free operant situation, in which there is no reason to suppose that the correct response will occur any more frequently than some other behavior. In the next chapter we will see that Guthrie attributed great importance to the idea that the correct response changes the situation.

The relation between Watson's theory and classical conditioning is somewhat more complex. In his 1914 book Watson described many techniques for studying animal learning, and Pavlov's procedure was treated as just another technique of investigation. It was not regarded as requiring a different type of learning process but was subsumed under the law of frequency. How this was accomplished is shown in Figure 3.1. Before the conditioning experiment the animal is equipped with two separate S-R connections. One involves the strong connection between the US and the UR. This is a simple stimulus-response reflex. The second connection is between the CS and an orienting response R_o, some other incidental behavior. Again

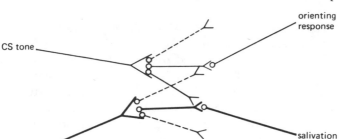

*Fig. 3.1 Watson's (1914) model of Pavlovian condi-
tioning. There are assumed to be latent connections
between virtually all stimuli and responses. Of this
multitude only that connection is strengthened
enough to become functional which feeds into a still
stronger reflex, namely, the unconditioned reflex.*

we have a simple reflex between the CS and R_o. But at the same time that
the CS elicits R_o it also *tends* to elicit a variety of other behaviors and
diffuse activities, including the UR. Because the particular association
neurons that would bring about this diffuse discharge have been little used,
no overt behavior occurs, and the CS produces only the R_o. During the
course of conditioning, however, the CS occurs and the UR necessarily
occurs because it is elicited by the US. Consequently, the pathway between
the two reflexes indicated in the diagram by the association neuron is
strengthened sufficiently so that the CS will produce the UR. Basically then,
according to Watson, what happens in a Pavlovian experiment is that the
CS occurs at approximately the same time that the UR is made to occur, so
the latent connection between the CS and the UR is strengthened.

Implicit in Watson's analysis are two additional and rather strange assumptions about how the nervous system works. One is that the exercise of
the US-UR connection can reduce the synaptic threshold of another neuron
feeding into that reflex. The second assumption, which is implicit in his
treatment of conditioning and especially in his treatment of the learning of
motor sequences, is that there must be latent connections between all
possible stimuli and all possible responses. If no new pathways can be
created, then all potential pathways must already be present in the brain.
Although neither of these assumptions appears really outrageous, both
should be recognized as assumptions required by a Watsonian type of theory.

Further Developments

Two events in the history of psychology contrived to change Watson's
relationship to Pavlov. No sooner was Watson's 1914 book published than
he was elected president of the American Psychological Association, and

he was therefore obliged to come forth with some shattering new development for his presidential address. At the same time, Bechterev's famous *Objective Psychology* was translated into French (Bechterev, 1913). Let us recall that at that time Pavlov's work was not available in English. But Bechterev had also developed, more or less independently of Pavlov, a variety of conditioning procedures such as shock to finger to elicit a motor response, finger withdrawal, rather than the salivary response Pavlov was working with. Although Bechterev presented very little data, his methods were described, and he presented a general philosophy that was just as mechanistic and reductionist as Watson's own view of behavior. So inspired, Watson set about to demonstrate classical conditioning in his own laboratory. He was, however, unable to accomplish salivary conditioning, according to the report of Lashley (1916). The finger-withdrawal conditioning procedure of Bechterev had also raised a host of problems (Hamel, 1919); nevertheless, a number of experiments did work, particularly when Bechterev's procedures were appropriately modified. Watson was therefore able to tell the APA that classical conditioning was a reality, the optimum way to study learning, and that classical conditioning was the prototype for all learning. American psychology had begun to close the conditioning gap.

What Watson had found in his successful conditioning studies was that a tone paired with shock came, after a few pairings, to produce both a defensive reaction such as leg withdrawal and emotional responses such as altered heart rate. Watson did not distinguish between these two different kinds of behavior, apparently because of a conviction that all behavior changes are brought about by conditioning. Henceforth Watson identified himself as a conditioning theorist and popularized the language and ideology of conditioning, so that when Pavlov's work ultimately became available in 1927 it must have already seemed vaguely familiar. American psychology thus entered a period of a decade or more in which everyone spoke of conditioning and paid homage to Pavlov, even though there was little or no understanding of Pavlov's own work. "Conditioning" had come to mean simply the acquisition of S-R habits as a result of the stimulus and the response occurring together a number of times.

Curiously, in his later works Watson backed away from the law of frequency as the universal mechanism of learning. His 1919 book, which was undoubtedly the most widely read and influential of all his writings, stressed the necessity for all behavior to be analyzed in S-R terms, emphasized the reality of the nervous system and the unreality of the mind, described the importance of learning, but offered no unifying interpretation of learning. Indeed, Watson said that the law of frequency is purely speculative, and he afforded it no more discussion than the law of effect!

But though Watson did not long remain an advocate of his own learning theory, he was constant in defense of his general view of behavior. For example, he steadfastly rejected the mind, granting no place in psychology to any mental activity. All mental events were reduced to simple physiological processes like internal stimuli. It is interesting to speculate on whether Watson's unusual treatment of subjective experience was a result of his own peculiar subjective world. Herbert Langfeld reported (in a personal communication) a conversation he had once had with Watson. Langfeld asked him how he could possibly deny the subjective reality of images. How could he, for example, dismiss the reality of visual images in a dream. Langfeld said that Watson had settled the issue in one short sentence. He asked, "What is a dream?" It was Langfeld's belief that Watson did not have visual imagery and that he therefore really did not know what some of his critics were talking about. Be that as it may, it is certainly clear that Watson emphasized kinesthetic stimuli and the theoretical part that they play in the determination of behavior.

In an early experiment (Watson, 1907) he had run rats that were either normal, blind, deaf, or asnomic (with no sense of smell) in a maze. He found that in each instance the animal showed essentially the same proficiency in learning the maze. He concluded therefore that none of these senses is an important part of the stimulus pattern involved in the maze habit. The critical stimuli therefore had to be from the one sense modality that he had not eliminated and that, for practical reasons, he could not eliminate: kinesthesis, the sense of the muscles. As Watson continued to develop the implications of behaviorism, unobserved kinesthetic stimuli were to play an ever-increasing part in his explanation of behavior. They were responsible, as we have seen, for the illusion of thought, for images, and indeed for virtually all of what we think of as mediated behavior in humans.

It is interesting to observe that, although Watson persistently demanded scientific objectivity in psychology, he had to rely increasingly on kinesthetic feedback, the existence and properties of which were highly speculative. But on the other hand, it should be noted that stimuli feedback are not unobservable in principle, as are the contents of the mind. They are unobservable only in the practical sense that we do not have, or at least in his time Watson did not have, the instruments for observing them. Although we are still not very advanced in the technology necessary for measuring kinesthetic stimuli, there have been in the intervening years a number of demonstrations of the possibility that small implicit responses may be correlated with subjective experience. Although we do not know if the subjective experience is caused by the muscle feedback, we do know that the requisite muscle activity is often present. For example, Jacobson (1932) measured muscle twitches in the arm and observed that they occurred in the appropriate muscles when subjects were instructed to "think about" throwing a ball. More recently McGuigan (1973) found that when a psychotic patient thought he was hearing voices, simultaneous muscle-action potentials were measurable in his throat. McGuigan suggests that the hallucinating psychotic may not be so crazy after all if he is, in some sense, actually hearing a voice. He is simply misinterpreting its source. The real test, of course, would be to stimulate the subject's arm muscles or throat muscles electrically in the appropriate fashion and to have him report thinking of throwing a ball or hearing voices. We are awaiting such evidence.

Watson discussed instincts at some length because they are the original behavior out of which learned behavior is built. Instincts are simply S-R connections, in some instances complex S-R connections, which have appreciable strength prior to their first use. The structure of all behavior was, for Watson, reflected purely and simply in the structure of the nervous system and the S-R connections that it contains. The human being is a *tabula rasa*, a blank slate, on which experience must write everything. The human is distinguished only by the fact that he has more latent S-R connections, so that he can display more different kinds of behavior and be responsive to more shades of stimulation.

The idea that man is essentially nothing but the sum of his experience is an old one and has been defended by a number of important philosophers like John Locke and the associationists. It is in one sense a very humanitarian and liberal point of view because it implies that we cannot blame a man for any defect we may find in him. We must find fault instead with the world that has produced his offensive behavior. This message has become familiar to many through a recent book by Skinner (1971). The unique aspect of this message as Watson gave it is that it is not only psychologically necessary, as others before and since have claimed, but also physiologically necessary. It is demanded by the nature of the nervous system that ultimately must be the source of explanation for all our behavior.

Probably Watson's most famous experiment was the one reported with Rayner in 1920 in which fear was classically conditioned in a child, the famous Little Albert. Little Albert was a healthy, normal infant who attended a day-care center. The CS was a white rat; Little Albert's initial reaction to it was curiosity. He looked at it and reached out as if to touch it. The US was the sound made by hitting a heavy iron rail with a hammer.[1] It evidently made an awful noise because the UR consisted of startle, falling over, crying, and crawling away. After three pairings of the rat and the frightening noise, the rat alone came to elicit various fear and defensive behaviors. After six conditioning trials the sight of the rat evoked a strong

---

[1] It appears from Watson and Rayner's report that the rail was struck only when Albert was reaching for the rat. Although the procedure was ostensibly conditioning, there appears to have been a response contingency; if so, it was actually a punishment procedure.

emotional reaction. Watson and Rayner then put Albert through a series of generalization tests. He was presented with a white rabbit, a dog, and a fur coat. In each case Albert showed considerable generalization of the emotional reaction that had been conditioned to the rat. When tested a few days later in a different situation, Albert showed little emotion, but one additional conditioning trial brought out the fear in the new situation. Watson and Rayner discussed a number of procedures that might be used to decondition or neutralize little Albert's fear. Although various kinds of therapy are discussed, Little Albert was unfortunately removed from the day-care center before any therapy could be carried out.

It was concluded that the experiments with Little Albert show conclusively that directly conditioned emotional reactions persist, though with perhaps some loss of intensity, for a considerable period of time. Conditioned reactions were said to persist and to modify personality throughout life. Finally, it was noted that Albert was a stolid and phlegmatic individual, and it was suggested that had he been emotionally unstable to begin with he would have demonstrated much more emotional behavior. All these assertions were made, of course, in the absence of any evidence, but they were consistent with Watson's view of personality development.

Characteristically, Watson could not resist poking a little fun at psychoanalytic theory. He suggested that some years later Albert might go to an analyst to seek help for his strange fears and that he might even come to believe that his problem was the result of an unresolved Oedipal situation. But, said Watson, taking us into his confidence, we would know that his trouble was entirely caused by conditioning. So Watson had slain all the dragons and made psychology a science.

Watson's career in psychology ended tragically and abruptly in 1920. Scandal over a personal indiscretion necessitated his leaving his position at Johns Hopkins and soon leaving psychology altogether. He later wrote a book (Watson, 1925) and revised it, but this publication presented little that was new for learning theory. In the meantime, he had acquired an important place in the advertising industry, and some of the slogans and advertising campaigns that can still be recalled were his efforts.

Watson's Contributions and Impact

In his short career Watson had an enormous impact upon psychology. Although the behavioristic revolution would undoubtedly have proceeded quite nicely without his help and guidance, it probably would not have occurred so quickly; it certainly would not have been so spectacular. It was Watson, more than Pavlov or any other one man, who convinced psychologists that the real explanation of behavior lay in the nervous system and that as soon as we understood the brain just a little better most of the mysteries would disappear. He also made us believe that learning was the all-important determinant of everything we are. Our behavior, our personalities, our emotional dispositions are all learned behaviors.

Watson's theory of learning gave us a third important theoretical position. His theory shared with those of both Thorndike and Pavlov the assumption that learning is to be analyzed in terms of S-R connections. But his position was vastly simpler than Pavlov's and much more systematic than Thorndike's. But then, paradoxically, it was largely because of Watson and his influence that much of the language and some of the experimental procedures originally proposed by Pavlov became a standard part of the learning literature. And it was mainly because of Watson that so many psychologists came to believe that what they called conditioning was so important.

References for Further Reading

Watson's own major works make provocative and enjoyable reading. Of his books, *Behavior* (1914) deals with animal and comparative psychology, *Psychology from the Standpoint of a Behaviorist* (1919) goes on to humans, and *Behaviorism* (1925) deals with developmental psychology. In all his writings Watson presented an uncompromising S-R associationism that later writers, with more data, could not match. Watson told a poignant tale of success and tragedy in his short autobiography (Watson, 1936). One of his major efforts was his defense of the mechanistic philosophy, and one of his strongest allies in this effort was Weiss (1925), who has made as good an argument for it as anyone. One of mechanism's staunchest and most sophisticated opponents is Kantor (1947).

CHAPTER
4

GUTHRIE

Edwin R. Guthrie (1886–1959) was an important contributor to the development of learning theory, even though he did very little research himself and his theory instigated very little research. Initially his theoretical position was much like that of Watson, but it evolved over the years and developed a unique character of its own. Guthrie was primarily a teacher, and for a period of forty-five years he devoted much of his effort to the indoctrination of undergraduates at the University of Washington in the ways of psychology.

Guthrie originally prepared to be a philosopher, but he became interested enough in the experimental aspects of psychology to see that many of the problems that had traditionally been regarded as philosophical could be better approached experimentally. He says of his own training (Guthrie, 1959) that he was much influenced by the teachings of the philosopher Singer. Singer had claimed that many of the traditional problems of the mind can be translated immediately into problems of behavior and analyzed at that level. But the behaviorist revolution was in full swing, and when Guthrie's first works appeared they were strongly mechanistic. Smith and Guthrie (1921) wrote an introductory psychology textbook that was built very largely on the foundation that had been laid by Watson. Simple behavior was explained in terms of simple S-R connections, and complex behavior was explained in terms of a multitude of simple S-R connections. There was little innate organization in the theory, and there were no motivational principles. The flavor of the work was strictly Watsonian. If there was any difference, it was that Smith and Guthrie had somewhat more appreciation than Watson did of the complexity of behavior.

Smith and Guthrie recognized two kinds of learning. One, which they called "positive adaptation," was simply a recasting of Watson's law of frequency: The more frequently a particular response occurs in a given situation, the more likely it is to be repeated in that situation. Relatively little was said about the underlying mechanism; recognition of this kind of learning was little more than acceptance of the traditional concept of habit, which traditionally reflected only the frequency of occurrence.

The second kind of learning was a little more interesting. Smith and Guthrie called it conditioning, but it bore little resemblance to the learning that Pavlov studied. As Smith and Guthrie described it, all responses are initially elicited by specific unconditioned stimuli, but a response can become "conditioned" to a previously ineffective stimulus. The essence of conditioning is thus the substitution of the CS for the US in eliciting a response. In one sense, all learning has to fit this formula. If a response formerly did not occur in a given situation, but now does, then the situation or some part of it can be regarded as a substitute stimulus. Today we do not call learning "conditioning" unless it involves particular kinds of responses and unless it occurs under particular conditions, for example, as a specific result of pairing CS and US. But such subtleties were not recognized in the 1920s, and for some writers, including Smith and Guthrie, conditioning was virtually synonymous with learning. The word did not mean a particular kind of learning; it was merely a label signifying the writer's faith in the objective method, the reality of the nervous system, and the explanatory power of the S-R association. All behavior was to be explained simply in terms of its eliciting stimuli; no other explanatory principles were to be allowed. Specifically, learning involved nothing more than a change in the eliciting stimulus.

Whereas many of our learning theorists developed their ideas in protest against prevailing ideas, Guthrie was more conservative. His first theory, written in collaboration with Smith, was little more than a restatement of Watson's behavioristic position. It was, let me add, an attractive and influential statement, but its main effect was to extend and prolong Watson's views of behavior in general and of learning in particular. This simple, S-R, and mechanistic view of behavior was also to provide the background for Guthrie's own highly individual theory of learning, which first appeared in 1935. Guthrie was thus in a curious situation: The conceptual background for his 1935 theory had been provided in part by his own earlier efforts, which had kept the mechanistic tradition going. As we look at the 1935 theory, we should see it as a direct descendant of the mechanistic tradition begun by Pavlov and carried on by Watson.

The Theory of Learning

One of the most distinguishing features of Guthrie's 1935 theory is that, whereas all other theorists before and since have emphasized the gradualness of learning and conditioning, Guthrie maintained that learning occurs all at once. A given response becomes connected with a given stimulus in one trial. This assumption clearly contradicts the obvious fact of gradual acquisition observed in most learning tasks, but Guthrie evaded this difficulty by redefining the stimulus. We may view the whole situation as a stimulus, but in reality the experimental situation consists of a mass of stimulus elements that change from moment to moment. Millions of nerves pour sensory information into the brain at every instant. Visual stimuli change as the animal moves about the apparatus. Olfactory and auditory stimuli that may be irrelevant to solving the problem are nonetheless present in the total pattern of stimuli. There are additional stimuli arising as kinesthetic feedback from the animal's own muscle contractions as it moves about. The total pattern of stimuli is thus constantly changing. According to Guthrie, when a response occurs, it immediately becomes conditioned to whatever stimuli are present at the moment. The formation of this connection constitutes the learning that occurs on that trial. On the next trial a quite different stimulus pattern may exist, and the response may not be elicited. But if the response occurs again for some reason, it will be conditioned to the stimuli present in the new pattern. Over a series of trials the response gradually becomes conditioned to an ever-increasing population of possible stimuli, and as this happens the response becomes ever more probable. After a number of trials, when the response becomes connected to virtually all the stimuli that can occur in the situation, then the response will be almost inevitable. The gradual improvement in performance characteristic of most learning experiments is thus seen to arise from the complexity of the stimulus world. The learning process itself is simple and certain; it is the world that is complicated and uncertain.

Just as there are different stimulus elements that appear on different trials, there are common stimulus elements that persist over trials. Let us suppose, for example, that we have an experimental situation in which the color of the apparatus is constant and irrelevant. Consider then the relationship between this constant stimulus element and the ongoing stream of behavior, the different responses the animal makes in the situation. As it walks, looks, orients, grooms, or explores, these responses become conditioned to the total stimulus pattern that exists when they occur. What this means in the case of an irrelevant stimulus such as the color of the apparatus is that if one of these responses is at one instant conditioned to the color, then at the next instant, when another response occurs, the prior learning will be undone and the new response will become conditioned to it. Thus we have the strange concept of learning occurring all the time; whenever the animal is engaged in any behavior, the response is becoming attached to prevailing stimuli. But much of this learning is promptly undone and replaced by the learning of the next response. In short, Guthrie viewed learning not as a special event that occurs once in a while but as a continuing stream of minute connections being formed all the time. Whenever we make any response, we are conditioning it to prevailing stimuli and unconditioning some prior response.

There is another important implication of Guthrie's analysis. Although Guthrie gave no actual figures, there are alleged to be a great many (perhaps a million) stimulus elements impinging upon the animal at any instant. This analysis of the situation into microscopic stimulus elements means that the theoretical stimulus (those elements to which the response becomes attached) cannot be equated with the physical things we call stimulus objects. Indeed, it is often difficult to determine from Guthrie's theory how the theoretical stimulus can be specified. So, in spite of the apparent objectivity of Guthrie's S-R analysis, there is a serious question about how objective the all-important S term is.

In all of the earlier theorists we can see a remarkable correspondence between the kind of process that was assumed to explain learning and the kind of experimental arrangements that were imposed upon animals. In each case the theoretical mechanism mirrors the experimental procedures. To illustrate the point, consider Thorndike's cat in the puzzle box. The experimental procedure could be described by an S-R-S* paradigm in which the stimulus, the response, and the "effect" of the response are all well defined as observable events. In Thorndike's theory the S* strengthens the connection between the S and the R. Thus the increased probability of the observed response in the experimental situation was assumed to be mirrored by an underlying neural connection between the stimulus and the response. Pavlov's experimental paradigm was different from Thorndike's, but Pavlov included the same kind of correspondence between experiment and theory. He paired stimuli until the response to one began to occur to the other; then the new reaction was explained theoretically on the assumption that, through pairing, the stimuli had become equivalent. The theoretical pairing mirrors the procedural pairing. In Watson's theory learning consisted of new S-R connections, and, again, if we watch what happens in a Watsonian experiment we see that a stimulus and then a response occur. The empirical fact that the response becomes increasingly probable in the presence of that stimulus was attributed to the strengthening of an S-R connection. Again, the theory reflects the data of the experiment. All these theorists had proposed theories that, in effect, simply redescribed their data. But Guthrie was different. He was describing not immediately observable events but a world of his own imagination. There are millions of stimulus elements, a few thousand of which become conditioned on any one trial.

Earlier theorists may have been overoptimistic about the simplicity of the learning process and of the various processes, such as learning, that they thought controlled behavior. But by the 1930s it had become apparent that behavior is really rather complex and is governed by many different kinds of determinants. It is as if behavior were intrinsically unpredictable, so that there has to be some part of any viable theory that is complex or uncertain enough to prevent us from making direct predictions of behavior with it! We may be able to predict the average case; we may be able to predict the rate of behavior that occurs over a period of time, but it seems unlikely that we can ever develop models that will tell us precisely what a particular organism will do at a particular moment. The remedy appears to be a theory that is intrinsically probabilistic or a theory that introduces unpredictability into the causal analysis of behavior.

Unpredictability may reside in the syntax of a theory (how the terms of the theory are hypothesized to relate to each other) or in the semantics of a theory (how the theoretical terms are related to observational data). Now the syntax of Guthrie's theory is simple and straightforward: Responses become conditioned to stimulus elements. That is all there is to it. The complexity and the inherent unpredictability appear in the semantics. Recall how important kinesthetic feedback stimuli were assumed to be to Watson's theory. They were necessary in his theory (for example, to explain awareness), but they were not observable. Guthrie seems to have taken this principle of unknowability one step farther. If no one can know what stimulus elements are going to impinge upon an animal at any instant, Guthrie can assert that, if the elements were known, then we would find them simply and directly related to the animal's observable behavior. In practice we do not know what elements are present, so behavior remains unpredictable. In summary, we can say that Guthrie retained the simple theoretical syntax of Watson, but he made the semantics complex enough, and perhaps untestable enough, to be consistent with the obvious complexity and unpredictability of behavior.

Applications of the Theory

One phenomenon that follows neatly from Guthrie's view of behavior is generalization. For Guthrie it was not necessary to think of the test stimulus as "similar" to the training stimulus or as related to it on some psychological dimension. Because all stimuli are constituted of a number of different elements, generalization can be attributed to the number of common elements shared by the training situation and the test situation. For example, if an animal is trained to respond in the presence of, let us say, a million discrete bits of sensory information and then encounters a stimulus pattern that contains only a half-million of the same elements, the probability of responding has to be somewhat reduced. In a test situation containing only a quarter-million of the original stimulus elements, the probability of the response must be further reduced. Thus, according to Guthrie, vague concepts like similarity are replaced by the precise notion of partial identity. Unfortunately, this precision is largely illusory because we have no way to quantify the number of identical elements. Our best approximation to such quantification is still in terms of stimulus similarity. But Guthrie's analysis had the conceptual advantage that generalization was not viewed as a phenomenon separate from learning itself. Generalization was part and parcel of the learning experiment, simply because from one trial to the next there could be only partial identity of the total stimulus patterns. In effect, any learning experiment really consists of a series of generalization trials.

The analysis of discrimination learning follows immediately. Discrimination is simply a case in which one response gradually becomes conditioned to one population of stimulus elements, while another response is becoming conditioned to another set. But there is an interesting complication here. Because an animal can produce some stimulation by means of its own behavior, particularly orienting responses that direct the eyes and the ears, these orienting responses may be a critical part of what the animal learns. The proper orientation of a rat in a black-white discrimination may be the essential part of the learning in this situation, and approaching the correct stimulus may be a trivial part of the task once the rat has learned to look at it.

There is no reinforcement mechanism in Guthrie's system; the consequence of a response is not assumed to have any direct influence on the strength of the response. The apparent response-strengthening effect of reinforcement is explained by Guthrie, as are many behavioral phenomena, in terms of change in the pattern of stimulation. Let us suppose that an animal is in a situation S_1 in which no response has been conditioned to enough stimulus elements to make it occur regularly. Under these conditions a series of different responses will occur, each one will become conditioned to the elements existing at the moment, and then each response will become unconditioned as it is replaced by the next response. (The different responses occur, of course, because they are elicited by new stimulus elements that appear often as the results of the animal's behavior.) This succession of responses can continue indefinitely. But let us suppose we have arranged the experimental situation so that when one particular response, R_1, occurs the situation is so changed that the animal is no longer in S_1 but in a new situation, S_2. Thus if R_1 is programmed to produce a dramatic change in the situation, the connection formed between S_1 and R_1 will be preserved. Further responses cannot be conditioned to the elements of S_1 because these elements, or at least a substantial proportion of them, no longer exist.

A reinforcer is therefore merely an event that produces a substantial change in the total stimulus pattern. Encountering food in the goal box or in the hopper of the Skinner box and opening the door of the puzzle box are presumably dramatic enough changes in the stimulus situation so that the immediately prior response remains connected to the immediately prior stimulus situation. Maze learning can be explained in the same way; a correct response moves the animal from one segment of the maze to the next where there are a number of different stimulus elements. So the correct response is learned. Let us suppose that, instead of making the correct response, the animal makes some competing response, such as grooming. Grooming would then be learned, but, when the stimuli that initiated the grooming are gone, it will stop and be replaced by some other response. Only the correct response can change the situation. Whereas other competing behaviors come and go, only the correct response will become gradually conditioned to more and more stimulus elements—because it is consistently the last response to occur in their presence. Because Guthrie's theory has no need for a reinforcement mechanism, because learning is assumed to depend only upon the stimulus and response occurring together, it is called a "contiguity" theory.

According to Guthrie's analysis, it should make little difference what kind of event produces the stimulus change; an electric shock, for example, should be just as effective a change as the presentation of food. But we know that, if electric shock is made contingent upon the animal's running into the goal box, it will quickly stop running. So there are instances in which stimulus change fails to protect the prior S-R connection and actually produces behavior that effectively competes with the response and prevents its further occurrence. Guthrie was well aware of this problem and dealt with it in his treatment of punishment. But he also considered the following mythical experiment (one that was discussed but apparently never run). An animal runs down an alley, and as it comes to a certain point a trap door opens, and the animal drops out of the apparatus and into a chamber that is wholly different from the original alley. Guthrie predicted that running in this situation would be learned, and he described a number of parallel situations, common in every-day life, in which we acquire habitual ways of responding even when the consequences of our behavior are undesirable.

Guthrie's conception of learning as a process that is continually going on and continually being undone leads very simply and directly to an explanation of extinction. Let us suppose that in a given situation, let us call it S_1, we require a certain response, R_1, to obtain food. We have just seen that the presentation of food so changes the situation (making it S_2) that the connection between S_1 and R_1 is preserved. In extinction there is no more food, so there is no more S_2; therefore there is no more stimulus change to protect the S_1-R_1 connection. Accordingly R_1 becomes replaced by other behavior like grooming and exploring. So the previously learned response is lost when food is withheld.

Motivation

Guthrie dealt with the phenomenon of motivation, which was becoming an important aspect of behavior by the 1930s, in purely associative terms. He had no motivational concepts *per se*, only a special new class of stimuli. For each physiological condition such as hunger or fear there are, he said, characteristic internal stimuli. These stimuli are unique in that they are persistent and cannot be changed by the animal moving about in space. They can only be altered by the animal engaging in some specific con-summatory behavior. For example, the stimuli arising from hunger can be eliminated only by eating. The animal must learn to eat when it is hungry because only eating can change the internal stimuli. The animal also learns to make any other responses that precede eating because the learning of these responses is also protected by the change that food makes in the situation. Similarly, many of the behaviors that makes an animal appear hungry—moving about, gnawing on the front of the cage, scratching at the apparatus, and many kinds of behavior that look like "eager anticipation" of food—occur because they too have become conditioned to the persisting hunger stimuli. Because these stimuli help maintain behavior throughout the learning task, Guthrie called them *maintaining stimuli*. With the postu-lation of maintaining stimuli, which persist and maintain whatever behavior becomes conditioned to them, Guthrie had no need for a concept of drive, instinct, or any other kind of motivational principle. Again we can see that a whole class of behavior phenomena—motivation—is explained in terms of the complexity of the total stimulus pattern.

We must consider one further application of Guthrie's theory. Suppose we have two situations, S_1 and S_2, in which the animal is required to learn R_1 and R_2 respectively. If the two situations are quite different, with few common stimulus elements, the animal will just acquire the two responses, each independent of the other. But let us suppose that there are many elements in common between S_1 and S_2. Then each response will tend to occur not only in its proper situation but in the other situation as well. Suppose, for example, that an alley is similar to the goal box and that R_2 is eating in the goal box. If food were suddenly introduced in the alley we would expect the animal to have a tendency to eat it because of the tendency for the eating response to be elicited by alley cues. In the absence of food in the alley there is still some predisposition for the animal to make the eating response or whatever other response occurs in the goal box. We can call such behavior anticipatory responses. They can result in a short-circuiting of a sequence of responses. Let us suppose that there is a long series of behaviors that the animal must produce, as in running a maze; then there will be a tendency for later responses in the sequence to move forward, so that the rat will make anticipatory errors. A number of writers since Guthrie have developed similar views of anticipatory behavior and the role that this type of short-circuiting mechanism can play in behavior. When we discuss Hull in Chapter 6 we will see that he and his followers have attached tremendous importance to such a mechanism. The principal use Guthrie made of it was in his interpretation of punishment.

Punishment

We have noted that earlier theorists had not come to any consensus on the mechanisms involved in punishment and that there was little understanding of why the punishment procedure was sometimes extremely effective and at other times quite ineffective in weakening behavior. Guthrie offered a plausible explanation of these discrepancies. His interpretation of punishment can perhaps best be illustrated by one of his own examples. Guthrie considers a modern, liberal young mother who decides to raise her child permissively; she will not use punishment unless she really has to. But, she decides, one rule is inviolate and must be backed up by punishment: The family lives on a busy street, and the mother decides quite reasonably that the one punishable offense will be the child's walking out on the street. So the mother coolly and rationally decides that such behavior will be punished in the child's own best interest (children are always punished in their own best interests). One day it happens. The mother sees her child running toward the street. She chases him and catches up with him just in time to slap him. Having established the rule, the mother has no question about whether to slap the child—that has already been settled; but there is one very important, crucial question, according to Guthrie. *Where* should the child be slapped? It is tempting to slap him on the rear end because that is convenient when the mother has run up behind him, but it would be exactly the wrong thing to do. Guthrie observes that what the young mother must do is to reach around in front of the child and slap him in the face. The reason is that a blow in the face will make him recoil, and the recoil response will then become attached to all the stimuli presented by the street. If the child is hit on the behind he is likely to lurch forward, and if that response is learned then sooner or later the child will be lost on the street.

Again we can think of the chaining of responses. The S_1 situation is the sight of the street in the distance, and there is some initial inclination to make R_1, approach, to this stimulus pattern. S_2 is the stimulus elements presented by the street up close together with the slap, and R_2 is the recoil reaction. R_2 is immediately attached to S_2 because of the great stimulus change. Now, to the extent that S_2 contains similar stimulus elements to S_1, the recoil reaction will generalize back to S_1 and will effectively compete with the originally elicited approach behavior. Guthrie thus tells us that punishment will be effective in weakening some behavior if and only if two conditions are met: First, the punishing stimulus itself must elicit a response, R_2, that is incompatible with the punished response, R_1, as recoiling from a slap is incompatible with running forward; second, S_2, the stimulus situation that elicits the competing response, must share a number of stimulus elements with S_1, the situation in which the punished response occurs.

As with most of the predictions from Guthrie's theories, the implications of his analysis of punishment have generated relatively little research. But one study, reported almost thirty years later by Fowler and Miller (1963), provides rather nice confirmation of his analysis. Fowler and Miller trained groups of rats to run in an alley for food. A control group simply ran and obtained food. The learning curve shown in Figure 4.1 reveals an orderly reduction in running time on successive trials. One experimental group received a mild electric shock to the front feet just as the animals reached the food cup. These animals showed retarded running relative to the controls; they seemed reluctant to run. The traditional view of punishment suggests that, with some positive reinforcement and some punishment, the rat should compromise and run more slowly. But the important group

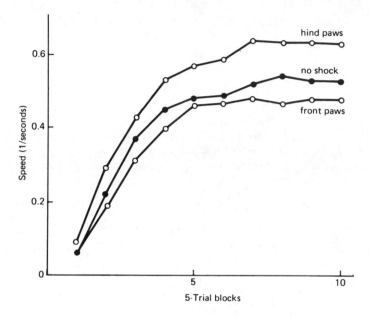

Fig. 4.1 Speed of alley running in groups of rats shocked near the goal. The groups received either hind-paw or front-paw shock; controls received no shock. (From Fowler & Miller, Facilitation and inhibition of runway performance by hind- and fore-paw shock of various intensities. Journal of Comparative and Physiological Psychology, *1963, 56, 801–805. Copyright 1963 by the American Psychological Association. Reprinted by permission.)*

Fowler and Miller ran gave results that defied the traditional view. These rats were shocked on the hind feet just as they reached the food cup. Their performance was facilitated relative to the controls. All conditions were the same for the three groups except whether they were shocked and where the shock was applied. It turns out that the rat's reaction to shock to the front feet is to recoil, to pull back. The slower running is predicted from Guthrie's theory, not because the rat is in conflict when there are both food and shock at the end of the alley, but merely because it is subject to response competition. It is partly running because of the food and partly pulling back because of the shock. On the other hand, the reaction to shock to the hind feet is to lurch forward. As the rat traverses the alley, it is partly running for food and partly lurching forward because of the shock. It should be emphasized that the results reported by Fowler and Miller probably depend upon using exactly the right kind and intensity of shock. Certainly a more intense punishing stimulus would inhibit all running. Nonetheless, the results provide nice confirmation of Guthrie's remarkable prediction.

Guthrian Experiments

Guthrie himself was not primarily an experimenter, but two noteworthy experiments have been conducted to test his theory, and produced good support for it. Learning should occur more rapidly in a situation in which there is great constancy of the total stimulus pattern from one trial to the next. A classical conditioning experiment in which all stimulus events are carefully controlled should therefore produce faster learning than a free operant situation in which there is more opportunity for random stimulus variation to occur. Voeks (1954) conducted a classical conditioning experiment and took special precautions to ensure the constancy of the stimulus conditions. Even the subject's internal stimulus environment was held constant; Voeks used a system of ready signals so that the subject could initiate each trial when he felt properly relaxed and ready for it. Using a bell as a CS and an eye blink as the CR, Voeks found very rapid acquisition of the conditioned response in each subject. A typical subject might show no conditioning at all for the first six trials and then on the seventh trial show the CR in full strength. Most subjects demonstrated at some point a sharp transition between no conditioning and full conditioning.

Voeks' results raise an interesting point. Let us suppose that we were to look at the performance of individual subjects in a learning experiment and we found that different subjects showed a sharp transition after different numbers of trials, as shown in Figure 4.2. Suppose that now we were simply to pool the results from the different subjects to determine the average performance for the group. We would obtain a group-average learning curve like that in Figure 4.2, which would look very little like the learning curve of any one subject. The rapid transitional learning found by Voeks suggests that the typical gradual learning curve may often be an artifact of statistically averaging the performances of subjects that are at different stages in learning. Certainly the average results for a group need not reflect acquisition in individual subjects.

A second experiment which provided direct support for Guthrie's theory was reported by Guthrie and Horton (1946). It was a variation of the old cat-in-the-puzzle-box trick. There was a box with a door that had to be opened, and food was just outside. Projecting up from the center of the floor was a pole, which was ingeniously arranged so that when it was tilted

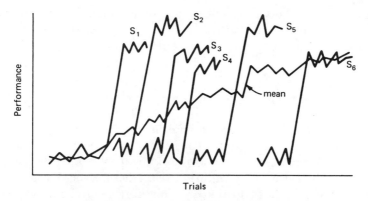

Fig. 4.2   Diagram showing how a number of sub-jects all showing one-trial learning, and some vari-ability, could produce a relatively smooth and con-tinuous group learning curve.

in any direction two things would happen: The door would open so that the cat could go out and eat, and the animal was photographed at the instant the criterion response was made. The data from the experiment con-sisted of a series of pictures of the response that occurred on each trial. These pictures showed a peculiar fixity or stereotypy to the animal's be-havior. If we know how the cat moved the pole on trial 13, then we can make a very good guess how it will move the pole on trial 14: It will make precisely the same response. In one series of trials the cat might bump the pole with its shoulder. Suddenly the behavior changes, and there follows a series of trials in which the pole is hit with a paw. Then this pattern is replaced by bumping with the head. The interesting point is that when the pattern changes it changes all at once. There is no gradual transition, and there is no gradual acquisition of skillful movements. We do not know what produces the transitions. Why is a particular cat a shoulder bumper on one series of trials and a head bumper on the next series of trials? Pre-sumably the stimulus situation changes in some way. Although the shifts in response patterns were difficult for Guthrie to explain, the stereotyped nature of the behavior over a series of trials provided support for his unique view of learning.

Guthrie was inclined to emphasize the fixity of behavior both in reporting this research and in many of his popular writings. He appeared to be fascinated by the fact that we often do stupid and maladaptive things. Our behavior often fails to reflect our intelligence; often it appears to be stereo-typed and mechanical. The cat in the puzzle box does not come to respond with appreciably greater speed or greater efficiency or more finesse over a series of trials. We find instead that it makes the same muscle contractions on successive trials. This mechanical type of responding gave support to Guthrie's theory, just as the apparent flexibility and adaptiveness of behavior have given support to other psychologists' theories.

Guthrie's Contribution and Impact

Guthrie himself did little research, and he had few students to carry out research on his ideas. Although he taught great numbers of students, they were mostly undergraduates (there was no Ph.D. program at the University of Washington during most of Guthrie's years there). Nor did he have any real disciples to carry forth his ideas. A few former students became outspoken defenders of the theory (for example, Sheffield, 1949; Voeks, 1950), but their efforts initiated little further activity.

There are perhaps two main reasons why Guthrie's work had relatively little immediate impact. One was that it generated little research. The second reason was that when the theory was formulated in 1935 it stood well outside the mainstream of developments in behavior theory. In the 1930s many theorists had begun to attribute great importance to the phenomena of motivation; theorists such as Tolman and Hull could not conceive of principles of learning without supplementary principles of motivation (see Chapters 5 and 6). But while this new impetus was entering into behavior theory, Guthrie was boldly proclaiming that motivational concepts are not necessary for the explanation of behavior. Motives were said to be simply a different class of stimuli. During the 1930s Thorndike's law of effect was being reinstated as a powerful principle of learning; theorists such as Hull and Skinner were soon to make it the fundamental principle of learning. But while reinforcement was becoming theoretically important, Guthrie was proclaiming that we did not need a concept of reinforcement. A reinforcer is simply a change of stimulation. While other learning theorists were becoming increasingly concerned with semantic questions, for example, how to define stimulus and response, Guthrie was relatively unconcerned about these matters. He was not committed to any specific response unit; a response could be a small thing like the twitch of a muscle or a molar event like driving downtown. Theorists like Tolman and Hull were complicating the syntax of their theories in order to deal with the complexity of behavior, but Guthrie retained the simplest syntax and put all the complexity into the definition of the stimulus.

Thus Guthrie's theory had an anachronistic quality when it first appeared in 1935, and this quality was more striking when the second edition of his book appeared, with little change, in 1952. In some respects it stood as a direct continuation of a theoretical program initiated by Pavlov and continued by Watson. Guthrie shared with these earlier theorists the conviction that all behavior is to be explained purely in terms of S-R associations. He included no motivation, no reinforcement, nothing mentalistic-sounding, nothing but Ss and Rs, especially Ss.

But in some respects the theory has had considerable impact. Guthrie's analysis of extinction, punishment, and other phenomena in terms of competing responses has been widely accepted. His theoretical formulation remains the definitive statement of a purely S-R interpretation of behavior and of a pure contiguity theory of learning. As such it has considerable intellectual interest, regardless of how effectively it can be applied to practical problems or how adequately it can be applied to theoretical problems. And, as the definitive statement of the contiguity position, Guthrie's theory has provided the framework for further theoretical development of contiguity theory; that is, it has provided the background for subsequent theoretical models in which learning is attributed to contiguity rather than to reinforcement. Let us consider two examples.

Later Developments

William K. Estes was not a student of Guthrie's (he originally worked with Skinner), but in 1950 he proposed a mathematical model of learning that embodies a number of Guthrian learning principles and that has had the effect of greatly expanding and clarifying Guthrie's original position and generating a good deal of research. One of the basic assumptions in Estes' model is that there is a large population of potentially effective stimuli that can impinge upon the organism but that at any one time only a small proportion of these stimuli is actually present. The subject, in effect, is constantly drawing samples from the population of stimuli. Estes assumed that this sample constitutes a fixed proportion of the total (usually designated by the Greek letter θ) and that these samples are drawn randomly, so that the probability of sampling a given element on one trial does not depend upon what happened on the previous trial. Another basic assumption in Estes' model is that a response is immediately conditioned to all stimuli that are sampled when the response occurs, that is, on each trial.

Suppose then that on the nth trial there is some definite probability P_n that the subject will sample one of the stimulus elements to which the response R has already been conditioned. This probability, P_n, also has to be the probability that R will occur on the nth trial. Certain specific implications about what will happen on the $n+1$st trial follow. There will be an increase in response probability, that is, $P_{n+1} - P_n$ will be positive, if the response occurs on the nth trial and a randomly sampled element is not already connected to R. The probability of R will then increase by the amount $P_{n+1} - P_n = \theta (1 - P_n)$ if R occurs on the nth trial. If R fails to occur on the nth trial, there will be a loss in the probability of the response if the subject samples an element to which R is already conditioned. This loss will be $P_{n+1} - P_n = -\theta P_n$ if R does not occur on the nth trial.

These two equations constitute the body of Estes' model. The underlying psychological principles are basically Guthrian, but the use Estes makes of the model is quite unlike a Guthrian analysis. The probability of a response at a particular time is an objective datum, and the data of an experiment may or may not be consistent with the equations, so Estes' model is empirically verifiable. It sometimes turns out that θ is not constant; it sometimes turns out that P_n does not increase in the predicted manner; sometimes the model does not predict accurately what happens following a correct and an incorrect response. Furthermore, Estes' equations can be manipulated to yield a variety of implications that go far beyond the kind of situation from which they were derived and that are therefore not intuitively obvious. Thus, Estes has teased out a variety of deductions about discrimination learning in which two responses to two classes of stimuli must be learned, and about probabilistic learning when two responses are reinforced with different probabilities. In the latter case Estes' theory leads to the prediction that the response probabilities should match the reinforcement probabilities. Such matching is often (but not always) found. The results thus sometimes confirm the basic assumptions and the mathematical derivations.

Although Estes' basic psychological assumptions about the learning process are very Guthrian, his method of developing these assumptions gives him two enormous advantages over Guthrie's original method of theorizing. (Consider how the probability-matching outcome could possibly have been predicted from or explained by Guthrie's original theory.) One advantage is quantification. By sticking to the basic equations and derivations from them, Estes can make precise quantitative predictions; he can also check the predictions against the data and test the various parts of the theory. There is a peculiar untestability to Guthrie's own formulations. Often they appear to be little more than affirmations of his faith that responses are caused by stimuli. If a response persists, then there must be a persistent core of stimuli; if the response changes, then the stimulus pattern must have changed. In short, Estes' approach is by its very nature quantitative, whereas Guthrie's approach had been qualitative.

The second advantage of Estes' method is that all the terms that enter into the theory are either directly observable (like P_n) or easily estimated from observable data (like θ, which is estimated by finding the best-fitting function for the data). In Guthrie's formulations many of the responses and most of the stimuli that enter into theoretical discussion seem to be not empirical events at all but hypothetical events in the nervous system. In

Guthrie's time one had to take a stand on the issue of mentalism versus mechanism, and Guthrie's stand was well over on the mechanistic side. But, by presenting a mathematical model that merely *describes* learning, Estes remains neutral on this issue. Both P_n and θ are obviously descriptive of the subject's behavior and nothing more. We see clearly, perhaps for the first time, that a mathematical model must necessarily be neutral on the issue of mentalism versus mechanism. For this reason mathematical representation of a learning experiment is perhaps the ideal way to avoid all the troublesome problems of mentalism and mechanism.

A model, any kind of model, is supposed to represent the thing being modeled in some particular way, and no one expects it to represent the real thing in all respects. If it did, it would be the real thing itself and not a model. For example, a model airplane is like the real thing in that it is the same *shape*. It "looks like" the real thing, but upon closer inspection it is found to be quite different from the real thing. It is a lot smaller, and it is made of paper and balsa wood instead of aluminum. But these differences are acceptable; as long as the toy plane looks like a real plane it is an acceptable model. The point of a model, however, is that, in being like the real thing in one respect, it may surprise us and give us "additional benefits" by being like the real thing in ways that we had not anticipated. For example, if we put a rubber band in our toy plane and wind it up, we may discover that it also flies. It may not fly in precisely the same way or make as much noise as the real plane, but nonetheless it flies, and this fact may be a very useful additional benefit. For example, if we put the model plane in a wind tunnel, we may discover that it shares a variety of aerodynamic properties with the real airplane. In other words, the surprising similarities, the additional benefits, of a model may turn out to be very great benefits indeed.

And so it is with a mathematical model of learning. We can work with the model with pencil and paper and derive predictions that could not, or would not, have been readily made from observing real subjects in real learning experiments. And this fact, too, may be a very great benefit. Estes (1958) also extended Guthrie's analysis of motivation in terms of maintaining stimuli in a much more nearly complete and satisfying way than Guthrie had been able to achieve. Although Estes has recently gone on to other kinds of theoretical models, for many years he renewed interest in Guthrie's principles of learning.

Another offshoot of Guthrie's contiguity theory is elicitation theory, as it is designated by M. Ray Denny and his colleagues. The first theoretical statements (Denny & Adelman, 1955; Maatsch, 1954) were primarily concerned with an interpretation of extinction based on competing responses. In an experiment reported by Adelman and Maatsch (1955), two groups of rats were trained to run into a box for food, and then extinction was begun;

that is, food was withheld. One group was permitted to jump through the top of the box to escape the presumably frustrating situation, whereas the other group was required to back up through the door and out of the box. The back-up group stopped running almost immediately, whereas the jump-out group continued to run to the box and jump out of it for many trials. Adelman and Maatsch argued that in each instance the animal learned to make that response in the alley that it had made in the goal box, jumping out on one hand and backing out on the other. Because the jump-out response is compatible with running, running continues to occur. But the back-up response is incompatible with running, and, because it generalizes from the goal box to the alley, its occurrence in the alley effectively competes with the running response.

Denny and Adelman (1955) have raised the more basic question of why in such a situation the running response was acquired originally. Their answer, which constitutes the fundamental premise of elicitation theory, is that approach behavior, or going forward, is elicited by food in the goal box. It is not that food is literally a reinforcer, a special kind of event that stamps in an S-R connection, or that it provides a goal to which the animal's behavior is directed. Reinforcers are simply events that initially elicit particular kinds of behavior like approach. Approach then becomes conditioned to other stimuli in the situation. This interpretation of reinforcement has been applied to a variety of phenomena, including the reinforcing effect of electrical brain stimulation, by Glickman and Schiff (1967).

Denny's elicitation theory is related to Guthrie's learning theory in the sense that it is a contiguity interpretation of learning in which reinforcers have no special properties other than that they elicit particular behaviors. A second point of similarity is the emphasis given to the generalization of a later response in a chain to earlier stimulus situation. For example, elicitation theory predicts that the extinction results of Adelman and Maatsch would be quite different if the alley and the goal box had been perceptually distinctive. If one had been painted black and the other white, both the persistence of running in the jump-out group and the rapid loss of running in the back-up group should have been much less marked.

Recently Denny has extended elicitation theory to deal with the very challenging problem of avoidance learning (Denny, 1971). The basic concept is that after some period of time following the termination of shock the rat will relax, and that once relaxation responses have become conditioned to a particular set of environmental stimuli the rat will approach such stimuli. In effect, the safe part of the apparatus will appear to be a positive reinforcer. What makes avoidance learning difficult in many avoidance situations is, first, that relaxation behavior may generalize back to the danger situation and interfere with running away and, second, that running away may generalize to the safe part of the apparatus and compete with relaxation. Avoidance performance has been shown to be influenced by the similarity between the danger area and the safe area and by the period of time in which the animal is permitted to relax in the safe area (Denny, 1971). This ingenious interpretation of avoidance learning seems to have considerable viability, and, in Denny's hands, it can explain a variety of phenomena that have been extremely troublesome to other theorists. A major point of difference between elicitation theory and its Guthrian ancestor is that Guthrie always emphasized the stimulus. Elicitation theory emphasizes the response and requires little detailed analysis of the stimulus elements contributing to a given situation. Attention is directed to the animal's response in a given situation because it is, after all, the response that is generalized from one situation to the next, and it is ultimately the response that we must explain.

In conclusion, we can observe that Guthrie's learning theory is built around one simple idea: Behavior is explained when the eliciting stimulus is found. When the stimulus cannot be found, then an appropriate stimulus, or even class of stimuli, is postulated to exist. The intrinsic appeal of Guthrie's theory and perhaps the reason that it has endured, even if it has not been very popular, is its conceptual parsimony. The theory occupies a unique place in our narrative because it is clearly a logical extension, almost a necessary extension, of the earlier theories of Pavlov and Watson, yet, subjected to only slight modification, it provides forty years later the substance of contemporary positions like those of Estes and Denny.

References for Further Reading

In contrast with our other theorists, Guthrie did not separate the experimental explication of his theory from its practical application. His theoretical writings draw heavily upon everyday experience and the casual observation of behavior. Thus, *The Psychology of Learning* (1935) and *The Psychology of Human Conflict* (1938) are easy reading and convey a sense of relevance. The main substance of the theory can be found in two short papers (Guthrie, 1930; Voeks, 1950). There is little biographical material on Guthrie, but in his last theoretical statement (Guthrie, 1959) he provided some insight into his background and a rather personal last look at his own contribution. The best short introduction to mathematical learning theory is the chapter on this topic in Hilgard and Bower (1974).

CHAPTER
5

TOLMAN

Edward C. Tolman (1886–1959) stood with Guthrie well outside the mainstream of learning theory. But he did not stand with Guthrie. Their theoretical positions were antithetical at many points. Tolman's view of behavior was molar rather than molecular. He was strongly opposed to S-R associationism and tried to replace it with a system emphasizing the adaptive, creative, and intelligent aspects of behavior. His system was therefore characterized as cognitive. Tolman was so opposed to mechanism that he was often accused of being mentalistic. Nearly all of Tolman's professional career was spent at the University of California at Berkeley; his writings and the mass of research that came out of the Berkeley laboratory made it the center of cognitive psychology for a number of years.

The major impetus to Tolman forming his view of behavior was the rising popularity of Watsonian behaviorism. The early behaviorists, Pavlov, Watson, and Guthrie, had all sought to dispel mentalism from psychology and to make psychology into a scientific discipline with objective methods. They admonished us not to speculate about what is going on in the mind of man or animal. The data of psychology were to be just the observations of behavior. Tolman was always sympathetic with this strategy, but he observed that the early behaviorists had all confused the objective method of science with a mechanistic philosophy. One does not have to be a mechanist in order to study behavior, to be objective or deterministic, or to follow the precepts of science.

The S-R association, which has been endorsed and advocated by almost all behaviorists except for Tolman, is in no sense an empirical fact; it is not an objective datum. It is an inference or conjecture about the physiological machinery that produces behavior. So, although Tolman could go along with the early behaviorists' emphasis upon behavior, he saw the introduction of the mechanistic philosophy to explain behavior as unwarranted and undesirable. Behavior is no better or more scientifically explained by S-R connections than by thinking and willing. In either case a philosophical doctrine about the underlying reality is superimposed upon the systematic observation and analysis of behavior. The philosophy must even bias how we observe behavior. To be a behaviorist all one has to do is to look at behavior and to try to discern its lawfulness. Tolman was thus a different kind of behaviorist. He believed in the elucidation of behavioral principles but rejected the mechanistic framework in which behaviorism had been cast. He rejected the S-R unit as a means of describing or explaining behavior and rejected most of the other assumptions characteristic of the associationistic approach.

Tolman's Perception of Behavior

In his first theoretical papers Tolman (1920, 1923) argued that the observation of behavior reveals that it is generally directed toward some goal. The hungry rat directs its behavior toward food. Its behavior appears to have a purpose. This appearance of purpose does not mean that the animal has a conscious purpose, a plan or intention, or that it is aware of its goal. It is simply to say that behavior itself appears to be focused on some end, like food. Because the animal's behavior looks as if the animal has a purpose in the more traditional sense of the word, Tolman coined a new term "purposive" to describe it. Literally it is *as if* the animal had a purpose. "Purposive" thus describes behavior, whereas "purpose" is a hypothetical mental event. When we watch animals going about their daily business, their behavior seems to be directed to certain outcomes. It is as if the behavior were guided by the outcome, and Tolman often spoke of this view of behavior as a kind of descriptive teleology.

One of the chief things that Tolman saw in behavior was its flexibility. Behavior is not invariant. There are, to be sure, fixed reactions to certain stimuli, which we call "reflexive," but they constitute a relatively small and uninteresting part of an animal's total behavior. Most of the time the details of behavior are unpredictable. We do not know what response will be made at the next instant. Behavior has an intrinsic flexibility or looseness; to use Tolman's expression, "behavior is docile." The idea that stimuli elicit responses implies a kind of necessity, compulsion, or mechanical action that simply is not characteristic of behavior except in certain situations, such as a Pavlovian experiment, that are not representative of behavior in general. For example, if we watch a bird building a nest we see that it flies off and finds a twig, carries the twig back to the nest, and adjusts it in many different ways until it is just right. Then it flies off and obtains a different twig, comes back, and adjusts it again in a somewhat different way. In picking out twigs the bird may sort through a half-dozen before it selects one. All this time the bird's behavior appears to be extremely flexible; it does not look reflexive. The bird flies to a place where there are appropriate twigs, then selects and carries the right twig back to the nest. All this time it is avoiding predators, flying around obstacles, and taking time out to eat and to defend its territory. Tolman (1923) argued that the only thing that seems fixed about instinctive behavior is the end product, the finished nest, mating with the female, eating the food, or whatever. In instinctive behaviors, Tolman tells us, the end is fixed, but the means toward the end is variable, flexible, docile.

According to Tolman, behavior can be understood only if we look at a whole sequence of varied behavior that has some fixed predictable end. Behavior is only to be understood by looking at the whole to see how the total pattern is put together and how the animal achieves the end. Previous learning theorists had all been atomists, who believed that complex sequences of behavior could always be analyzed into a multitude of simple S-R units. This strategy is essentially that of the chemist, who reduces the uncountable number of compounds in the universe to various combinations of about a hundred different types of atoms. To the associationist, the S-R is the atom out of which everything is built. But Tolman saw behavior as holistic. To continue the analogy, Tolman told us that we can have little appreciation of the properties of water—its wetness, fluidity, various physical and chemical properties—if we regard it simply as oxygen and hydrogen atoms in combination. Behavior, too, must be regarded and explained in terms of its observable molar properties.

Had Tolman merely stated his point of view, few psychologists would have paid very much attention, but he did much more. He had a unique facility for translating his own individual perception of behavior into laboratory experiments, the interpretation of which seemed amenable only to his own cognitive kind of interpretation. Let us look at some of these remarkable experiments.

Some Representative Experiments

An interesting example of how Tolman's different perception of behavior could be translated into new kinds of learning situations is a study reported by one of his students, Macfarlane (1930). Macfarlane trained rats to swim in a maze. It was an ordinary maze filled with several inches of water, and the rats had to paddle their way past the several blind alleys to reach the goal box, where they could climb out of the water and obtain food. Granted that the animals learned to reach the food, there remained the question of whether they had learned something cognitive about the maze—how to get to the food—as Tolman claimed or had learned a series of stimulus-response connections as almost everyone else would have argued. To address this question, Macfarlane drained the water out of the apparatus, so that the maze was dry. Rats were put back into it so that they could run through it instead of swimming through it. Macfarlane found almost perfect transfer from swimming to running; that is, the animals were immediately able to run the maze with virtually no errors. Notice that completely different responses and even muscle systems are involved in swimming and running. The stimuli are different, too. The maze was dry instead of wet, it was warm instead of cold, and there was a floor underneath instead of a supporting body of water. It appears that what was learned in Macfarlane's maze was not a series of movements in response to specific stimuli but something much more abstract and holistic: the spatial layout of the maze itself. The rats had acquired a map of the maze. Tolman coined the phrase "cognitive map" as a label for the learned representation of the experimental situation. It is as if the rat learns where it is, where food is, where the blind alleys are, and where the open pathways are. Once this information has been assimilated into some kind of central map, the animal's task is simply to go from where it is to where the food is, and it need not do so by means of any fixed kind of locomotor system. If Macfarlane's rats could have been outfitted with wings, they presumably would have flown through the maze without making any errors.

There is another series of studies, conducted mostly in the 1940s, called the "place-learning experiments." The basic situation is a simple T maze, as shown in Figure 5.1. The rat starts at the south end of the maze and

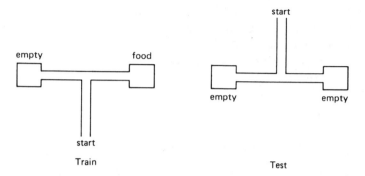

Fig. 5.1   Typical arrangement for a place-learning experiment.

must learn to go, say, east to obtain food. After a few trials the rat learns this task and performs quite consistently. We might conclude that a right-turning habit has been learned. But perhaps again the animal has learned a map, and what it is really doing is running to the east, where food is located. We do not know whether the rat has learned a response (turning right) or a place (where the food is). This question can be answered by conducting, as Macfarlane did, a transfer test. The rat is started at the north (see Figure 5.1). Now, if it has learned a response, it should go west, but, if it has learned a place, it should still go east. Most of the place-learning experiments done at Berkeley have shown that the rat learns the place (e.g., Tolman, Ritchie & Kalish, 1946).

In other laboratories the results have often come out somewhat differently. It seems that under some circumstances rats are place learners but that under other conditions they are response learners. Thus the whole series of experiments produced no simple overall conclusion. But the fact that place learning can occur at all poses a considerable challenge for the traditional S-R learning theorist. There is a way out; it is based on the kinds of cues provided by the experimental situation. All cues may arise within the apparatus itself, so-called "intramaze cues," or there may be a rich supply of cues from outside the apparatus, generally called "extramaze cues." If the animal is trained and tested under conditions that minimize extramaze cues, then it has to respond to stimulus patterns provided by the apparatus and perhaps also the proprioceptive feedback from its own behavior. Under these conditions we have to find response learning. But, if there are extramaze cues, so that the animal can orient in space, then we may find place learning. If the situation provides information about where north, east, west, and south are, the animal can, and sometimes does, respond in terms of this kind of information. The day seems to be saved for the S-R position, for the results of different experiments can be explained in terms of the availability of different kinds of stimuli. But there are some problems with a straightforward application of this S-R analysis. For one thing, when there are only intramaze stimuli, the animal approaches them or makes a right turn in their presence, both simple S-R associations from the S-R point of view. But these simple associations are apparently not formed when there are extramaze cues. Why not? Why does the rat use the information provided by distant extramaze cues when it can use cues close at hand?

A further complication in place learning was noted by Kendler and Gasser (1948). They found that if rats were given fewer than twenty trials on the original T maze, they showed place-learning in the test situation. But if they were given more than twenty trials they learned the response. Again we may conclude that, although the rat can and sometimes does learn the response, Tolman was apparently right in emphasizing the importance of place learning. The rat's initial and preferred mode of responding is place-wise. Kendler's results indicate, too, that once the rat has learned to solve the problem, there is further learning that resembles the old-fashioned idea of habit acquisition. The behavior becomes automatic in the sense that it no longer depends upon the stimuli that controlled it originally.

Tolman denied that reinforcement is necessary for learning. Behavior changes, Tolman admitted, when there is food in the apparatus, but this change should not be taken to mean that the food causes learning. In Tolman's view, the animal learns about the layout of the maze, where the blind alleys are, and so on, simply by running around in it and exploring it. Learning consists of the incorporation of information about the environment. Once this information is incorporated, the animal will use it to obtain food if it is hungry. To test this view of learning, Tolman and his students conducted a long series of studies that have become known as the "latent-learning experiments." In a typical experiment (Tolman & Honzik, 1930b) three groups of rats were trained in a complex maze. One group was run under normal conditions, with food always available in the goal box. The second group was run with no food in the apparatus. The critical third group had no food at first, but food was introduced on the eleventh day. The results for each group are shown in Figure 5.2. Performance was poor when there was no food present; little learning was evident. (There is some question about whether these groups showed some gradual improvement in error reduction.) But when food was introduced in the critical group performance improved dramatically. The rapid reduction in the number of errors in the next trial or two brought this group up to the level of the group that had received food all along.

Tolman and Honzik suggested on the basis of these results that the learning was actually identical for all three groups but that, for the non-reinforced animals, the learning was "latent." Learning was not manifest in

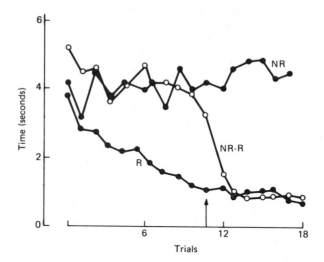

Fig. 5.2   Results of the Tolman and Honzik (1930b) latent learning experiment. Control group NR received no reward in the maze; control group R received reward on all trials. The critical group (NR-R) had reward introduced on the eleventh trial. Animals were run one trial a day in a 14-unit maze. (Originally published by the University of California Press; reprinted by permission of The Regents of the University of California.)

behavior until food was presented in the goal box. All animals had presumably learned a cognitive map of the maze in the early trials, but there was no reason to manifest this learning until the goal was made valuable. In Tolman's own language, good performance requires that the animal not only have "knowledge" about the layout of the maze but also have a "demand" for the goal object. Performance is then a joint function of knowledge, like that contained in a cognitive map, and a demand (or motivation) for a particular object, like food. An important implication is that learning is not necessarily manifest in behavior. Often it is, of course, but only when the appropriate motivation conditions, reinforcing conditions, or incentive conditions are present. In general, learning is something other than a change in behavior.

The original latent-learning experiments done by Tolman and his students at Berkeley have been replicated and carried out with many variations in a number of other laboratories. It is now apparent that there are conditions under which latent learning is likely and other conditions under which it is difficult to obtain. But, even with these difficulties, the latent-learning phenomenon is extremely important. The fact that it occurs at all indicates that changes in performance are not synonymous with learning; learning is something else.

Let us consider another experiment reported by Tolman and Honzik (1930c). Rats were trained in the apparatus diagramed in Figure 5.3. There were three paths from the start box to the goal box. The straight path A was the shortest and most preferred route. The animals were given a number of trials in which they were forced to take paths B and C, somewhat longer and less direct routes to the goal. After this experience and after a preference had been developed for path A, the path was blocked at point X. The question that concerned Tolman and Honzik was how the animals would detour around this block. The preferred detour was path B, the next shortest path. But then a block was imposed at point Y, requiring animals quite near the goal to run all the way back to the starting point to take another detour. The question then was how accurate was the animals' cognitive map. Would they again take detour B, or would they choose the only effective detour, path C? They did not take the next most preferred route, path B, but apparently had the "insight" to take the only path leading to the goal, the least preferred and most roundabout route, path C.

A common assumption underlying most S-R associationist accounts of behavior is that the S-R association is built up gradually and automatically.

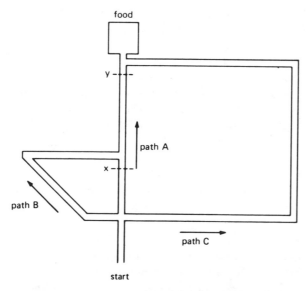

Fig. 5.3 *Apparatus used by Tolman and Honzik (1930c) to demonstrate "insight" in rats. (Originally published by the University of California Press; reprinted by permission of The Regents of the University of California.)*

Even Guthrie admitted that the response to the total stimulus situation gradually increases in strength. Tolman was skeptical of this interpretation on two counts. One was that it made behavior seem much too passive. For Tolman the animal was always engaged in doing something, directing its behavior toward some goal. The second point was that, for Tolman, the principal determinants of behavior were basically perceptual: the reading of maps, the perception of signs, and so on. Behavior also depends upon such perceptual mechanisms as attention. The idea that S-R associations are gradually built up was endorsed by those who thought of attention as too mentalistic to have a place in psychology. Learning had to be automatic and mechanical.

Both these propositions were tested in a series of experiments by Krechevsky, who was first a student and later a colleague of Tolman. In one experiment Krechevsky (1932) used an apparatus that presented the animal with a series of four choices. At each choice point the animal might go either left or right, or to a light or dark stimulus, or it might perseverate on or alternate from the previously correct response. Krechevsky programmed the series of choice points so that no one stimulus was consistently correct; the problem was objectively unsolvable. No matter what aspect of the choice-point situation the animal responded to, it had just a 50-50 chance of being correct on a given trial. Note that when an animal responds in a particular way at a particular choice point, we cannot know what it is doing, but over a series of choices we can identify behavioral strategies such as alternating or always going to the left side. Krechevsky discovered that his rats did not respond at random but instead responded systematically first to one aspect of the situation, then to another. For example, a rat might run consistently to the left for perhaps a dozen trials, then switch to the black side for a number of trials, then perhaps revert to left-going behavior for a third series of trials, and so on. Krechevsky labeled these systematic response tendencies "hypotheses." He said that it is as if the rat had a tentative hypothesis about how the problem might be solved and then proceeded to test the hypothesis by running consistently in a certain manner. Having disproved one hypothesis, it would then proceed to test another and then another and would sometimes revert to retesting a previously tested hypothesis.

In other experiments, Krechevsky used the same kind of analysis to study the solution of solvable problems. He found not gradual acquisition but rather 50 percent responding to the correct stimulus as, apparently, the animal tested different irrelevant hypotheses. Then suddenly a string of correct responses would occur as the animal tested the correct hypothesis and, confirming it, stayed with it. It is interesting to note that Krechevsky found in these experiments that, although the rat was evidently "intelligent" enough to form and test hypotheses, it was not generally intelligent enough to test hypotheses by the acquisition of incidental information; a direct test appeared to be necessary. For example, let us suppose that the situation is arranged so that going left is correct, and let us suppose that a particular animal starts by testing the black hypothesis. What will happen is that going to the black stimulus will be correct when it is on the left but not when it is on the right. The animal ought to be able to learn something incidently about the correctness of the left by testing the black hypothesis, but evidently it does not.

In a dramatic test of the noncontinuity of discrimination learning, Krechevsky (1938) found that it was even possible to change which stimulus was correct, and if this change was accomplished fairly early in the course of discrimination training it made no difference in how quickly a group of rats would ultimately learn the discrimination. In other words, Krechevsky has shown in another way that nothing was learned about the correct cue while the rat was testing an irrelevant hypothesis. Other experimenters (for example, Spence, 1945) rose to the challenge and found results contradictory to those of Krechevsky, and for many years the question went back and forth. Indeed, it is still not clear what conditions lead to continuous learning of the sort that Spence and other S-R theorists require, and what conditions lead to the noncontinuous discrimination learning that Krechevsky had discovered. But, however the issue is finally resolved, it seems safe to conclude that there are at least some conditions under which discrimination learning is an extremely active process and does not consist simply of gradually strengthening S-R associations. The rat can direct its behavior toward particular stimuli to test particular hypotheses.

Tolman's Theory of Learning

We have described some parts and pieces of Tolman's theory of learning. Let us now see if we can put these pieces together into a coherent picture. Tolman started from the premise that all behavior is directed toward some goal, that the rat has a "demand" for some object such as food, a mate, safety, or whatever. In the laboratory the situation is often arranged so that the rat is hungry and the goal is obtaining food. This situation is brought about intentionally by the experimenter to give him better control, but the same purposiveness of behavior is apparent when the animal's goals are less insistent. In short, we work with animals that are highly motivated, and we provide a goal object because this guarantees that the animal's behavior will be directed toward the goal that we provide.

In instrumental-learning situations we arrange that the animal must produce some particular behavior. It must run a certain path, press a certain bar, or make some other specific response to obtain food. As we order the rat's world by programming this contingency, we are making one event necessarily follow another. What learning involves is the meaning of these different ordered events. An early event such as a stimulus in the apparatus becomes a *sign* for the final event, food. If one event invariably follows another, that is, if food always follows the occurrence of a particular sign cue, then what the animal learns is just that: food follows the sign. It was convenient to introduce a new word to describe this kind of learning, and Tolman's word was "expectancy."

Over a series of trials the rat's behavior becomes more predictable, more orderly, and better organized. The rat comes to behave as if it expects food when it sees the sign cue. Note that just as Tolman's definition of purposive had an "as if" quality to it, so does the definition of expectancy. Expectancy does not reflect a guess about what is going on in the animal's mind; it is a term that describes the animal's behavior. Expectancy had been a mentalistic term, but Tolman did not mean to imply that the rat is thinking about or is conscious or aware of the goal. To say that the rat expects food is really to say only that its behavior is organized "as if" it expects food, in the conventional sense. If we put food in a certain place in the apparatus, then the animal will behave as if it expects food in that place: It runs toward that place. If we impose a particular task that must be performed to obtain food, the rat acts as if it expects the performance of the task to produce food: It presses the bar or whatever. What learning consists of, then, is the expectancy that a particular event will have a particular consequence. The most general formula for an expectancy is S-R-S*. The animal expects that in the presence of a particular sign (S) a particular behavior (R) will have a particular consequence (S*).

In Tolman's own experiments information about the environment was ordered spatially; his rats had to learn spatial signs indicating where food was, how it could be reached, and so on. It is also possible to order information in time. For example, in a Pavlovian experiment the CS becomes a sign for the US: The bell becomes a sign for food, and in the hungry animal the bell arouses an expectancy of food. That is why the animal salivates.

Tolman saw stimuli as serving several different functions. A stimulus can arouse an expectancy. It can convey, in effect, that, if the animal would respond in a certain way, a certain consequence would be forthcoming. A stimulus can also serve a purely informational function, as in a classical conditioning experiment where the animal is required to make no particular response. The CS can signify that food is coming. In an instrumental situation a cue can signify that food is down at the other end of the alley, or it can signify that the path has been blocked and that the animal must take a detour. But, whatever information a stimulus conveys, Tolman assumed, the rat is probably capable of learning what it is. In conducting any kind of experiment, we are establishing signs and enforcing contingencies. We put the rat in a T maze, and it has to turn left in order to obtain food. That is how we perceive the experimental arrangement. What Tolman was saying is that that is how the rat perceives it too. The rat is simply perceiving the regularities in the experimental world that we create for it, and it responds on the basis of its demand for a certain goal object such as food, again, because we have deprived it of food.

Motivation

Tolman was one of the first psychologists to treat the problem of motivation in a systematic manner. He proposed that an animal is stirred to action when it has a "demand" for a particular goal object. Demand was assumed to be governed by two kinds of factors: deprivation and what we may call incentive. One of the most interesting and dramatic demonstrations of incentive motivation was reported in an early experiment by Tinklepaugh (1928). Tinklepaugh trained monkeys to work at a discrimination task. While the monkey was watching, Tinklepaugh placed a small piece of highly preferred food like banana under one of two containers; then after a brief delay the monkey was allowed to approach and pick up the container in which it had seen the food placed. Tinklepaugh's animals quickly learned to play this game. Then from time to time Tinklepaugh would trick them. The container would be loaded with the highly preferred food, and surreptitiously an acceptable but less preferred food such as a piece of lettuce would be substituted. On these occasions the monkey would typically refuse the food and start looking carefully all around inside and outside the container. It would look on the floor and around the room. Occasionally, it would become upset enough to shriek at the people in the room. It is clear that the normally cooperative subject was disturbed both behaviorally and emotionally.

According to Tolman's interpretation, the monkey had an expectancy not just of food but of a particular kind of food. The results of switching food objects show that the animal's behavior is governed not by the immediate consequences of its acts but by what it expects its behavior to produce.

The importance of an expectancy for a particular food object was also demonstrated in Tolman's laboratory by Elliott (1928). Elliott trained different groups of rats to run in a maze for food. For one group the food was sunflower seeds, for another group bran mash. The performance of the two groups, shown in Figure 5.4, indicates that bran mash was much preferred. On the tenth day Elliott shifted incentives for the mash group. When the animals were switched from the more preferred to the less preferred food, they showed a sharp deterioration of performance. There was even

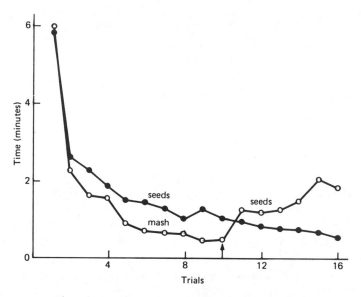

Fig. 5.4   Results of the Elliott (1928) study in which rats switched from mash (preferred) to sunflower seed (less preferred) performed more poorly than rats rewarded all along with the seeds. (Originally published by the University of California Press; reprinted by permission of The Regents of the University of California.)

what has become known as a "contrast effect," animals shifted to the less preferred food performed more poorly than those receiving the less preferred food all along. Elliott's results provide a further demonstration of the fact that a worsening of reinforcement conditions, in this case a failure to confirm an animal's expectancy, produces not only a loss of behavior but also an active disruption of behavior.

The results obtained by Elliott with foods of different values can be duplicated by using animals that are more or less hungry. Such a study was reported by Tolman and Honzik (1930a). The results are shown in Figure 5.5. It is apparent that by far the best performance in eliminating errors in the maze was shown by animals who were both rewarded and also hungry.

So there are evidently two factors that contribute to an animal's motivation and to its use of expectancies about the environment. One of these motivational factors is deprivation or drive, and the other is the incentive value of the goal object. Both factors together determine the animal's overall demand for the goal object and the extent to which its expectancies about the world, its cognitive maps, or other kinds of cognitive structures will be used and manifest in adaptive behavior.

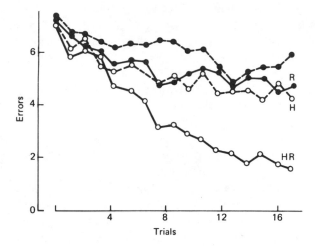

Fig. 5.5   Results of the Tolman and Honzik (1930a) experiment in which groups of rats were either hungry (H), Rewarded (R), neither, or both (HR). The animals were run one trial a day in a 14-unit maze. (Originally published by the University of California Press; reprinted by permission of The Regents of the University of California.)

The Language of Cognition

One of the things that sets Tolman's theory apart from all other theories of learning is that its syntactical rules are of a quite different order from those that we have seen. We note that all our other theorists shared a simple syntactical principle: Learning occurs when an S and an R become connected. A rat responds to a particular situation because an appropriate S-R connection has been strengthened or reinforced. In other words, all our theorists have had a single kind of syntactical unit that has been assumed to be very simple and universal. But Tolman said, on the contrary, that behavior is determined by a much looser and more flexible kind of system. The detour problem, for example, is solved not by an appropriate response to a particular stimulus but by a process like looking at a map and seeing what route to the goal remains open. However we may conceptualize the rat as reading its map, this process is intrinsically much more complex than simply connecting an R to an S. The syntactical rules are flexible and loose, and they are basically perceptual in character. If we want to understand how the rat solves a particular problem, therefore, it will do us no good to know how one neuron is connected to another or how a response becomes connected to a stimulus. Instead, we must find out something about how maps are constructed and how they are read. Tolman not only emphasized the flexibility and richness of behavior; he also built a theory in which these aspects are produced by the complexity of the syntactical rules. These processes, which are very like perception, are not easy to understand. The best way to understand them is simply to run a number of experiments to find out how they work. What kinds of expectancies can rats have? How do they perceive the world around them? What kinds of problems can they solve? At one level Tolman's principles of behavior are very simple: The animal acts in a certain way because it expects that its behavior will have certain consequences and because simultaneously it has some demand for those consequences.

Much of the language with which Tolman described behavior, and certainly much of the language in his theory, was frankly mentalistic. Largely on that account, Tolman has been widely criticized as unscientific, unbehavioristic, and subjective. Guthrie, for example, made this criticism. But the criticism is unfounded. We have seen that such essential terms in Tolman's theory as "expectancy" and "demand" are defined behaviorally. We know an expectancy from the fact that the animal's behavior is disrupted when the conditions of the experiment are changed, as in Tinkelpaugh's study. We know that the animal has a demand for a goal object by the vigor with which it runs to the goal. We should thus not be deceived by the kind of language Tolman used. It has to be viewed in historical perspective; it was no doubt introduced as a kind of antidote to the heavily mechanistic language of Watson. Actually, we may ask of the early behaviorists, like Watson, whether their concepts and language were any more scientific or any more objective. Is it any better to speak of behavior in terms of reflexes and inferred neural machinery? Tolman's use of mentalistic language merely dramatized his claim that a purely mechanical model cannot adequately explain animal behavior.

In the 1930s psychologists became much more sophisticated in their conceptions of the relationship between data and theory. We have noted in previous chapters the tendency of earlier theorists to regard behavioral phenomena as direct expressions of underlying mechanisms. The observed correlation between a stimulus and a response was assumed to reflect, somehow, a neural connection between them. We have seen that, although Guthrie appeared to use this strategy, in practice he assumed that the underlying mechanism was more complex than the data, in the sense that it involved a vast number of simple S-R connections. Thus Guthrie introduced a gap, a lack of correspondence, between the data and his theoretical terms. Tolman widened the gap. Guthrie had made no verbal distinction between observational data and his theoretical terms; when he referred to strengthening an S-R association it was not always easy to know whether he meant the increased probability of a response in the experimental situation or a stronger neural connection. Tolman recognized the importance of the distinction and tried to make it explicit. He has told us (Tolman, 1936) that his empirical terms are all objective data and that his theoretical terms are "intervening variables."

Tolman's theory was therefore quite different from those of his predecessors in that he made no pretense that his explanatory terms, intervening variables such as demand and expectancy, have any reality or can be located somewhere inside the organism. The intervening variable is essentially an abstract property of behavior itself. It is much like the mathematical construct discussed in Chapter 4. Intervening variables are so called because they are hypothesized to intervene conceptually between stimulus input and behavior output, not because they are assumed to be located somewhere in the animal. Expectancy is assumed to be a determinant of behavior in any simple situation, as when the rat runs in an alley for food, but it is not clearly manifest in behavior except in experiments, like those of Tinkelpaugh, that are especially contrived to reveal it. Demand is assumed to operate in many situations but is most clearly observed in a latent-learning experiment. The intervening variable is in turn assumed to be dependent upon antecedent conditions like environmental information in the instance of expectancy and deprivation in that of demand. But this dependence is not simple or direct. If an experimenter arranges for a sign to signify food in a particular situation, the rat may or may not incorporate and use this information. Its response depends largely upon the ingenuity of the experimenter in demonstrating the assumed relationships between observable events and intervening variables.

Essentially the intervening variable is a psychological kind of explanatory device. It has reference neither to physiological nor to mentalistic events. Like all concepts in Tolman's theory, it is merely a way of making useful abstractions about behavior and explaining behavior in that sense.

Tolman's Impact and Contribution

Tolman was an eclectic theorist. He gathered ideas from here and there and often did not combine them very systematically. In a number of different theoretical statements spanning a quarter-century he emphasized this, that, or another aspect of behavior but did little systematic organizing of his theory after 1932. Over the years his emphasis changed, and the language he used to describe his unique perception of behavior often changed dramatically. Tolman was also eclectic about the kinds of laws that he sought to incorporate within his theory. At one time he emphasized the capacity of animals for particular kinds of learning or for processing certain sorts of information (Tolman, 1932). At other times he observed that behavior might have an intrinsic probabilistic character because the world in which animals live is not itself completely predictable (Tolman & Brunswik, 1935). But Tolman was steadfast in emphasizing the purposiveness and docility of behavior, and he always emphasized that what is learned is an expectancy or the value of signs, rather than S-R connections.

In short, Tolman was too open to new ideas and not systematic enough in integrating them to build a precise, formal theory. His unique and enduring contribution was primarily to relate his perception of the behavior of animals, rather than in any systematic statement of learning principles.

The success of Tolman's theory was due in large part to his own efforts, specifically, to his theoretical papers of the 1930s and 1940s and to the mass of provocative research reported around 1930. As Tolman himself became less active, about 1950, there seemed to be few students or disciples to carry his work forward. Others have, however, made some important extensions of his learning theory. For example, Osgood (1950) showed how easily an expectancy theory can be applied to the difficult problem of avoidance learning. In Chapter 10 we will see that there is renewed interest in the expectancy concept at the present time just because it provides a powerful approach to troublesome phenomena like avoidance. Rotter (1954) developed a quite influential social-learning theory in which Tolman's basic concepts were extended to the case of human motivation in everyday kinds of situations. This development has continued in a number of different directions, so that the conception that behavior is a joint function of something like expectancy and something like demand has become a central part of many contemporary theories of human motivation.

It should be obvious that Tolman stood outside the mainstream of behavioristic psychology. And perhaps his greatest contribution has been his indirect influence on those who have been in the mainstream. Initially he stood in opposition to Watson's simple S-R connectionism and mechanistic philosophy. In later years his chief opponent was Hull, and it is a great tribute to Tolman that Hull was forced to hypothesize some very sophisticated S-R devices to explain such phenomena as latent learning and place learning. Hull also had to incorporate motivational concepts within his system. In other words, the complexity and sophistication of Hull's system were largely a response to the challenge posed by Tolman. And that, as we shall see, was a very large contribution indeed.

After Tolman had his say it became impossible for anyone to take seriously a simple mechanistic S-R interpretation of behavior, it became impossible to ignore motivational principles in any complete account of behavior, and it became impossible to ignore the great flexibility, adaptiveness, and apparent intelligence of animal behavior.

References for Further Reading

The early research that gave substance to Tolman's theory is described in *Purposive Behavior in Animals and Men* (Tolman, 1932). The main features of the theory laid down at that time remained relatively unchanged, but the details of the theory and the language Tolman used to describe it varied considerably over the years. Tolman wrote a minor book on motivation, *Drives toward War* (Tolman, 1942), and a number of theoretical papers that have been reprinted in his *Collected Papers in Psychology* (Tolman, 1951). The latter are his most readable and perhaps most important works. Tolman wrote with a lot of spirit and wit but not much systematic style or formal precision, which makes his work entertaining but hard to grasp. MacCorquodale and Meehl (1954) tried to systematize the theory, but the results were not very satisfactory. Tolman's last papers include a retrospective view of his life's work (Tolman, 1959) and a short autobiography (Tolman, 1952).

CHAPTER
6

HULL

Clark L. Hull (1884–1952) was able to synthesize into a unified system many of the achievements of earlier theorists. He did, in fact, stand on the shoulders of his predecessors, building on their strengths and avoiding some of their pitfalls. Hull's system of behavior was in the S-R tradition, but it was deductive and mathematical in form, and it was almost purely behavioristic, with hardly a taint of mentalism or mechanism. Hull's theory was explicit and highly testable, and it was tested. For years it was subjected to systematic experimentation both by those who sought to attack it and those who rushed to its defense. During Hull's lifetime and for some years after his death his ideas dominated the animal-learning literature; he founded an empire with Yale University as its capital. More than anything else, Hull generated research.

Although Hull was nearly the same age as Tolman, his commitment to the study of learning came approximately a decade later. During the intervening years Hull had distinguished himself by his research in such diverse areas as concept formation (Hull, 1920) and aptitude testing (Hull, 1928). In 1929 he went to Yale to head a group at the Institute of Human Relations, whose mission was to study the place of learning in the conduct of human affairs. Hull's original orientation was strongly Pavlovian. He was evidently impressed with the systematic nature and scientific aura of Pavlov's work, and he depended almost exclusively upon the principles of Pavlovian conditioning to account for learning. Of course, he was not alone in this commitment; most theoretical statements in the early 1930s were made within a conditioning framework.

Hull's first papers on learning theory in 1929 and 1930 were attempts to show that purposiveness in behavior could be explained with Pavlovian S-R associations. In other words, Hull sought to extend the Pavlovian framework from the original conditioning situation to the kind of situation in which behavior appears highly flexible, adaptive, and intelligent. Hull did not deny these descriptive attributes of behavior. He sought rather to derive them from simple conditioning principles. The argument was like that made a few years later by Guthrie (see Chapter 4). Hull argued that there is a tendency for the consummatory response to be elicited not only by goal-box stimuli but also by stimuli similar to those in the goal box that arise in other parts of the apparatus.

Then there was an important new development. Thorndike had returned to the study of learning and was vigorously defending the idea that learning occurs as a result of reinforcement. By the mid-1930s a confrontation between Thorndike's reinforcement position and the better-established conditioning position seemed inevitable. The crisis for Hull apparently came when he wrote a long analytical review of a new book by Thorndike (Hull, 1935). In this review Hull noted a major inadequacy of conditioning theory: its failure to deal convincingly with the phenomena of motivation. Hull saw that motivation may be viewed as either a learned aspect of behavior (as Guthrie regarded it) or a behavioral determinant quite independent of learning (as Tolman regarded it), but one way or the other, it had to be given more status than it was afforded at that time.

A final factor that gave form to Hull's theory came not from the intellectual environment but from the man himself. He was greatly impressed by the elegance and power of quantitative and deductive methods in science. In his early theoretical papers Hull proclaimed that the proper strategy for science would be to start with certain specific, testable postulates even if they would have to be based upon minimal evidence. Concrete, empirically verifiable deductions could then be derived from these postulates. When these deductions were tested, the system of postulates would then be either confirmed or shown to require modification. The task of the theorist would therefore be to formulate postulates in such a way that they would lead to unequivocal deductions. If there were no question about what inferences the theory led to, the deductions from the theory could be tested by anyone who cared to test them. The worth of a theory must then ultimately reside in how much research it generates and how consistent with its theoretical deductions the resulting findings are. We may note that applying this strategy to predictions about behavior necessarily requires us to be behaviorists. We cannot be concerned about the mental or physiological events giving rise to behavior if the postulates themselves are framed in behavioral form, as they were in Hull's work.

To summarize the several factors that formed the conceptual background for Hull's theoretical synthesis, first was the challenge presented by Tolman, both by his view of the purposiveness and goal-directedness of behavior and by his emphasis upon motivation and the important part that it plays in behavior. Second was Thorndike's concept of reinforcement, which came to the fore to challenge classical conditioning as the universal learning process. The third factor was Hull's desire to create a quantitative and deductive system to put behavior theory on a strong scientific footing. Hull struggled for years to establish a postulate system that he thought would account for what was then known about learning and motivation. When the final system was presented in his major book, *Principles of Behavior* (Hull, 1943), it embodied all the characteristics that we have described. It was a system of intervening variables, most of which were put in mathematical form. It incorporated distinct motivational and learning mechanisms, and learning was said to be based on reinforcement, rather than just on contiguity. Let us look at this 1943 theory.

Hull's Theory

The ultimate function of behavior in an animal, according to Hull, is to enable it to solve its biological problems. Consider an animal that has a need. Perhaps it has a need for food. A useful reaction to such a problem would be for the animal to become active. It does not matter too much what kind of behavior the animal engages in; as long as it does something, it is likely to improve its chance of survival. Let us suppose further that while the animal is engaged in this increased activity it accidently makes a response that leads to food; the food eliminates the original need and solves the animal's immediate biological problem. What an elegant system we would have if this event, the reduction in need, were to serve as reinforcement and produce learning of the lucky response! The animal would then be, in effect, an automatic problem-solving system. Need would produce behavior, and the particular behavior that reduced the need would be gradually learned. Animals would thus come to adapt to the special requirements of their environments in solving their particular problems. This is precisely the kind of system that Hull postulated.

First, there is drive. The animal's need state, whether it be hunger, thirst, sexual arousal, pain, or some other type of biological problem, produces a state of motivation that Hull called "drive." Drive activates and generates behavior—no particular behavior, just behavior. Second, there is reinforcement, which occurs whenever drive is reduced so that there will be learning of whatever response solves the animal's problem. Over a number of trials, the animal's behavior will become increasingly efficient and more highly adapted to its environment. The animal will become increasingly adept at solving its problems in a given environment.

The same mechanism works in the laboratory. An animal in a box is suddenly in pain because of an electric shock applied to the grid floor. The animal displays a lot of behavior; it scrambles around and jumps and cries. In the course of this disorganized behavior it happens to press the bar in the box and terminates the shock. How elegant it would be if the bar-press response were automatically strengthened; then the next time the rat was in such a difficulty (on the next trial) it would be somewhat more likely to press the bar again. Hull's scheme predicts that animals will learn to solve their problems both in the laboratory and in nature. Hull's system provides a basic concept of need-related motivation, drive, and S-R learning produced by reinforcement. The S-R connection was called "habit." Let us see how these basic concepts were developed in more detail.

Hull (1943) postulated that drive and habit multiply together to determine the strength of behavior. This proposal was based upon a pair of experiments conducted by two students, Williams (1938) and Perin (1942). Williams trained groups of rats to press a bar for food, each group being given some fixed number of reinforcements ranging from five to ninety. Immediately after acquisition the response was extinguished in all animals. The resistance to extinction that Williams found in each group is shown in Figure 6.1. Perin's experiment was conducted in exactly the same way. Different groups of animals were given a fixed number of reinforcements for pressing the bar and then extinguished. Perin's results are also shown in Figure 6.1. The major difference between the two experiments, and presumably the reason the results came out differently, is that Williams' animals had been food-deprived for twenty-two hours at the time of testing, whereas Perin's animals had been deprived for only three hours. Hull noted that the strength of behavior depends upon both the animal's motivating conditions

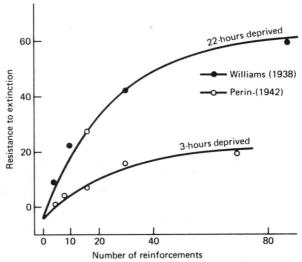

Fig. 6.1 *The famous Perin-Williams data showing how the strength of behavior, as measured by resistance to extinction, depends on both current motivation conditions (drive) and prior learning (habit). (From Perin, Behavioral potentiality as a joint function of the amount of training and the degree of hunger at the time of extinction.* Journal of Experimental Psychology, *1942, 30, 93–113. Copyright 1942 by the American Psychological Association. Reprinted by permission.)*

at the time of testing and the amount of prior learning. He analyzed the data further and found that it was possible to fit a mathematical learning curve to the results of each experiment. In each case the equation came out in this form:

$$\text{Behavior strength} = A(1 - 10^{-BN})$$

When A indicates the level of performance ultimately reached with a given deprivation condition, B is the "growth constant" that indicates how fast the habit is formed, or how fast the animal approaches the ultimate level of performance, and N is the number of prior reinforcements.[1] Once these equations were obtained for Perin's and for Williams' data, Hull discovered that the term B was almost identical in the two experiments; the only real difference in the two sets of results was in the constant A. Hull therefore

[1] This equation describes the growth over time of a great variety of biological systems. It is likely to be applicable to any system on which there is some limit to how much growth can occur. It is based on the assumption that the rate of growth is proportional to the amount of growth still possible.

tentatively identified the factor $(1 - 10^{-BN})$ with habit and emphasized that it was not dependent upon deprivation; it seemed to depend only upon the number of prior reinforcements. Similarly, Hull identified the constant A with the animal's motivational state, or level of drive, which seemed to depend only upon deprivation conditions. The strength of behavior then becomes motivation times learning, or drive times habit, or $D \times H$.

Here we have a mathematical equation, an approach toward quantification, that describes behavior as a function of the two factors that it is supposed to depend upon, motivation and learning. We note, too, that, according to this equation (and in accordance with common sense) neither motivation nor prior learning by itself will tell us how much behavior we will obtain from an animal. Thus, if we have an animal running rather slowly in an alley, we cannot tell whether it is not motivated but has a well-learned habit or is highly motivated and is just beginning to learn. The same response strength can be produced in either way. Consequently it is impossible to assess either drive or habit from a single observation. It takes a series of observations, together with some assumption, such as the $D \times H$ equation, to establish what is determining the behavior in a particular instance.

The principles of quantification that appear in Hull's theory were rather elaborate and, as it turned out, rather prematurely formulated. Hence we do not have to be concerned with his mathematical formulations. But it is important to understand the kind of deductive system that Hull attempted to create. According to Hull, science depends upon systematic observation and measurement, but in addition science requires that sooner or later there be basic laws, preferably in mathematical form, from which it is possible to deduce theoretically what the results of experimental observations should be. Let us digress briefly to see how this deductive process works in the well-established science of classical mechanics.

In the seventeenth century Isaac Newton observed that if a pendulum was swung back and forth, it moved with a fixed period; it was therefore possible to determine how fast a particular pendulum swung. Newton did a number of experiments to see what determines this fixed period, and some of these experiments were rather interesting. If a heavy weight was put on the pendulum, it swung at precisely the same speed; weight was not a determining factor (which is rather interesting because the results are counter to intuition, or at least to some people's intuition). The amplitude of the motion—how far the pendulum swung—did not affect the period either, which is also a rather interesting negative result. But Newton discovered that the period of the pendulum did vary with its length. In fact, length turns out to be the only variable that affects how fast the pendulum swings. Having established some facts about the simple pendulum, Newton proceeded to derive an equation to describe his results. He assumed that the force of gravity always operates downward, and with a little mathematical manipulation he was able to conclude that the acceleration of the pendulum is $a = \dfrac{F}{m}$, when F is the force of gravity and m the mass of the pendulum. Then, happily, when this equation is solved to determine the period, the m term drops out, so that this deduction is consistent with the observation that the mass of the pendulum is not a factor in determining its period. Indeed, all of Newton's observations were consistent with the equation. He rewrote the equation as $F = m \times a$, and in this form it was the basic postulate that summarized pendular motion. But, as with many mathematical models, there were a few additional benefits. The $F = m \times a$ equation turned out to describe not only the behavior of pendulums but also the behavior of cannon balls, falling stones, celestial bodies, and the motion of the earth about the sun. Observation of an immense variety of phenomena revealed that Newton's equation was almost universally valid. Now we know of situations in which Newton's equation fails to describe scientific observations, but for more than two centuries it met all experimental challenges.

Hull attempted to follow the Newtonian model. He started with a few simple experiments like the studies by Perin and Williams and summarized these results in terms of a simple equation:

$$\text{Behavior strength} = D \times H$$

This equation then serves as a postulate or tentative hypothesis about the determinants of behavior in general. Its generality is tested by means of a variety of experiments the outcomes of which are deduced from the postulate. If the deductions are consistent with observation, well and good; the postulates have gained in generality. If the results are inconsistent with the postulates, then the postulates must be modified. In what follows we will examine some of Hull's postulates.

Motivation

Hull (1943) attributed a number of specific properties to drive. We have already seen that he related drive to the animal's biological needs, considering it an immediate, unlearned physiological reaction to need. According to Hull, drive does not contribute to the direction of behavior. For example, a hungry animal is not motivated to do anything about its hunger *per se*; it is just motivated. The different needs can be regarded as different sources of drive (Brown, 1961), but in each instance the same kind of motivation, that is, drive, is produced. Different sources of drive simply multiply the existing habit structure without biasing the animal to engage in any particular behavior. One prediction from this postulate is that, after a hungry animal has learned a particular response, such as pressing a bar, the execution of this response should not be dependent upon the animal being hungry. If the rat were suddenly shifted from hunger to thirst, the behavior ought to persist because it would be motivated by the new source of drive. Of course, extinction would occur unless the source of reinforcement were shifted at the same time from food to water, but the point is that there should be no sudden loss of behavior when the animal is first motivated inappropriately. Some early experiments tended to confirm this remarkable prediction (for example, Webb, 1949), but a number of more recent experiments have failed to find such motivation transfer when proper care has been taken to use sources of drive that can really be manipulated independently. Food and water deprivation are inappropriate, it turns out, because when an animal is deprived of water it is both thirsty and hungry (Grice & Davis, 1957). For many years Judson Brown was the chief spokesman for the idea that different sources of drive are interchangeable, but recently he has reported that in a hunger-fear conflict situation, the behaviors motivated by hunger and by fear appear to be motivated relatively independently (Brown, Anderson & Brown, 1966).

There is another implication of Hull's concept of generalized drive: An irrelevant source of drive should contribute an additional increment of drive, leading to greater strength of behavior. For example, a hungry rat should be more likely to press a bar for food if it is also a little thirsty, a little frightened, or has some other source of irrelevant drive. Again, some early experimental reports suggested that this was the case (for example, Perin, 1942), but more recent and careful experimentation has shown that the summation of different sources of drive is very unpredictable. The effect can be found with some sources of drive and in some situations, but it appears to have little generality (this literature is reviewed by Bolles, 1975). Evidently, the motivation of behavior cannot be attributed to a completely general kind of mechanism, as Hull originally postulated.

Of course, Hull knew that animals make specific responses when satisfying particular needs. As early as 1933 he had shown that the rat can learn to make one response to obtain water when it is thirsty and another response to obtain food when it is hungry. But in formulating his principles of behavior Hull retained the notion of drive as a generalized energizer and added an additional postulate, that specific stimuli (equivalent to what Guthrie called maintaining stimuli) are characteristic of each need state. These stimuli were said to have no motivational function; they were simply stimuli to which adaptive behavior, like behavior to satisfy the need, could be conditioned. This postulate therefore contained virtually the entire substance of Guthrie's motivational principles, but Hull had, in addition, all of the other hypothetical properties of drive.

Learning

The basic construct involved in learning is habit, according to Hull. Whereas he assumed drive to be quite generalized and unable to direct behavior, he proposed that habit was very specific. In fact, all the specificity of behavior was attributed to habit; he emphasized the point by placing subscripts S and R around the symbol H. Thus $_sH_R$ indicates the tendency of a specific stimulus to evoke a specific response. In his 1943 postulate system Hull treated habit as a function of the number of reinforcements (see Figure 6.1) and, in addition, the amount and delay of reinforcement. For example, the rat should learn to press a bar more quickly if it has received a large, immediate food pellet. But in 1952, when Hull revised a number of the postulates, he said that habit depends only upon the number of reinforcements.

Another basic postulate that was altered in detail but remained essentially the same over the years was Hull's famous postulate 4, which asserted that habit is built up as a result of drive reduction. Relief from pain and relief from hunger are obvious instances of reinforcement by drive reduction. In the last experiment reported from Hull's own laboratory, a dog was prepared with a fistula in the esophagus so that it could only "sham eat." That is, food taken into the mouth would pour out through the fistula in the neck without ever reaching the stomach. Hull and his collaborators (Hull *et al.*, 1951) tested the dog in a T maze where going to one side permitted sham eating and going to the other side resulted in no food but did permit the animal to have its stomach filled via a tube. The first choice offered the animal the possibility of consummatory behavior; the second choice gave it the possibility of need reduction and presumably drive reduction. It was reported that the animal showed an initial preference for sham eating but after a few trials switched to the side that reduced drive. Drive reduction therefore appeared to produce learning of the new response. These results therefore provided nice confirmation of Hull's postulate.

There are now, however, a number of lines of evidence to support alternative interpretations of reinforcement. Let us just briefly note some of this evidence. Miller (1957) has summarized a series of experiments similar in concept to the study of Hull and his colleagues (1951). These carefully controlled experiments clearly indicate that placing food directly in the stomach is reinforcing but that food in the mouth is much more reinforcing. Other researchers have developed techniques by which the rat maintains itself without eating. A bar-press response activates a pump, which puts a small amount of food directly into the stomach through a surgically implanted tube. The results of these experiments (for example, Holman, 1969) indicate that it is extremely difficult to elicit new learning with this procedure.

The rat typically does not maintain its body weight, and even when the procedure does work it is not certain that there are not sensations in the head that accompany the passage of food on its way to the stomach. Thus it appears that some kind of mouth or head stimulation may be a much more important factor in reinforcement than placement of food in the stomach and the reduction in drive that it produces.

Another problem connected with the drive-reduction hypothesis is the discovery by Olds and Milner (1954) that electrical stimulation of certain areas of the brain is reinforcing. Since the initial discovery of this phenomenon there have been many studies that show learning reinforced by brain stimulation in a variety of situations. In some cases this source of reinforcement is enormously effective and preferred by the rat to eating, mating, or any other kind of more natural consummatory response. But, if learning occurs under these conditions, then we have to ask where is the source of drive that is being reduced? Where is the "need" for the stimulation? There are also a number of more natural situations in which learning occurs in the absence of an apparent need and in which there seems to be no possible drive reduction. For example, it was discovered that the rat would learn a maze problem in order to get into a complex situation which it could explore. Exploration thus seems to be a kind of consummatory response the occurrence of which is reinforcing. Again we may ask where is the drive that is reduced? Some writers have gone so far as to invent a new source of drive, claiming that the rat becomes bored in a familiar situation and that exploration reduces this new source of drive. But again we may ask what is the underlying need that produces boredom? How does boredom threaten the biological integrity of the animal? It can be argued that animals have to explore their natural environments if they are to survive, so there is a need in some sense, but this long-term and subtle need is very different from the brutal necessity of having food or water. The same argument could of course be made about mating as a source of drive. It, too, is a need in a biological sense, but it is not the kind of need and does not have the kind of time course that Hull was thinking about when he postulated that need gives rise to motivation.

Perhaps the most straightforward and convincing demonstration of reinforcement in the absence of drive reduction was reported in several early studies by Sheffield and his associates. Sheffield and Roby (1950) found that rats would learn to run in an alley if they could drink saccharin in the goal box. It was found that it was the vigor with which the consummatory response occurred, rather than the nutritional benefit to the animal (saccharin contains no calories and cannot reduce need), that made saccharin reinforcing. Sheffield proposed that it is not reduction in need or drive or any variant of this idea discussed by Hull that constitutes reinforcement; it is simply the occurrence of a consummatory response that produces learning. The rat learns a response when this response permits it to eat, mate, explore, or whatever else it is motivated to do. The occurrence of the consummatory response undoubtedly increases the animal's level of arousal momentarily. Sheffield (1966) therefore suggested that reinforcement may be thought of as more like drive induction than drive reduction.

The evidence against the drive-reduction hypothesis was just beginning to turn up at the time that Hull died. But he had already begun to question the validity of the hypothesis (Hull, 1952a). He was impressed with Sheffield's work and was evidently aware of other mounting problems connected with his theoretical position. As more negative evidence became available, would he have attempted to defend the drive-reduction hypothesis? Would he have accepted some alternative view of reinforcement such as Sheffield's? Would he have abandoned the reinforcement principle altogether and tried to explain learning without it, as Guthrie and Tolman had done? We do not know, but we do know that for several years, when Hull's work was being carried forward and defended by a number of colleagues, former students, and independent parties who had been won over to the Hullian persuasion, the reinforcement question became the all-important issue of the day. All during the 1950s the question of what constitutes reinforcement and whether or not reinforcement is necessary for learning received a great deal of research attention. It is not clear why this particular issue should have become such a battleground, but it did. Ultimately the battle was lost by Hull's followers. Later in this chapter we shall see that the drive-reduction hypothesis has been abandoned by one after another of those who had attempted to defend it.

Inhibitory Factors

So far we have been talking about excitatory factors that lead to the production of behavior. Both D and H contribute positively to the expression of a response. But Hull also postulated the existence of factors that inhibit behavior and subtract from its expression. He proposed that there are two kinds of inhibition. One type, which he designated "reactive inhibition," or I_R, is specific to a particular response. It is as if the response mechanism becomes fatigued when the response occurs. This fatiguelike-type of inhibition dissipates in time, however, and, as the inhibition dissipates, response strength returns to the full potential given by the basic formulation $D \times H$. Hull introduced reactive inhibition into his system to explain the Pavlovian phenomenon of spontaneous recovery. The same mechanism also helped explain the fact that performance is poorer under massed than under distributed trials. The argument is that under massed trials I_R does not have the opportunity to dissipate from one trial to the next, so that the expression of behavior is always somewhat less than if it were determined just by the strength of $D \times H$.

Hull's second kind of inhibition also had a strong Pavlovian flavor. It was called "conditioned inhibition" and was symbolized $_sI_R$. It was also hypothesized to subtract from the strength of behavioral expression. As the symbol indicates, $_sI_R$ was supposed to be specific to a particular stimulus and a particular response. As the basic mechanism was postulated, when a response occurs in a particular situation and reinforcement does not follow, there will be a build up of $_sI_R$ in a manner parallel to the buildup of $_sH_R$ when a response is reinforced in a given situation. In effect, there are two learning mechanisms, one that makes reinforced responses more probable and one that makes unreinforced responses less probable. As we have noted already, the spontaneous recovery often found after extinction is caused by the dissipation of I_R during the long intertrial interval. But at the same time repeated extinction trials will ultimately lead to the cessation of responding, and this permanent inhibition of behavior is caused by the build up of $_sI_R$. Hull's basic equation was thus modified to read:

$$\text{Behavior strength} = D \times {}_sH_R - I_R - {}_sI_R$$

Hull was one of the few theorists to give explicit recognition to the fact that behavior is essentially probabilistic. He noted that, even when an experimenter has done his best to maximize habit strength and drive level and to minimize inhibitory factors and distracting stimuli, he still finds a disconcerting amount of variability. He finds to his consternation that response strength varies widely over a group of animals and varies from trial to trial in an individual animal. To deal with this variability Hull postulated the existence of an oscillation mechanism. He proposed that the overt expression of any behavior requires that the factors, D, H, and I, produce a tendency to respond that is greater than some threshold value. A subthreshold response tendency is simply not overtly expressed. Then Hull assumed that the threshold of response evocation varies randomly in time according to an oscillating function, $_sO_R$, which can sometimes lead to the expression of a weak response tendency but at other times may inhibit the overt expression of a strong response tendency. This oscillatory function $_sO_R$ is subtracted from the other determinants of response strength. The complete equation is therefore

$$\text{Behavior strength} = D \times {}_sH_R - I_R - {}_sI_R - {}_sO_R$$

The idea of an oscillating threshold was not entirely new; it had been applied to sensory-detection thresholds for many years, but Hull's system was unique in postulating the existence of such indeterminacy on the behavioral side of the organism. It was an admission that behavior can be predicted only on the average, over a period of time, or over a group of animals.

We would seem to have all the conceivable determinants of behavior gathered before us, but there is still one more consideration. The tendency to make a particular response can be measured in different ways. It is possible to measure the vigor or amplitude of a response, that is, the speed or force with which it is executed. It is also possible to measure the rate or probability of responding. The two measures may be correlated, but often they are not. We might have a very frequent response of low amplitude or a rare response of great amplitude. Which are we to say is the "stronger" response? Clearly what is needed is some sort of mathematical formulation that will convert the equation for the strength of behavior directly into feet per second, occurrences per minute, or whatever other response measure we actually record in the laboratory. Hull tentatively postulated different mathematical equations for the different response measures, but none of them proved to be entirely satisfactory. But there is one response measure whose treatment within Hull's system has proved to be both widely accepted and highly convenient. Spence (1954) proposed, after reviewing a variety of data, that the probability of a response can be best measured directly in terms of the reciprocal of its latency. For example, if we think of a response as having such strength that it occurs on the average in four seconds, then, according to Spence's analysis, the equation describing the strength of behavior, $D \times H$ . . . , is equal to .25. If the behavioral tendency were twice as strong, so that $D \times H$ . . . $= .50$, then the response would occur in two seconds on the average. Spence and his students have been quite consistent in analyzing their data in terms of such reciprocal time scores, or speed scores. This consistency is based partly on the conviction that such scores can be directly related to $D \times H$ . . . and partly on the additional benefit that such scores have desirable statistical properties. Over a series of trials if an animal gives a number of fast starts and a few slow ones, the frequency distribution may be so badly skewed as to be virtually useless for statistical purposes. Taking reciprocals typically makes such distributions much more nearly normal.

Implications of the Theory

Earlier associationists had hypothesized syntactical elements that corresponded precisely in form to their data. Typically, the correlation between the observed response in a particular experimental situation was assumed to be mirrored by a corresponding S-R connection in the nervous system. Hull's theory had a much more elaborate syntax. The effective or hypothetical, internal stimulus was said to be related to the external stimulus situation by means of additional postulates that we need not discuss here. And then this hypothetical stimulus enters into the structure of the theory at two points. It enters into $_sH_R$ on reinforced trials and into $_sI_R$ on nonreinforced trials. There will be a tendency to respond when there is an appropriate habit—if there is enough drive and if there is not too much inhibition. And the tendency to respond is finally transformed according to some mathematical function into observable behavior. The value of this type of approach was its extreme flexibility; it enabled the Hullian theorist to apply the system to a tremendous range of behavioral phenomena.

All the theoretical relationships that we have discussed here have been presented mainly in verbal language. Hull also described them all in tentative mathematical equations. Each syntactical link was spelled out formally and precisely in tentative equations. It was thus possible to make rather precise predictions from the theory, and some of the research originating from Hull's own laboratory was extremely mathematical in character.

We could indulge in physiological fantasizing about where various parts of the learning system are located in the central nervous system. We might identify drive as physiological arousal and locate it in the reticular activating system. We might put habit in the cerebral cortex and inhibition in the hippocampus. Hull himself was inclined to such speculations from time to time. But they play no part in his system *per se*. All the constructs are primarily intervening variables (or hypothetical constructs, as Hull preferred to call them). The theory is basically descriptive, each part of it being based upon certain critical experiments. Hull maintained that the proper use of his theory was to predict the outcomes of new experiments and check the outcomes of such experiments against the predictions. Because of the explicitness and relative precision with which Hull's theory was stated, it has been possible to test most of his theoretical assertions. Most of those pertaining to the drive concept, including the famous drive-reduction hypothesis of reinforcement, have now been shown to be either wrong or inadequate. Other parts of Hull's theory, such as his treatment of inhibition, have fared somewhat better, but they have been extensively modified by both Hull and his followers. Between 1943 and 1952 Hull made a great many minor changes in the postulates. For example, reinforcement was no longer attributed to reduction in need or drive, but to the reduction in the stimulus correlated with drive. The amount-of-reinforcement variable was no longer considered to affect the rate of learning but was made a motivational variable (a development that we shall consider in more detail shortly). The oscillation function was altered. All these changes came about as a result of evidence that accumulated in a few years after Hull's theory was first announced in 1943.

It might be inferred from all the changes that Hull made in his theoretical system that its initial form must have been quite inadequate. But this conclusion misses the point of what Hull was trying to do. What mattered to Hull was not whether the details of his postulates were right or wrong but rather the *method* for building a theory. Hull no doubt expected all the specific details to be modified, corrected, or discarded. The details were originally based on very little evidence, but that did not matter. What was important to Hull was that his conjectures could be tested and changed or rejected as the evidence necessitated. Hull's willingness to be wrong was a remarkable, perhaps unique, virtue. It is a virtue that is, unfortunately, not shared by many of us.

The Secondary Learning System

So far we have considered what may be called the "primary learning system." Hull had, in addition to this $D \times H$ system and superimposed upon it, what we may call the "secondary learning system," which adds another whole dimension of flexibility and power to his theory. Hull was aware that many instances of learning found both in everyday life and in the laboratory occur in the absence of any apparent reduction in need. He therefore assumed that learning can be obtained by means of secondary reinforcers. He postulated a class of primary reinforcers, the effectiveness of which is not dependent upon prior experience; food for the hungry animal, relief from pain, and similar events are typical examples of primary, or unlearned, reinforcers. But there is, he assumed, a class of events, like social approval and money for the human subject, and getting to a box where food has been located for the rat, whose effectiveness as reinforcers depends upon prior experience. These events are secondary, or conditioned, reinforcers. Hull paid relatively little attention to secondary reinforcement, but he included it among the postulates. He also speculated about what is necessary to establish a stimulus as a secondary reinforcer. The necessary condition was said to be pairing of the stimulus with primary reinforcement. It is interesting to note that secondary reinforcers are established through a Pavlovian procedure. Hull accepted Pavlov's claim of higher-order conditioning (using an established CS as if it were a US), and viewed it as equivalent to secondary reinforcement. The CS becomes a US, according to Hull, in the same way that a previously neutral stimulus becomes a reinforcer. It should be noted that what is learned under these circumstances is not a response but rather a new functional property of the stimulus.

Hull formulated another important principle of secondary or learned motivation. Hull's primary motivator was drive, but in addition he recognized a source of learned motivation, which he called "incentive." The phenomenon is best illustrated by the classic experiment of Crespi (1942).

Crespi trained three groups of rats to run in an alley for food. Different groups received different amounts of reinforcement. One group received a single pellet of food in the goal box, the second group received 16 pellets, and the third group received 256 pellets, virtually a full day's ration. After twenty trials under these different conditions, the three groups evidenced very different levels of performance in the runway, as shown in the left part of Figure 6.2. At first, Hull (1943) suggested that such differences in behavior reflect differences in habit; more food means more reinforcement, which means a faster buildup of habit. But Hull changed his interpretation because of other results reported by Crespi. After the twentieth trial Crespi equalized the amount of reinforcement for all groups at sixteen pellets. As Figure 6.2 indicates, there were rapid changes in performance following the shift in amount of reinforcement, all groups quickly adopting a running speed that was appropriate to the new conditions. Notice that the shifts in performance of the 1-pellet and 256-pellet groups were much more rapid than the changes in performance in the original learning. Crespi therefore concluded that the amount of reinforcement variable does not affect learning (habit) but does affect performance through some kind of motivational variable. Hull (1952a) accepted Crespi's argument and designated with the

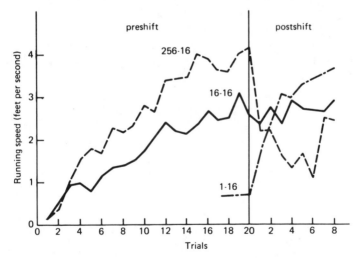

Fig. 6.2 *The effect of giving rats different amounts of reward, either 1 or 16 or 256 pellets. Starting with the twentieth trial, all animals were given 16 pellets. (From Crespi, Quantitative variation of incentive and performance in the white rat,* American Journal of Psychology, *1942, 55.)*

letter K a new construct, which he called "incentive motivation." Hull simply inserted K in the behavior equation, so that

$$\text{Behavior strength} = K \times D \times {_sH_R} \ . \ . \ .$$

Hull now had two kinds of motivators, the old primary drive factor and the new secondary incentive factor. He also had, in effect, two kinds of learning: the primary S-R learning embodied in ${_sH_R}$ and the learning involved in establishing secondary reinforcers and incentive motivators. In the first instance it was clearly an S-R connection that was learned, but in the second what appeared to be learned was a new property of a previously neutral stimulus. Hull made everything consistent, however, by assuming that the secondary learning system was based upon the learning of a response—a special kind of response, to be sure, but still a response—which followed the same laws of learning that he had elaborated in the primary system. Hull's argument was that a unique response, such as eating, occurs in the goal box. This goal response, designated R_G, is assumed to become associated with the stimuli present in the goal box. This argument is very much like that noted in our discussion of Guthrie's interpretation of motivation. One difference was that Hull invoked drive reduction for the learning of all responses, including R_G, but the rest of the argument is the same.[2] Then, if other stimuli in the apparatus are similar to those present in the goal box, there will be a tendency for the goal response to generalize forward to other parts of the apparatus. Of course, there is no food anywhere except in the goal box, so the R_G cannot really occur. Certain fractional parts of R_G can occur, however. Specifically, responses such as salivation can occur anywhere in the apparatus. Hull designated this hypothetical response a "fractional anticipatory goal reaction." He expressed it r_G (pronounced "little ar-gee"). Thus r_G is elicited by stimulus generalization by stimuli similar to those present in the goal box where R_G occurs.

There is one more step to the argument. The occurrence of r_G was assumed to provide incentive motivation, which Hull designated with the symbol K. How can the occurrence of a response produce motivation? The answer in Hull's system is that r_G has stimulus consequences. The exact

[2] When Hull first developed the R_G concept in 1930, he believed in Pavlovian conditioning as a universal learning mechanism. But in 1943, when he had switched to drive-reduction reinforcement as the basis for all learning, he invoked this new mechanism for the explanation of R_G learning. At this point Hull had no use for a Pavlovian conditioning mechanism. He argued, for example, that the food used in a Pavlovian experiment was a drive reducer and might be expected to reinforce salivation, and produce learning in that manner. Later theorists, as we shall see in Chapter 8, have tended to follow Spence (1951) in returning to the older view that R_G is a classically conditioned response. It is said to be the pairing of goal-box cues with food that conditions R_G, and produces incentive motivation in the manner about to be described.

identity of these stimuli was never established, so that we must think of them as hypothetical. These stimuli are designated with a symbol s_G. The occurrence of r_G thus introduces a new stimulus, s_G, into the total stimulus pattern. Then this additional stimulus s_G could, like any stimulus, have the correct response associated with it. The rat thus runs in an alley, partly because running is associated with alley cues but also partly because alley cues produce r_G, which produces s_G, to which running is also associated. Hull's final explanation (1952a) of Crespi's experiment was that animals receiving a larger amount of food have a more vigorous r_G conditioned to the goal box (or perhaps have the same r_G conditioned more strongly). In either case, r_G will be more strongly elicited by alley stimuli, and there will be a more prominent s_G to provide additional stimulus support for running. It was this additional source of stimuli that Hull designated "incentive motivation," or K, and assumed to produce multiplication of D and H. When the amount of reinforcement was suddenly shifted in Crespi's experiment, a different r_G became rapidly conditioned to the runway stimuli so that different amounts of r_G and s_G were produced, and a different magnitude of K was generated.

The development of the r_G aspect of the theory, and indeed the whole secondary learning system, may seem unwarranted and unnecessarily complicated in view of the power and flexibility of the primary system. But during the 1950s a variety of facts began to be discovered that simply could not be dealt with in terms of the primary system alone. Much of the research reported earlier by Tolman and his students had also proved extremely embarrassing to S-R theory. The r_G mechanism provided a convenient if not very simple explanation of many of these findings. Consider again the latent-learning experiment in which rats performed poorly on the first few trials when there was no food in the goal box, and then showed a dramatic improvement in performance when food was introduced. Tolman had argued that learning had been occurring all along but that it became manifest in behavior only when the goal box contained an object for which the animal had a demand. Hull's explanation of the same data was that learning had indeed been occurring all along (we may note that there was some decline in errors by both the control animals and the experimental animals before the introduction of reward) but that, although $_sH_R$ had built up, performance was very poor because incentive motivation was so low. When the rat encountered food in the goal box, an appreciable amount of K was suddenly established, and it "multiplied" the previously established habit.

For another illustration of the incentive-motivation principle, consider the place-learning versus response-learning experiment, in which rats trained to run from the south to the east for food continue to run to the east when they are tested from the north. Tolman had maintained that such behavior indicates that the animal has learned where food is and is simply going to the food place. Hull's interpretation was that during training, whenever the animal looks to the right (east), it will encounter stimuli, perhaps extra-maze cues like those present in the goal box, and that these stimuli will elicit r_G and produce s_G. Then, when the animal runs to the right and eats, this drive reduction will strengthen the running response to these s_G stimuli. Later, when the animal is tested starting from the north, it will again run to the choice point and look in both directions; when it looks to the left (east), these s_G stimuli are reinstated and they tend to control the behavior. In short, the r_G-s_G mechanism permitted the Hullian theorist to explain a variety of phenomena that could not be explained by the primary learning system alone.

Hull formulated an additional secondary learning mechanism. He postulated that a stimulus that is paired with drive will itself come to serve as a secondary source of drive. For example, a rat should become hungry if placed in a box where it has been hungry. It should become frightened if placed in a box where it has been frightened. Hull did not pursue the implications of this principle or do any research on it, but others did. During the 1950s an enormous amount of research was addressed to the idea of secondary or learned drive. The only instance in which the mechanism appeared to work as required by the theory was that of fear conditioning. But the results of these experiments were subject to a variety of interpretations and provided little support for the learned-drive concept. We shall consider this complex subject in more detail in Chapter 9.

Applications of the Theory

The 1943 version of Hull's theory was boldly proclaimed as a new scientific program and as a set of postulates to encompass all behavior. Recall that Hull's earlier research had been done with human subjects and that he had brought to his major theory-building efforts a background in human learning. Actually, his first attempt to build a formal mathematical model was related to human verbal learning (Hull *et al.*, 1940). But the research conducted during the 1940s to test Hull's 1943 theory was done almost exclusively with rats, and in 1952 Hull admitted that at that time his behavior system was probably applicable only to hungry rats. But few can resist the temptation to apply a limited system universally. All of our earlier theorists, and particularly their followers, were quite ready to extend their systems to the explanation of social behavior, abnormal behavior, developmental psychology, and the remotest frontiers of psychology. Much of the appeal and popularity of Hull's theory were no doubt due to the programmatic promise of handling problems in these far-flung areas, but its greatest success was in accounting for the data in the area in which its basic postulates had been derived: the study of the rat in the laboratory.

Hull's theory was designed to handle a much wider variety of learning phenomena than any prior theory had been. We have already seen applications of the theory to a number of behavioral phenomena, but two other basic phenomena must be mentioned. One is generalization. Hull treated generalization in terms of stimulus similarity, and he recognized that the question of similarity is basically a perceptual problem. But he also recognized that many perceptual problems can be dealt with quantitatively by using psychophysical techniques. In an early experiment Hovland (1937) had done psychophysical experiments with human subjects and had found that response strength varied in a systematic way (see Figure 6.3) with the distance of the test stimulus from the training stimulus. The distance was measured psychologically in terms of just noticeable differences, that is, the number of detection thresholds separating the stimuli. Thus, similarity did not have to be judged subjectively; it could be measured along particular physical dimensions, and generalization gradients could be derived from

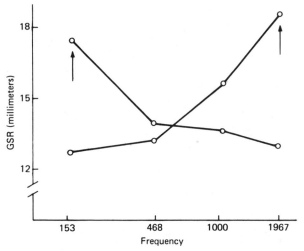

Fig. 6.3 Amplitude of conditioned galvanic skin response (GSR) when tested with different frequency tones. The arrow indicates the frequency at which each group was initially conditioned. The frequencies were selected to be equally discriminable, but are plotted here on a logarithmic scale. (From Hovland, The Journal of General Psychology, *1937, 17, 125–148, by permission of The Journal Press.)*

such measurements. In short, it was possible to provide a quantitative analysis of stimulus generalization along any stimulus dimension on which one cared to measure the generalization gradients. These gradients were assumed to be an intrinsic property of the sensory receptors.

Discrimination was easy to deal with in terms of the opposing $_sH_R$ and $_sI_R$ constructs (Spence, 1937). The $_sI_R$ builds up to the negative stimulus and generalizes throughout the stimulus dimension; $_sH_R$ builds up to the positive stimulus, and there will again be generalized habit strength to other stimuli along the stimulus dimension. The resulting strength of behavior is assumed to be the difference between the positive $_sH_R$ and the negative $_sI_R$ components. The scheme is illustrated in Figure 6.4.

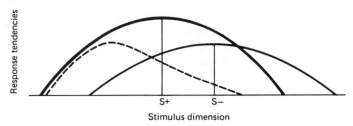

Fig. 6.4 Illustration of Spence's (1937) theory of generalization and discrimination. The higher, heavy line represents the tendency for the excitatory effects of training with S+ to generalize to other points on the stimulus dimension. The lower, lighter line represents the generalization of inhibition resulting from training with S−. The broken line, which is the difference between the two, represents the resulting tendency of the response to occur to different stimuli.

Further Developments

During the critical years of the 1930s and 1940s, when Hull was putting together and modifying his behavior system, he had the immense advantage of being the center of an extremely active and capable group of students and colleagues. He had the further advantage that many of these coworkers were more than willing to contribute generously to the broad enterprise that became known as Hullian theory. Even as these individuals matured and went their own ways and even as some of them came to develop their own strong theoretical convictions, their efforts continued to contribute to the enterprise. When Hull died there was a new generation of exceptionally able men to carry forth the program he had started. These men tested his ideas, as well as their own, and continued to modify the basic postulates and refine the whole theoretical structure. Many of these men had able students of their own who provided a third generation of Hullian or neo-Hullian theorists. Thus the enterprise that Hull began at Yale spread around the country in just a few years. Even psychologists who were not dedicated to Hullian theory itself found themselves caught up in such issues as the nature of reinforcement and the nature of incentive motivation.

Space does not permit analysis of all the work or the issues involved, but we may survey some of the highlights. Some of the basic assumptions of Hull's 1943 theory had been anticipated by his colleagues. The importance of motivation as a codeterminant of behavior (along with habit) had been stressed by O. Hobart Mowrer. In two important theoretical papers Mowrer (1938, 1939) showed the inadequacy of a purely Pavlovian approach to learning, and he began to build a specialized theory of avoidance learning, an extremely challenging phenomenon that no one but the Hullians, and particularly Mowrer, was able to deal with at all adequately. In these same papers Mowrer had also urged that learning by reinforcement be substituted for learning by contiguity, which was still in vogue at that time. Mowrer began to part company with Hull in 1947 and continued to go his own way. He soon began to emphasize the importance of the secondary learning system, and in his 1960 book there was almost no vestige of Hull's original primary learning system.

In 1941 Neal Miller and John Dollard presented a systematic and comprehensive behavior theory that anticipated many features of Hull's 1943 system. The presentation was not as formal or as detailed and complex. The habit construct was essentially the same. The drive-reduction hypothesis of reinforcement was there, but drive was treated considerably differently, not as a separate kind of construct. According to Miller and Dollard, any strong stimulus can have motivating or drive properties without being tied to the needs of the organism. Complications such as inhibition and oscillation were missing from their theory. Extinction, for example, was explained by means of competing responses rather than by inhibition. This simplified version of, or preview of, Hull's theory was shown to have great potential applicability to human social learning. In subsequent years Miller came to dominate both theory and research in the area of conflict (for example, Miller, 1959). He, together with Mowrer, clarified and attempted to codify the difficult areas of learned drives and learned rewards (Miller, 1951). These developments are so important for understanding the subsequent history of learning theory that we will devote more space to them in Chapter 8. In the 1950s Miller turned his attention to the relationship between drive and need and the relationship between drive reduction and reinforcement. Much of his work on these problems is summarized in an important paper

(Miller, 1957), in which he concludes that the drive-reduction hypothesis can be defended, provided that drive is not tied as closely as Hull tied it to biological needs. In recent years Miller has focused his attention on the physiological bases of learning and motivation (Miller, 1969).

A few theorists have attempted to follow the principles that defined Hull's primary learning system. For example, Judson Brown (1961) defended the concept of drive, and with considerable success, but his definition of drive was somewhat different from Hull's original definition, in that it was expanded to include learned sources of motivation, such as incentive. But in recent years most Hullian theorists have followed Mowrer in abandoning the primary learning system in favor of the secondary learning system.

The man who was mainly responsible for the early development of the secondary system was Kenneth Spence. In some important early papers Spence had contributed to the Hullian enterprise in such ways as analyzing discrimination learning (Spence, 1937) and clarifying the logic of the mathematical deductive approach (Spence, 1944). But it was Spence who explicated the r_G theory of incentive motivation (Spence, 1951) and stressed the importance of secondary reinforcement (Spence, 1947). His last major theoretical statement (Spence, 1956) retains so much of the programmatic spirit and scientific philosophy that had characterized the Hullian enterprise that it constitutes, in effect, a final status report on Hull's theory. But at the same time Spence shifted the emphasis so much and broke so much new ground that his book stands apart from Hullian theory and perhaps marks the end of the era. For example, Spence gave a great deal of attention to such phenomena as amount of reinforcement and delay of reinforcement. Much of the relevant research had been done by his own students, and its explanation seemed to require the secondary learning system. The old $D \times H$ equation was of no use in describing these phenomena.

Hull's impact was immense. During the 1950s his ideas completely dominated the research literature. Thus he accomplished what he wanted to do, which was to generate research that would test his theoretical conjectures. Virtually every behavioral conjecture that Hull made has now been shown to be wrong. But that is not important; what is important is that, because of Hull, we now know a great deal more about the hungry rat than we did just a few years ago.

References for Further Reading

Hull's major works, *Principles of Behavior* (1943) and *A Behavior System* (1952a) are tough going and require extraordinary commitment from the reader. His shorter works are more rewarding but typically present only part of the total theoretical system. Spence (1956) is the best spokesman for both his own and Hull's position on many theoretical issues; there is also an excellent analysis by Logan (1959). Their common philosophy of science is further described in several of Spence's collected papers (Spence, 1960). Hull's motivation principles are discussed in some detail by Brown (1961). For biographical material we are fortunate to have, first, an autobiographical chapter (Hull, 1952b) and, second, the "idea books," a sort of personal intellectual diary (Hull, 1962).

CHAPTER
7

SKINNER

From the outset of his professional career, B. F. Skinner (born 1904) has used his own methods for studying behavior, his own apparatus for observing it, his own techniques for analyzing it, and his own ideas about how it should be explained. Gradually at first and then at an accelerated pace, Skinner's methods and his approach to the problems of behavior have become popular. Their success is apparent not only in laboratory situations but also in a broad range of practical applications. Over the years Skinner has attracted an increasing number of followers who, if not willing to call themselves Skinnerians, are at least happy to call themselves operant conditioners and who vigorously extol the virtues of Skinner's experimental analysis of behavior.

Our earlier theorists had all struggled with the basic term "stimulus." For Guthrie the stimulus was not a manipulable object in the environment; it was a mosaic of hypothetical events whose existence was inferred from the occurrence of some behavior. Hull tied behavior to stimulus objects but only through a tortuous path of intervening variables and a number of postulates, including one postulate that could make the effective stimulus almost totally unrelated to physical stimulus objects. For Tolman it was not the stimulus object itself but how the animal perceived it that mattered. In his first theoretical paper, which had been part of his doctoral dissertation, Skinner (1931) observed that the terms stimulus and response had both come to acquire a double reference. Even the relationship between stimulus and response, the reflex, had a double meaning. On the one hand, there was the hypothetical physiological entity, the "reflex arc," which was assumed to necessitate a given movement when a given receptor was stimulated. On the other hand, there was the fact that we can often elicit a reliable response by presenting an appropriate stimulus object. Difficulties arise when we confuse the behavioral S-R with the assumed underlying physiological S-R.

Consider that when Pavlov first discovered his dogs salivating in the absence of any physiological event that could cause the secretion, he found it necessary to coin the anachronistic phrase "psychic reflex." Here the behavioral events were clear, but the underlying mode of operation was obscure, and Pavlov merely assumed that it was like a physiological reflex. Skinner tells us that a single basic observation gives rise to both the psychological concept of reflex and the physiological concept of the reflex arc. The observation is that certain specific responses are very reliably correlated with certain specific stimuli. The empirical or behavioral reflex is, then, nothing more than the correlation of a response with a stimulus. The neurological machinery that produces it is partly speculative and partly the result of further empirical correlations that have been discovered by the physiologists. Skinner (1931) concluded that the basic datum for the student of behavior is simply an observed correlation of stimulus and response.

> When we say, for example, that Robert Whytt discovered the pupillary reflex, we do not mean that he discovered either the contraction of the iris or the impingement of light upon the retina, but rather that he first stated the necessary relationship between these two events. So far as behavior is concerned, the pupillary reflex is nothing more than this relationship. Once given a specific stimulus-response correlation, we may, of course investigate the physiological facts of its mediation. The information there revealed will supplement our definition but it will not affect the status of the reflex as a correlation. (Skinner, 1931, p. 439)

Sometimes the observed correlation is extremely high, and we are all pretty well agreed on using the word "reflex" when it is high enough. Skinner proposed, however, as Pavlov had proposed many years before, that we use the word "reflex" to describe any kind of correlation, even a weak one, between stimulus and response.[1] Thus we see Skinner indicating quite early that for him the explanation of behavior is to be found in the conditions with which the behavior is correlated. The science of behavior should concern itself not with either postulating or attempting to discover underlying mechanisms but with devising experimental arrangements that will make our observations more lawful and orderly.

In a further analysis of the concept of stimulus, Skinner (1935a) addressed the problem of the relationship between stimulus objects and the determinants of the animal's behavior. His answer was again essentially empirical. We have to recognize that the physical energies change from one trial to the next and that, as Guthrie observed, what we like to call the stimulus is in reality a vast population of potential stimulus elements. There is, in short, an indefinitely large class of events that the response may be correlated with. But how large this class is can only be determined empirically. If we vary the stimulus situation we will always find that some subclass of elements is relevant, in the sense that it maintains the correlation with the response, whereas another subclass is irrelevant, in the sense that it can be modified without altering the correlation. The same argument can be applied to the response side. There is a large class of muscle movements that may be effective in depressing a lever sufficiently to operate the food magazine in a Skinner box, but there is only one relevant subclass that changes in probability when the stimulus is changed, and this subclass defines the response for us. In effect, then, the stimulus is whatever environmental events produce a given correlation with a response, and the response is defined as whatever motor activities maintain a given correlation with the stimulus. Later, when Skinner (1938) developed the concept of the operant, it proved more convenient to define a response in terms of some fixed consequence, so that in the Skinner box, for example, a response was defined as whatever motor movements produce a depression of the lever and a food pellet. Here we find a different correlation, but the idea is the same.

So, from the beginning, Skinner did not confine himself to any anatomically defined unit of analysis. The stimulus, the response, and later the reinforcement—all of the terms that enter into Skinner's analysis of be-

---

[1] Pavlov called all behaviors reflexes because for him that was the only way to ensure that they be thought of as determinant mechanistic entities. Skinner (1931) wanted to call all behaviors reflexes because to him it must have seemed the best way to indicate that they are simply S-R correlations. For Pavlov the mechanistic interpretation was the only way to satisfy his requirement that the stimulus *necessarily* produces the response, whereas for Skinner necessity itself is only a matter of observation. Causation does not require a mechanical system; it requires only that the correlation between observed events be perfect or nearly perfect.

havior—were defined in terms not of an *a priori* conception of what these units must be but simply of classes of observable events that maintain the observed correlations between them. If we find that we can control a minute movement like the twitch of an individual muscle fiber (see for example Hefferline, Keenan, & Harford, 1958), then for that purpose that movement becomes the response. If we find that we can control a molar act like going to the movies with contingent reinforcement, then that behavior is appropriately defined as the response.

By the mid-1930s something of a crisis had arisen because Pavlovian conditioning could no longer be viewed as either the universal method or the universal mechanism for producing learning, yet the term conditioning had become virtually synonymous with learning. A learned response was likely to be called a "conditioned response" whether the learning was obtained by means of a Pavlovian or a Thorndikean procedure. In an attempt to settle the matter equitably, Skinner (1935b) observed that there are two types of conditioned reflexes—two types of learned S-R correlations—and that they are produced by different experimental procedures. Then, partly because of the different procedures and partly because of the different kinds of responses that are subject to learning with them, there are certain other technical differences. For example, the important event S* must necessarily follow the learned response in the reinforcement procedure; but S* precedes the response and usually elicits it in a Pavlovian procedure. A second point of difference is that the classically conditioned reflex may have zero strength initially, but the operant cannot because it has to occur at least once before it can be reinforced.

In this 1935 paper Skinner mentions the stimulus that he assumed must necessarily be correlated with the operant response. He said that it was unimportant, but he included it in his diagrams. But Skinner must have seen the inconsistency of including a hypothetical, or at least unobserved, stimulus in his otherwise highly empirical analysis. The elicitor of the operant began to disappear in 1937 and was totally absent from his 1938 book. A new and much more fundamental difference between the two learning procedures was discovered. The classically conditioned response is correlated with and controlled by an antecedent event, an eliciting stimulus, which is initially the US and subsequently the CS. But in the reinforcement-learning paradigm there is no antecedent; behavior is controlled by its consequence, S*. Although there may actually be an internal, unobservable elicitor, the task of the behavioral scientist, we recall, is not to speculate about or search for such things. His task is to discover what environmental events control behavior. In the case of the operant response it is correlated with its consequence. The operant is emitted, rather than elicited, and it is controlled by its consequences. In the Pavlovian procedure the response, now called a "respondent," is elicited and is controlled by its eliciting stimulus. This then became the fundamental difference in the two procedures.

Skinner (1938) was perhaps the first to observe that different kinds of responses seem to be peculiarly subject to learning with these two procedures. The operant is typically a skeletal response, and in earlier days it had been called voluntary. Such behavior is readily observable because it is external. It is, in fact, that behavior with which the organism operates on its environment (which is why it is called operant), and because it is external it is behavior that the environment can control by reinforcement and punishment. Respondent behavior is internal and has a secret, or personal, quality about it. Feelings, glandular secretions, or emotional reactions are not very effectively communicated to the environment, and our fellows do not very often bother to reinforce or punish these kinds of reactions.[2] Thus we have a picture of two classes of behavior: The respondent class is internal and consists primarily of emotional and glandular reactions (like salivation); the operant class is more public and consists of skeletal behaviors that operate upon the environment and frequently meet with particular consequences. The respondent class seems peculiarly subject to classical conditioning, and the operant class seems peculiarly subject to modification and control by environmental consequences. Two kinds of behavior: two kinds of learning.

The Operant Experiment

While Skinner was developing his philosophy of behavior, he was also rapidly developing his own methods for studying it. If we are to believe his own account (Skinner, 1956), the Skinner box evolved rather quickly. The chief evolutionary pressure was expediency: how to obtain a lot of behavior in a short period of time and ensure that it would be orderly and lawful. Ultimately Skinner had his rats working for food in a small enclosure so that their time, and Skinner's time, was not wasted by a lot of running around. A response that required little effort was chosen, so that the rat could work for long periods of time without showing any apparent fatigue. The response was pressing a small mechanical lever, or bar, which defined the response without Skinner having to judge if the response had occurred, if it was correct, or if it was the response that was desired. Indeed, Skinner did not have to be there at all because he used a mechanical response-

---

[2] We will see in Chapter 8 that, if someone takes the trouble to monitor these private reactions and bothers to arrange consequences for them, they are both reinforceable and punishable and can be made voluntary.

recording system. Skinner (1956) has indicated that the cumulative record was also developed primarily as a matter of expediency. The rotating food-delivery mechanism he was using at the time had a central spindle, and all that was necessary was to put a string around the spindle and allow it to wind up as the food magazine rotated. A pen attached to the string pressed against a rotating paper drum so that the results of an experiment were immediately presented as the cumulative number of responses made after a given passage of time (see Figure 7.1). The cumulative record is simply one of many ways in which the occurrence of the response in time may be recorded, but it enables the experimenter to see perhaps more easily than with any other presentation the rate at which the response occurs.

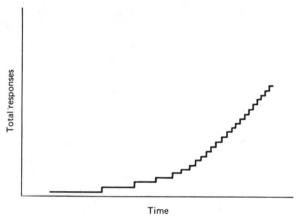

Fig. 7.1 *A small sample of a cumulative record showing how the total number of responses increases with time, slowly at first and then at a higher rate. Typically the record is constructed on such a small scale that individual responses cannot be seen; therefore only the resulting overall rate is apparent.*

So the basic Skinnerian experiment was born. The methods of obtaining data and analyzing it were introduced in Skinner's doctoral dissertation and have been used with little further modification in the bulk of operant-conditioning experiments from that time to this. What was at first a convenience after a while became routine and eventually a ritual. Skinner and his followers rarely look at behavior except as it emerges in their cumulative records. They rarely look at any aspect or dimension of behavior other than the rate of responding. Other measures of response strength such as amplitude, latency following the onset of a cue, or the percentage of time a response is made to one stimulus rather than another are usually ignored.

There is another feature of the ritual. Skinner has frequently argued that to be useful a law of behavior must be applicable to an individual subject. Empirical generalizations that apply only to the average performance of a number of subjects are likely to have little power or generality. The experimental strategy is therefore to establish and demonstrate a particular kind of control in a single subject. Typically, a stable base-line rate of responding is first established. Then some experimental parameter is systematically altered, and the resulting change from the original base-line rate of responding is carefully noted. Then the experimenter returns to the conditions under which the original base line was obtained, and, it is hoped, the behavior returns to the initial rate. This process of systematic departure from the base line and return to it is repeated as often as necessary to convince the experimenter that he has gained control over the behavior, that he can manipulate it in the same way that he manipulates, say, an electric light with a switch. Then, to show that there is nothing exceptional about that subject, the same phenomenon is obtained in one or two others. Once the experimenter has found how to control a particular subject's behavior, the technique can be verified with other individuals, but lawfulness itself is said to reside in the individual's behavior; it is that lawfulness that must be sought in an experimental analysis of behavior.

Does this mean that we have finally arrived at a truly deterministic psychology? Can we leave behind the uncertain semantics of Guthrie, the loose syntax of Tolman, and the oscillatory function of Hull? Yes we can, according to many Skinnerians. Behavior is determined in the sense that it is lawful, they say, and if we find variability in behavior it is because we have not yet learned how to control it fully. The force of this optimistic argument is largely lost, however, because it is based on two special considerations that are often not recognized. One consideration is that behavior appears to become lawful when it is analyzed in terms of rate of responding; it is the number of responses per hour that is highly predictable. But is not such a measure itself based upon a kind of averaging? An animal might respond consistently a thousand times an hour and still show a great deal of moment by moment variability. When examined in detail, a cumulative record may show an animal pausing after one reinforcement for ten seconds before resuming bar pressing, then pausing for thirty seconds after the next reinforcement. There may be nothing particularly lawful or predictable about these pauses, and this unpredictability is obscured by looking only at the overall cumulative record. In fairness to Skinnerian researchers, it should be emphasized that they have extensively studied local rates, short-term effects, and the fine details of their cumulative records generally. But it should also be noted that these details of behavior often prove peculiarly unpredictable. The fact remains that the moment by moment behavior of an animal in any situation is very likely to be unpredictable and this difficulty can be easily obscured by summarizing a great number of behavioral events in a cumulative record.

The second consideration upon which the argument of lawfulness often depends is the conviction that it really does not matter how long it takes the experimenter to produce stability, to gain control over behavior; it is the final stable performance of asymptotic behavior that matters. A Skinnerian may not find the kind of behavioral control he is looking for or the kind of lawfulness he seeks until his animal has been run for 50 or 100 sessions in the Skinner box. During this long time the behavior may reveal a variety of changes, some systematic and of great potential interest for what they may reveal about learning and others that appear to be unsystematic and more or less random. But with sufficient training all the changes in behavior caused by learning, as well as the more subtle factors interfering with effective control, become stabilized, and the behavior becomes predictable.

The development of Skinner's approach to behavior can be summarized with the following points. On some of the toughest theoretical issues of the mid-1930s Skinner took a firm stand on the side of an objective, empirical approach. His approach has been both sophisticated and practical; he tells us that we should not confuse philosophy with data collection. On the difficult question of how to define the stimulus and the response, he tells us again to let the data be our guide. If there is a class of events that is consistently correlated with behavior then we may call it the stimulus, and if there is a class of events produced by the animal that can be correlated with the experimental situation then we may call it the response. There seem to be two kinds of learning because there are two kinds of procedures with which learning can be demonstrated; that is, there are two ways to make behavior predictable.

Skinner discovered quite early that it is possible to obtain a great deal of systematic data using certain methods. He selected a response, bar pressing, that the animal can make easily and frequently, and he confined the animal in a simple apparatus in which there was little else to do except press the bar. Then he proceeded to watch all the different ways in which it was possible to control the rate of responding. Sometimes control is achieved quickly, and sometimes it requires a great deal of training, but this difference is relatively unimportant as long as the behavior of individual subjects can ultimately be controlled.

The Concept of Reinforcement

Any environmental event that is programmed as a consequence of a response that can increase the rate of responding is called a reinforcer. This definition is strictly empirical; it makes no assumptions about the underlying process. Skinner has stayed relatively free of the question of what is learned when learning occurs. For Skinner, reinforcement is a procedure for controlling behavior, not a hypothetical device that produces S-R connections, habits, or expectancies. Reinforcers are simply events that increase the rate of responding.

We all know from our own efforts to control the behavior of other organisms that some kinds of events are rather consistent reinforcers, whereas others are not. For the hungry rat, dog, or pigeon, food is usually very effective. But, whereas reinforcers like food have great generality across species, others are much more specific. Petting a dog can be reinforcing, whereas petting an adult human or a rat is usually not. In the case of the human subject, social approval, praise, or getting the right answer to a problem is often effective. Giving a gerbil pieces of paper that it can tear up for nest material is reinforcing.

It should be noted that reinforcers do more than affect the preceding response; they also tend to elicit particular behaviors (recall our earlier discussion of elicitation theory). Food elicits eating, petting may elicit tail wagging, and paper may elicit shredding. It is clear that such elicited behaviors compete with the execution of the reinforced response. For example, if we want a rat to press a bar at a high rate, then we have to be concerned about the fact that the rat may spend more time eating food pellets than pressing the bar. Skinner provides a characteristically practical answer to this problem: Reinforcement is not given after each response in a continuous manner (so-called continuous reinforcement, or CRF); it is given intermittently, so that the animal is obliged to make a large number of responses to obtain a small number of reinforcements. The cumulative record will then reflect primarily time spent pressing the bar rather than time spent eating.

Reinforcers can be classified in two large categories: those whose presentation increases responding, as food does for the hungry rat, and those whose removal increases the rate of responding, as does electric shock. The latter are called negative reinforcers. If we set up such a contingency between behavior and shock and obtain increased responding, then we have an effective escape-training procedure. There is another procedure, punishment, in which the presentation of an event such as shock is made contingent upon a response. If the response is weakened, then we have an effective punishment procedure. The human tendency to judge all things as good or bad may bias us toward thinking of punishers and negative reinforcers as equivalent in some way (perhaps as being equally bad), but they are defined by different kinds of procedures. Ordinarily the same kinds of "bad" stimuli can be used either as negative reinforcers to strengthen behavior or as punishers to weaken it, but there are some interesting exceptions (see Bolles & Seelbach, 1964).

There is a fourth logical category: the removal of a positive reinforcer. A common procedure in contemporary research is the time out (TO). An animal may be making one response to obtain food; whenever it makes a second response a brief TO is introduced during which the first response no longer produces food. Under these conditions it is usually found that the rate of the second response is reduced. In these cases the removal of the positive reinforcer reduces the rate of responding.

Some reinforcers are effective without prior experience. Food and shock are assumed to be typical examples. These events are therefore called primary reinforcers. But, as Skinner discovered quite early in his career, it is possible to establish a completely neutral cue such as a light or a buzzer as a reinforcer. That is, we may have a conditioned reinforcer; Skinner introduced this concept several years before Hull did, and he also investigated it experimentally considerably earlier. Before describing conditioned reinforcement, it is necessary to make an important digression to describe discrimination. In everyday life we require that a response occur under particular conditions and not willy-nilly. As the administrators of reinforcement for other organisms, we reinforce their behavior on some occasions and withhold it on others. A stimulus in the presence of which behavior is reinforced is called a discriminative stimulus, S^D. The presence of S^D therefore defines when the reinforcement contingency is in effect. The complementary stimulus in the presence of which the particular behavior is not reinforced is usually designated S^Δ. When discrimination training is carried out, what happens sooner or later is that the animal comes to respond almost exclusively in the presence of S^D and withholds its behavior in the presence of S^Δ. As in other aspects of his analysis, Skinner does not speculate about the underlying mechanisms. He does not appear to be concerned with whether some form of inhibition reduces the rate of responding in S^Δ. It is simply an empirical fact that discrimination training is frequently, though not invariably, effective in making animals respond in the presence of one stimulus and not respond in the presence of another.

When discrimination training is successful, we can say that we have brought the behavior under stimulus control or under discriminative control. There is an interesting paradox here, because operant behavior is defined partly by the fact that we do not know, or usually care, what stimulus elicits it. But at the same time most operant behavior is under some kind of discriminative control, and if this control is strong enough we have the illusion of eliciting an operant by presenting the appropriate S^D. But it is not proper to use the word "elicit" in this context. Primary or unlearned control of behavior is "elicited," whereas learned stimulus control is typically called just "stimulus control." The phraseology is awkward, but it emphasizes an important distinction.

Consider now the following experiment originally reported by Skinner in 1936. Rats were trained to press a bar for food, and then this behavior was brought under discriminative control in which S^D and S^Δ were presented during alternate three-minute periods. After a number of sessions the behavior became highly predictable, with a high rate of responding in the presence of S^D and virtually no responding in the presence of S^Δ. At this point, Skinner changed the experimental situation so that the duration of S^Δ was not fixed. The rat could terminate S^Δ and begin the S^D period by pressing the bar. Soon bar pressing began to occur in the S^Δ. It is clear that making the onset of S^D contingent upon bar pressing increased the rate of bar pressing. By definition, therefore, the onset of S^D is a reinforcer, but because it was not originally a reinforcer it must be a conditioned reinforcer (Skinnerians say "conditioned" reinforcers; Hullians say "secondary" reinforcers). At this point, Skinner made one of his relatively rare theoretical conjectures: S^Ds are conditioned reinforcers.

Conditioned reinforcement is readily demonstrated in the Skinner box using the conventional method of initially training rats to press the bar. First, the rat is put in the box, and the magazine that holds the food delivers a free food pellet from time to time. The presentation of food is accompanied by a characteristic "click" from the food magazine. After a while this click becomes an S^D for approaching the food cup (because food reinforces approach following the S^D but not other times). The click can be established as a very effective S^D, so that no matter what the animal is doing or where it is located it will run over to the food cup when the click occurs. Now the bar is introduced for the first time, and the experimenter can sit back and wait for the animal to make its first response. When it does, the click occurs, and the rat runs over for its food as before. But now a new phenomenon appears. The rate of bar pressing rises dramatically. The argument (there is very little direct evidence to make it more than an argument) is that, just as food reinforces the approach response, so the click reinforces the bar-press response. Of course, food provides additional delayed primary reinforcement for bar pressing, but the initial contact with the behavior is made by the immediate conditioned reinforcer.

All of the behavior that ultimately becomes integrated into the unit called bar pressing consists of a series, or chain, of responses. The animal must approach the bar, touch it, press it, go over to the food cup, obtain the food, eat it, and return to the bar. Each response in the chain is said to be reinforced partly by the ultimate delivery of food but also partly by the new stimulus configuration that each response produces because each of these stimulus patterns serves as an S^D for the next response in the chain. The first few times the chain of behavior occurs it is not executed efficiently, but the repeated action of the series of secondary reinforcers tightens up the behavior, speeds up the whole sequence, and produces what amounts to a single unit of behavior that occurs rapidly enough so that the whole unit can then be almost immediately reinforced by the food. Again we have the summary theoretical statement that S^D is a conditioned reinforcer.

One way to control the specificity of behavior is to bring it under discriminative control. But there is also another kind of response specificity. We may wish to have a rat press a bar with between 15 and 20 grams of force, not any less and not any more. We may wish a child to say "daddy" instead of "dada." This can be done by a technique of differential reinforcement that is similar to discrimination training. Rather than specify particular stimuli under which the contingency is in effect, we require a particular form of response, a particular subclass of the organism's total behavior output. We restrict reinforcement to just those responses that we want. If the appropriate subclass has some reasonable operant level, so that the total generation of behavior will survive the reduction in reinforcement density without extinguishing, it should gradually become stronger as the reinforcement contingency goes into effect. If the original operant rate of the desired behavior is too low to survive the new requirement, then we can introduce a new trick: We can "shape" the behavior. For example, if the rat is pressing the bar with a force that ranges only from 5 to 10 grams, we may reinforce responses that lie in the upper half of this distribution, that is, from 7.5 to 10 grams. As we do so, the mean response strength will increase, and, if the variance stays the same, the animal will soon be showing a distribution of forces ranging between 7.5 and 12.5 grams. If we reinforce only the stronger half of these responses, the distributions should soon shift to a range between 10 and 15 grams. Soon the animal should be giving us precisely the behavior we want.

Schedules

There is another mechanism that introduces further specificity into behavior. Skinner noted that reinforcement in the real world is typically intermittent rather than invariant. So, if we are to understand behavior in the real world, we must study different schedules of intermittence (we have already noted that intermittent schedules serve the experimenter by generating lots of behavior). Different schedules of reinforcement produce their own characteristic alterations in the rate of responding. For example, if we reinforce every fifth bar press, we typically find the rat giving us five quick responses and then a brief pause while it consumes its food pellet, as in Figure 7.2. If we reinforce every twentieth response, we are likely to find a very high rate of responding during a run, but we are also likely to find longer pauses following reinforcement. If we train an animal up to a ratio

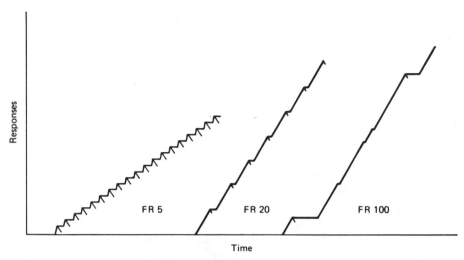

Fig. 7.2   *Illustrative records showing typical patterns*
of responding on different FR schedules. The little
hash marks indicate delivery of reinforcement.

of 100, we may expect to find breaks in the run and long, variable pauses
after reinforcement. These characteristic patterns under different schedules
of reinforcement suggest that the animal learns something about the specific
response requirement or that different schedules introduce their own subtle
S^Ds (for example, perhaps on a long ratio some feeling of fatigue becomes
an S^D for continued responding). Whatever the underlying mechanisms are,
they are clearly dependent upon the particular schedule of reinforcement.
More specifically, these details of behavior can be modified by making the
schedule intrinsically unpredictable. If we train animals on a schedule that
pays off irregularly, after a variable number of responses (a VR schedule),
the breaks under high fixed ratios tend to disappear. A VR-100 schedule
will still produce postreinforcement pauses, but it tends to yield long steady
runs.

Reinforcement can also be scheduled to occur only after a fixed lapse of
time. For example, we may decide to reinforce the first response that occurs
one minute after the last reinforcement. When such a fixed interval (FI)
schedule is first introduced, we tend to obtain extinction curves during each
minute. But after a few sessions a new phenomenon is discovered: The
animal responds at a low rate immediately following reinforcement and
at an increasing rate as the time for the next reinforcement comes due.
This characteristic pattern is called a "scallop." It is as if the lapse of time
from the last reinforcement acquires discriminative control over responding.

Short postreinforcement times constitute an S^Δ, and times approaching one minute become an S^D. Again, if the time for reinforcement is made unpredictable, for example, if we have a variable interval (VI) schedule, then scallops do not develop, and the animal gives us, as in the case of the VR schedule, a quite steady, continuous rate of responding.

Consider again the schedule of reinforcement that Skinner used in the secondary-reinforcement study already cited. His animals were pressing a bar for food for a period of time in the presence of one stimulus and were in extinction for a period of time in the presence of a second stimulus. Such a program is called a "multiple schedule." A similar schedule that includes two or more components but without correlated stimuli to indicate what is happening at a given moment is called a "mixed schedule." An animal may also be subjected to two reinforcement schedules at the same time, a so-called concurrent schedule in which two different schedules, two different kinds of reinforcers, or reinforcement for two different responses may be programmed simultaneously. It should be clear that schedules of reinforcement can be enormously complicated. Ferster and Skinner (1957) wrote a very large book just to describe the different patterns of responding found with different kinds of schedules.

Applications of the Theory

Extinction is the procedure of withholding reinforcement following the occurrence of a previously reinforced response. If a stable rate of responding is first established, then withholding reinforcement produces a characteristic flattening out of the cumulative curve, as shown in Figure 7.3. Skinner is usually more interested in producing behavior than in extinguishing it, and he characteristically does not speculate about the mechanisms underlying extinction. Is it due to loss of incentive motivation? Is it due to loss in strength of the previously learned S-R connection? Is it produced by inhibition of some type? But these Hullian-flavored questions are never raised. Skinnerians do note, however, that extinction proceeds more rapidly under some conditions than under others. In general, the less predictable reinforcement is on the base-line task, the more slowly extinction occurs. For example, extinction is slower following training on an FI schedule than following continuous reinforcement, and it is slower still after training on a VI schedule.

Reinforcement was defined earlier as an event that increases the rate of responding. But here we have discovered a somewhat different property of reinforcement: It is also assumed to maintain a given rate of responding. If behavior collapses as a result of the manipulation of some consequence of

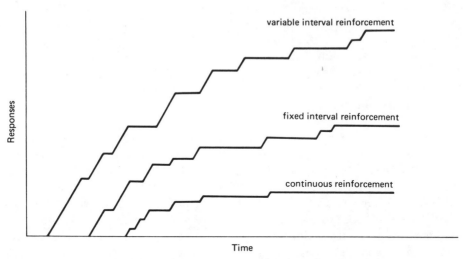

Fig. 7.3 Extinction of responding following three kinds of prior reinforcement experience.

the response, then we are obliged to conclude this manipulation has removed reinforcement. It is important to note the shift in emphasis here. For Hull, a reinforcer was basically a strengthener of connections, an event that produces learning. For Skinner, a reinforcer may produce learning, but that is not its fundamental property. Basically, a reinforcer is an event that gives us control over operant behavior. It makes relatively little difference whether the behavior is originally quite weak and brought up to strength through reinforcement or is simply maintained at a constant rate with reinforcement. If some programmed consequence of responding is found to have the property of maintaining behavior, then it must necessarily be a reinforcer. We saw this logic applied to Skinner's original definition of conditioned reinforcement, and it can be applied as well to primary reinforcement. The old question that so fascinated Tolman and Hull, whether reinforcement is necessary for learning, is therefore answered logically, rather than empirically. If the rate of responding is maintained by some consequence of the response, then the consequence must be a reinforcer.

The topic of motivation receives relatively cursory treatment from Skinner. The principal reason for depriving an animal of food is simply to ensure that the presentation of food will be an effective reinforcer. The object is apparently to produce some fairly severe level of weight loss, like 15 or 20 percent, and hold it at this value. What is wanted is a level of deprivation that will be as high as possible without risking the eventual debilitation of the animal. A few investigators have looked systematically at the effects of deprivation upon rate of responding, and some of the results

show interesting interactions between reinforcement schedules and deprivation level. For example, Clark (1958) has shown a systematic relationship
between the response rates of rats on different VI schedules and the strength
of hunger motivation (see Figure 7.4). On the other hand, Powell (1971)
found that when pigeons are trained on VI schedules their motivation
seems to have little if any effect on scalloping, on overall rate of responding,
or on the postreinforcement pause. Behavior on an FI schedule appears to
be dependent almost entirely upon the pigeon's experience with the schedule
and to be relatively independent of its motivation.

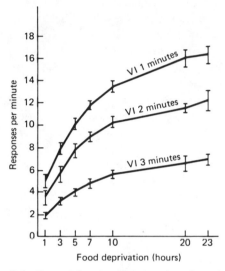

Fig. 7.4 *Rate of bar pressing as a function of motivation and schedule of reinforcement. The variance
under each condition is indicated. (From Clark, The
effect of deprivation and frequency of reinforcement
on variable-interval responding, Journal of the Experimental Analysis of Behavior, 1958, 1, 221–228.
Copyright 1958 by the Society for the Experimental
Analysis of Behavior, Inc.)*

Some of Skinner's early research was addressed to these kinds of questions. For example, his dissertation reported a study of how the rate of
responding declined during the course of a long session as motivation was
decreased by the food that was consumed. But he soon turned his attention
to other determinants of behavior that seemed more interesting or more
predictable or that led to more stable responding across time.

There is some question about whether or not Skinner really has a theory
of behavior. At one point, he explicitly denied having one (Skinner, 1950).

It is certainly clear that he does not have a theory if by that we mean a set of conjectures about an underlying reality. Skinner has held steadfastly to the view that the lawfulness of behavior is to be found in behavior itself. He does not mean that there is no nervous system or mind; he means that these other realms add nothing to the lawfulness found in behavior.

But theory can also mean a systematic orientation toward data. It can mean simply having a particular bias toward what kind of observations to make and how to order and describe them. Skinner typically looks only at asymptotic performance; he is not particularly interested in the transitions that fascinate the majority of learning theorists. He tends to look at behavior in situations in which it can occur at very high rates over long periods of time, and he tends to look only at cumulative records. In other words, Skinner has a strong commitment to finding particular kinds of lawfulness. Are not such prior assumptions about how behavior should be analyzed just as constraining, and may they not have just as much influence on the kind of data that are obtained as the prior assumptions made by Hull, for example, in postulating a set of intervening variables? Skinner makes prior assumptions about how behavior should be collected and analyzed. Hull merely made prior assumptions about how it should be explained.

Skinner also tends to overgeneralize on the basis of available data. This tendency afflicts all of us from time to time, but it is chronic in and diagnostic of the theorist. Some of Skinner's generalizations are clearly theoretical. For example, he noted that many reinforcers that are effective in controlling human behavior are not tied to any specific motivating conditions. The human does not have to be hungry, thirsty, or frightened in order to be reinforced by money or social approval. These events are assumed to be conditioned reinforcers (a theoretical assertion), but, in addition, Skinner suggests that, when a particular reinforcing event such as social approval has been established as a conditioned reinforcer under a variety of different motivation conditions, it then becomes independent of any motivation condition. It becomes a generalized conditioned reinforcer. This formulation is clearly a theoretical statement, one that is probably wrong.

In explaining superstitious behavior, Skinner (1948a) observed that, when food was presented at a fixed temporal interval independently of the animal's behavior, the animal (a pigeon) developed a great deal of stereotyped and rather bizarre behavior. The pigeon would walk around in circles, scratch the floor, wave its head this way and that, and engage in long sequences of these behaviors during the interval between food presentations. Skinner argued that whatever behavior an individual happened to make just before food presentation would quite likely increase in rate and be caught up in a positive-feedback arrangement in which the more often it occurred, the more often it would be reinforced, and the more often it was reinforced the more likely it would occur. Ultimately each animal must develop a large amount of individualistic behavior, none of which is necessary for producing food, of course, because food is not contingent upon any particular behavior. Such behavior can be called "superstitious." It is clear that Skinner has presupposed, as Thorndike did years before, that events like food have an automatic response-strengthening effect, and he has presupposed further that this effect increases with the contiguity between the response and reinforcement. Both these suppositions are defensible on the basis of other data, but in the context of the superstitious experiment they are clearly theoretical commitments and not just statements of fact.

Still, the work of Skinner and his followers is relatively nontheoretical. Their concern with nothing but behavior, their generally inductive attitude toward the accumulation of data, their empirical accounts of their own experiments, their preoccupation with reliable and consistent control of behavior, their emphasis upon empirical rather than conceptual resolutions of problems all indicate that Skinner's theory is the least theoretical of the theories that we have examined. Furthermore, over the years there has been a clear trend away from learning theory in Skinner's writing. *The Behavior of Organisms* (1938) was obviously a contribution to learning theory. It presented much of the author's early thinking related to philosophical and methodological questions. It contained a wealth of data too, but its main contribution at the time was to the better understanding of animal learning in simple situations. In effect, the theoretical questions in animal behavior had been solved, at least by common consent among Skinner's followers; their attention then turned to the complex problem of applying their methods to human behavior. Here the behavior was more complex, the data were sparse, and there was renewed freedom for theoretical developments (for example, Skinner, 1953).

It is also apparent that over the years Skinner has not only moved from simpler to more complex organisms, he has also moved from theoretical to more practical questions, from laboratory situations to real life situations. He has made a "flight from the laboratory" (Skinner, 1961). Operant-conditioning principles have been applied to an ever-increasing number of human-behavior situations, and Skinner has shown, accordingly, less interest in the problem of learning and more interest in the maintenance of behavior. Acquisition of new behaviors and new kinds of stimulus control is viewed as less important in the long run than simply regulating and maintaining (in short, controlling) behavior. To the extent that current emphasis is upon applications of behavior-control techniques, there has been a lessening of concern with learning mechanisms *per se*; to that extent

Skinner's theory of learning becomes less theoretical and, of course, less pertinent to learning. Skinner's attitude has become increasingly that of an engineer rather than that of a scientist: practical rather than theoretical. We may start with some idea of how to control a particular behavior; so we try it. If it works, it works. If it does not work, then we must search about for another technique that is more effective.

At times it appears that control is of value simply for its own sake. Skinner and many of his followers show a peculiar and perhaps revealing fascination with controlling behavior by means of very "lean" reinforcement schedules. Fixed ratios of 50 to 1 and 100 to 1 are common; but how high can the ratio be pushed? For some time the record was the ratio of 192 reported by Skinner in his 1938 book. But, as the technology developed and the number of enterprising Skinnerians increased, the record kept going up. It is apparently now held by Findley and Brady (1965), who managed to train a chimpanzee to respond 120,000 times in order to obtain its food.

It might be fair to say that Skinner has a philosophy that most behavior, probably all behavior that affects other individuals, is controlled by its consequences. And if we program consequences in appropriate ways, we can control the behavior. We can make behavior occur if we want it to, and we can make it not occur if we do not want it to. According to Skinner, that is really all we ought to be concerned with.

Further Developments

Soon after developing the methods and a conceptual framework for studying behavior systematically in simple laboratory situations, Skinner turned his attention to other matters. One was the training of animals for such work as being assembly-line inspectors and missile pilots (Skinner, 1960). As soon as he began working with pigeons, Skinner discovered that they have very fine vision; their behavior can be controlled by extremely subtle visual displays. They will also peck keys almost endlessly for a little food. The pigeon in the missile therefore needs only to be given a visual display showing how the projected path departs from its target and occasional reinforcement for minimizing this discrepancy. One well-trained pigeon could direct a missile more accurately and more cheaply than any complex mechanical system then available.

Skinner also turned his attention to human applications. One distinctive feature of humans is that they talk so much; the obvious strategy is therefore to apply operant-conditioning principles to verbal behavior. Skinner's 1957 book, *Verbal Behavior*, gives a detailed analysis of such behavior. His general argument is that speech is not a means we have been blessed with for "expressing our ideas"; it is simply verbal behavior. It is behavior that, like any operant behavior, has come under stimulus control through differential punishment and reinforcement by other people in the community. People teach us to speak, and we in turn teach others by controlling the consequences of speaking. Speech becomes partly a way to obtain reinforcement from others and partly a way to reinforce others in our verbal community. Skinner sees no special problem in creative or artistic behavior. What we call literature, poetry, and other forms of creative writing follow the same principles; they are only exaggerated extensions of verbal behavior acquired and maintained by the same reinforcement principles that control all our operant behavior.

Can reinforcement principles explain the relationship of man to society? This is perhaps the ultimate goal of any behavioral science. Skinner's novel *Walden Two* (Skinner, 1948b) boldly answers this question in the affirmative. We can construct any kind of society we wish, he has said. Skinner paints a picture of a utopian society that he feels is far superior to our own. The difficulty with real, naturally evolved societies is that the control of behavior is haphazard and disorganized. The contingencies that control us are inconsistently applied. Often behavior that is reinforced by one part of the community is punished by some other vested interest. Even the same people give reinforcement inconsistently. Sometimes it seems that no matter what we do we cannot obtain reinforcement. Skinner argues, however, that the greatest failing of our own poorly designed culture is that much of our behavior is controlled by punishment and by threats of punishment. This type of control is not only relatively ineffective and unpredictable in its results, as has been shown by several laboratory studies; it degrades the quality of life. What makes Walden Two a utopia is quite simply that all behavioral control is effected through positive reinforcement schedules. Walden Two is designed so as to increase the rate of desired behavior rather than to decrease the rate of undesired behaviors. Skinner assures us that we already have most of the principles we need to establish such a utopia. Most important, we have an experimental methodology so that we can find out as we go along how to build into the culture just those behaviors we want in its people. If we put a positive value on artistic creation, then we can reinforce creativity. On the American scene a person who is reinforced for being creative by a few is punished in various ways by many others. The difficulty in establishing Walden Two is that we have all become so accustomed to using punishment and other kinds of aversive control and so used to defending against this kind of control that it might not be possible to make the transition to a system in which all reinforcement is positive.

Skinner's Impact

In recent years Skinner has had a tremendous influence; his impact during the 1960s was probably even greater than Hull's was during the 1950s.[3] Several aspects of his approach have been particularly appealing. One is his atheoretical emphasis. During the 1960s a number of psychologists became disenchanted with theory in general. Hull's own theoretical statements were not well supported empirically, and when his followers and defenders had little success in patching up the old theory or extending some part of it, there gradually developed a feeling that something might be inherently wrong with Hull's type of theory. Perhaps it was too early to attempt quantification or to develop a deductive postulate system. Perhaps some of the fundamental assumptions underlying Hullian theory were intrinsically untestable. Whatever the specific source of disenchantment, Skinner does not require us to make any theoretical commitments. We can simply go into the laboratory and collect masses of systematic and highly reliable data. The theorist can retire for a time, and the empiricist can seek the safety of an inductive approach.

Another dimension of Skinner's success is his emphasis on methodological considerations. The use of automated equipment is not logically necessary, but it becomes a practical necessity. Automation brings with it the attendant promise of good environmental control and a ready-made system for analyzing data. The need for expensive equipment was met by Federal granting agencies, which appeared for a time willing to supply Skinner boxes, clocks, and relays to anyone who promised to do something interesting with them. Everyone could be a real scientist like Pavlov and could control everything to his heart's content.

Much of the appeal of the Skinnerian enterprise in the past few years is the great promise of applying operant-conditioning principles to practical problems of behavior management. Skinner was by no means alone in seeking to extend his laboratory-derived ideas to everyday problems. But none

---

[3] It seems that there was a decade in which the contribution of each of our theorists had its greatest impact and in which his work dominated what was going on in learning theory. The 1900s clearly belonged to Thorndike and the 1910s to Watson. Pavlov then emerged as the big name in the 1920s. Guthrie never really had his own decade because he never overwhelmed those who preceded him, but his impact was felt mostly during the 1930s. The most important years for Tolman were the 1940s, the era of the latent-learning experiment and cognitive psychology generally. But the Hullian hordes were rising fast, and they took over in the 1940s and dominated the 1950s. Skinner and his band of followers took charge in the 1960s. Whether they will retain their preeminence in the 1970s or will be replaced by others, or whether the present decade will belong to anyone in particular is not yet clear.

of the earlier extensions had turned out to be very fruitful; Skinner's approach put the practitioner immediately in contact with behavior. It is, after all, the control of behavior and not the explanation of behavior that ultimately matters to the practitioner. It is thus perhaps not surprising that there has developed an immense amount of interest in reinforcement techniques. Today teachers, parents, law-enforcement agencies—everyone, it seems—is trying to use reinforcement techniques to shape and control the behavior of their charges. It is well past time that psychologists made a useful contribution to the practical management of behavior, and it is a great credit to Skinner that he has provided concepts, techniques, and procedures that promise to be more useful than those of any of his predecessors.

Much of Skinner's success is attributable to other men devoting themselves, for one reason or another, to his cause. Skinner and his students at Harvard University were joined around 1950 by a powerful group of allies at Columbia University. Keller and Schoenfeld (1950) wrote an introductory textbook, they established an undergraduate operant-conditioning laboratory that was to prove a model for similar laboratories throughout the country, and they had a group of very able students who applied Skinner's approach to a variety of new problems such as secondary reinforcement and avoidance behavior. In time these enterprising men went forth to establish their own laboratories, train their own students, found their own journal, and promote the cause across the land.

References for Further Reading

The Behavior of Organisms (Skinner, 1938) is still of considerable value, even though much of the material is now dated. *Schedules of Reinforcement* (Ferster & Skinner, 1957) contains an oppressive amount of material on schedule effects. The best short account of operant conditioning is Rachlin (1970). Skinner is among the best of contemporary writers, and his *Cumulative Record* (Skinner, 1972) is a joy to read, as well as being highly informative. Most of the papers cited in the chapter are reprinted there. It tells us much about the man as well as his many intellectual adventures.

PART
II

THE
CONTEMPORARY
SCENE

In Part I we emphasized the differences among theoretical positions in order to stress their distinctive features and to focus on certain key theoretical issues. But history does not leap about; it flows. There has been continuity, there have been overall trends, and there has been a gradual accumulation of understanding about learning. In Part II the focus will be on the contemporary scene. We will try to make explicit some of these overall trends and to see if there is some consensus among contemporary views of learning. In Chapter 8 we shall focus primarily on different views of classical conditioning and on the important question of how classical conditioning interacts with instrumental, or operant, learning. We shall see that, although there is a working consensus on these matters, there are also some very difficult theoretical problems that remain to be solved. In Chapters 9 and 10 we will conclude our analysis of learning by pointing out some of the directions in which contemporary theory seems to be moving. We will see that contemporary approaches to learning have been enriched, first, by the inclusion of broad evolutionary principles and, second, by the revival of cognitive conceptions of animal behavior.

CHAPTER
8

THE STATUS QUO

Although our classical learning theorists have tended to pull us conceptually this way and that, there have been some gradual overall trends and continuities. Some of these continuities may be apparent to the discerning reader, but others must surely be difficult to perceive. For example, the concept of classical conditioning was first promoted by Pavlov, then discounted by Thorndike, altered by Watson and Guthrie, minimized by Tolman and Hull, and accepted by Skinner. The reader would have to be discerning indeed to perceive any trend here or to draw any conclusion about the current status of classical conditioning. In this chapter we will make current thought about classical conditioning more explicit. We will see how classical conditioning and instrumental learning together constitute the main framework for learning theories in the mid-1970s.

Basic Paradigms

Earlier chapters have revealed a diversity of views on the fundamental nature of the learning process. Thorndike and Hull proposed that learning depends upon a reinforcement mechanism, Guthrie proposed that contiguity is sufficient, and Tolman put forth a quite different proposal. The big question—What is the fundamental nature of the learning process?—is as unsettled today as it has ever been. There is, however, less concern today than there used to be about this ultimate question. One reason for this loss of concern may be a growing skepticism about whether the question can ever be answered. A second and perhaps more important reason is that, even though there is little agreement about the basic *processes* of learning, a good agreement about the *procedures* that produce learning has grown up. The procedures are relatively clear and useful, whereas the processes remain uncertain and rather conjectural.

The consensus is that there are two effective experimental procedures, two basic paradigms, for producing learning. The first is that discovered by Pavlov. It can be called Pavlovian conditioning, classical conditioning, or respondent conditioning. According to this paradigm, learning occurs whenever a relatively unimportant stimulus S is paired with an important stimulus S*, such as food or shock. The second paradigm is variously called trial-and-error learning, instrumental learning, reinforcement learning, or operant conditioning. According to this paradigm, learning occurs when an important event S* is made contingent upon a particular response. Because of the unanimity about the effectiveness of these procedures, the terms "operant conditioning" and "classical conditioning" have tended to become labels for the procedures themselves, rather than designations for the corresponding but still unknown learning processes. This relabeling is not altogether happy from a theoretical point of view, but it is workable enough for the empiricist because he can proceed with his experimental study of learning. He can study as thoroughly as he wishes the conditions under which learning is found.

This methodological, practical, or operational approach to learning also raises a number of questions, which, if not theoretical in the grand sense of seeking the ultimate basis of learning, are nonetheless theoretical in the limited sense of seeking general answers to methodological and practical questions. What type of responses are learned with reinforcement procedures and what type of responses are learned with classical conditioning procedures? What is the critical procedural aspect of classical conditioning? The CS and the US are always paired, but does learning depend upon pairing *per se* or upon some other kind of relationship between the CS and the US? In an operant conditioning procedure, the reinforcer is always contingent upon the response, but does learning result from this contingency or from some other aspect of the operant-conditioning paradigm? To what extent do classical conditioning and operant conditioning occur simultaneously in a given learning experiment? For example, if we attempt to reinforce a particular behavior, may we not also be inadvertently classically conditioning some other response?

In the present chapter we will attempt to summarize current thinking about these kinds of issues. We will grant, for the moment, that there are two basic paradigms. We will see how precisely these paradigms can be defined and how much we can find out about them. Then we will be better prepared to return to the big question of the ultimate nature of learning.

Two Response Systems

During the era of Watson and Guthrie, all learning was said to be classical conditioning, but the work of Tolman, Hull, and others clearly indicated that most responses are not readily classically conditionable. It was therefore suggested by Skinner (1938) and argued at some length by Mowrer (1947) that classical conditioning was applicable only to certain behaviors, a class of responses that Skinner called respondents, such as glandular secretions and reactions of the autonomic nervous system. The learning of behaviors such as running, bar pressing, and the like was assumed to require reinforcement. In short, we had operant responses subject to operant conditioning and respondent behaviors subject to respondent or classical conditioning.

This comfortable and convenient ordering of things was not acceptable to some of the earlier Hullians. Hull (1943) noted that if we were to undertake a classical-conditioning experiment on salivation we could not be sure that the dog did not salivate to the bell because the ensuing food pellet reinforced salivation. The same argument was applied to fear conditioning, most notably by Miller (1951). If shock is the US it must ultimately terminate, and, when it does, there has to be a large reduction in drive that should be effective not only in reinforcing operant behavior but also in reinforcing the fear reaction itself. In effect, the rat learns to fear the CS in much the same way that a man learns to bang his head against a wall: because it feels so good when it stops. In discussing this possibility Miller (1951) noted that it is contrary to common sense, but he also pointed out that common sense often proves to be wrong. Mowrer conducted a series of experiments to defend the idea of two basic learning paradigms by attempting to separate them experimentally. In a typical experiment, Mowrer and Solomon (1954) found that the strength of fear conditioning depended not upon the relationship between the CS and the termination of the US, as Hull and Miller argued, but seemed to depend instead upon the relationship between the onset of the CS and the onset of US, as the Pavlovian paradigm required. It was apparently the contiguity of these stimulus events that produced a fear reaction and not the subsequent relief from shock. Miller (1963) subsequently abandoned the idea that fear is learned by drive reduction, but he still did not accept the idea that there are distinct classes of responses that are ruled by distinct learning principles. His tactic was to abandon drive reduction for both operant conditioning and classical conditioning, which took a heavy burden off the drive-reduction hypothesis but left open the question of whether or not the two types of conditioning are uniquely applicable to the two kinds of behavior.

The story does not end here, however. For several years Miller has continued to investigate whether or not the distinction between the two response classes is valid. In the first reported study of this series, Miller and Carmona (1967) conditioned salivation using operant techniques. They had noted that during the course of a session there was spontaneous variation in the amount of salivation; so they simply made water reinforcement contingent upon the occurrence of a relatively high rate of salivation (water was used instead of food to eliminate the possibility that the reaction was merely a classically conditioned response). A companion group, necessary to control for various extraneous factors, was reinforced whenever it gave a lowered rate of salivation. In both cases salivation was found to be subject to control by its consequences.

In another experiment DiCara and Miller (1968) trained one group of rats to avoid an electric shock by increasing the heart rate. This finding in itself is not remarkable because heart-rate increase might be interpreted as a classically conditioned part of the fear reaction. To control against this interpretation, DiCara and Miller trained another group of rats to avoid shock by decreasing their heart rate (see Figure 8.1). It could be argued that the learning that occurred under these conditions was really produced by learned skeletal responses, perhaps running around to increase heart rate and holding still to lower it. But this interpretation was ruled out because no movement was possible—the experiment was conducted while the rats were deeply paralyzed with a curare-type drug. In a similar study Miller's student Trowill (1967) trained curarized rats either to increase or to decrease their heart rate in order to receive electrical brain stimulation. The results of a number of such studies (summarized by Miller, 1969) indicate that respondent behaviors, which are usually assumed to be involuntary and not subject to control by contingent reinforcement, actually are modifiable by using operant techniques. Operant control has been established with an impressive variety of such responses, including gastric motility, the formation of urine, temperature of different parts of the body, and localized changes in blood pressure.

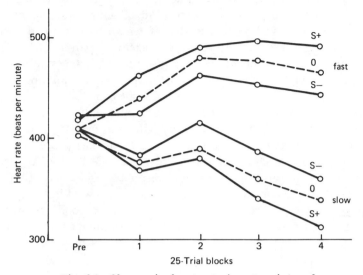

Fig. 8.1 Changes in heart rate in rats reinforced for faster or slower rates. Results are given for the response to S+ signaling shock, S— signaling no shock, and "blank trials" on which no cues were presented. The results indicate large overall changes plus smaller changes specific to the cues. (From DiCara & Miller, Changes in heart rate instrumentally learned by curarized rats as avoidance responses, Journal of Comparative and Physiological Psychology, 56, *1968, 8–12. Copyright 1968 by the American Psychological Association. Reprinted by permission.)*

There is an important practical application for this kind of training in psychosomatic medicine. It is possible that people can control their own blood pressure or heart rate, once they learn how. The argument is that such internalized responses are not commonly reinforced in our culture because they do not ordinarily affect anyone else. The community reinforces our verbal behavior and our overt movements because such behaviors affect them, but no one really cares about our internal emotional reactions, so they are not reinforced. Therefore, according to Miller, a myth has grown up that such behaviors are not subject to reinforcement.

Although this recent work by Miller and his colleagues has a number of interesting theoretical and practical implications, the only conclusion that we can draw in the present discussion is that while we may continue to think of two distinct paradigms and two separate classes of learnable responses, these two dichotomies can by no means be put into a one-to-one correspondence. The two dichotomies do not overlap perfectly. We cannot conclude that, just because responses like heart rate are subject to reinforcement, they are not also subject to some kind of nonreinforcement or Pavlovian learning process. The fact is that if we wish to control heart-rate changes in an organism it is much more efficient to pair a CS with shock and then use the CS to control the response than it is to establish control by means of the operant paradigm. Even though operant methods do work (see Figure 8.1), the changes in heart rate do not come about quickly. The effects achieved by Miller and others often require tedious and technically difficult procedures which contrast sharply with the speed and reliability of comparable effects that can be produced with Pavlovian procedures. Thus, there is good reason for continuing to believe that the Pavlovian paradigm, if not uniquely applicable to autonomic responses, is at least particularly effective with such responses. In effect, we still have two kinds of learning, we still have two kinds of responses, and we still have a good rule of thumb: Respondents are learned with respondent conditioning and operants with operant conditioning. For most purposes this conventional rule still holds good.

Two-Factor Theory

The two learning paradigms interact in another way that is theoretically very important. Suppose a rat has been trained to press a bar for food. We assume that the food pellet reinforces and maintains bar pressing. But we may also assume that, in accordance with the classical-conditioning paradigm, the food pellet is a US that classically conditions responses such as salivation to all the stimuli present in the Skinner box. In other words, there should be an interaction between operant and respondent procedures because, whenever we conduct an operant experiment, we can expect respondent conditioning to occur simultaneously.

Hull's secondary learning system was based upon just such an interaction, as we have already seen. Reinforcement learning was assumed to contribute to the strength of habit, and classical-conditioning processes were assumed to contribute to the strength of motivation. Let us recall the final form of Hull's equation:

$$\text{Behavior strength} = K \times D \times {}_sH_R \ldots$$

Here the habit is assumed to be motivated by both the primary motivator D and the secondary motivator K, whose strength depends upon how strongly the unconditioned consummatory response is elicited in the goal box and how strongly the conditioned response r_G is elicited by stimuli like those in the goal box. As Hull's secondary learning system was developed by Spence and his students, it provided a clear conceptual separation between operantly learned habit and Pavlovian learned motivation. We saw in Chapter 6 that this model was used to explain phenomena, such as latent learning, that were extremely difficult for Hull's primary learning system to account for. When the rat suddenly encountered food in the goal box for the first time, r_G was sufficiently conditioned to provide substantial motivation for the learned running response.

If we think of $_8H_R$ and K as acquired through independent kinds of learning—by the two different basic paradigms—then it ought to be possible to manipulate $_8H_R$ and K independently. More specifically, it ought to be possible to demonstrate the independent acquisition of the habit factor and the motivation factor in a latent-learning situation somewhat simpler than the complex mazes used by Tolman and his students. An attempt to do this was reported by Seward (1949).[1] Seward first let animals explore a T maze and become habituated to it (no food was present in the maze at this time). Then they were passively placed in one of the goal boxes with food. When the animals were then placed in the start box and allowed a single test trial, a significant proportion of them chose that side of the T maze where food had been located. Whether we think in cognitive terms (Tolman had interpreted a similar experiment by saying that the animals had learned where the food was in the apparatus simply by being placed there) or in Hullian terms (r_G is elicited by cues like those present where the animal was given food), there is a clear prediction that the animal will approach the previously positive goal box, and this is what Seward found.

There are some peculiar difficulties with this kind of experimental procedure, however. For example, it ought to be possible to show the same facilitation of performance in a simple runway following direct placement in a baited goal box. But this effect is evidently extremely difficult to obtain (Seward, Datel & Levy, 1952), and even the latent-learning phenomenon in the T maze does not always come out as theory predicts. Seward and Levy (1949), however, reported a technique that more effectively supports an r_G interpretation of instrumental performance. They reasoned that if an animal had first learned to perform in the apparatus until behavior had stabilized and then was given direct placement in an empty goal box, this experience should produce immediate deterioration of instrumental performance: a phenomenon aptly named latent extinction. The argument is that, just as r_G can become conditioned to goal-box cues independently of the running response itself, so this conditioning can be extinguished independently of the instrumental behavior. Although the original latent-learning procedure

---

[1] John P. Seward is an important theorist in his own right. Quite independently of the Hullian group, he wrote during the 1940s and 1950s a series of provocative theoretical papers in which he developed his own version of a secondary learning system, emphasizing the importance of a mediating reaction like r_G, which motivates and directs behavior. Seward (1956) provides a good summary of his thinking along these lines.

has proved generally difficult to work with and rather unreliable, the latent-extinction procedure has turned out to be much more effective and reliable, and, accordingly, it has been much more widely investigated.

But the latent-extinction effect is not entirely free of interpretive problems either. For example, sometimes the effect is not found (Koppman & Grice, 1963), and sometimes when it is found, it is not facilitated by increasing the similarity between goal-box cues and cues elsewhere in the apparatus—which it should be according to the r_G interpretation.

In spite of these and related difficulties, there has been growing interest in and acceptance of the idea that incentive motivation can be manipulated independently of the behavior it is supposedly motivating. One reason for optimism is that the interactive effects of Pavlovian and reinforcement paradigms have been demonstrated in a variety of situations besides latent-learning and latent-extinction experiments. One of the newest techniques is really a revival of a procedure reported many years ago by Estes. When Estes' study was published in 1943, it attracted little attention, but the general technique has been widely used in recent years. Estes trained rats in a Skinner box to work for food; then the bar was withdrawn and the animals were given a series of Pavlovian pairings of a buzzer followed by free food pellets. Then the animal was returned to the base-line task of bar pressing, and the buzzer was occasionally introduced as a probe on the base-line task during extinction.[2] Estes found that when the buzzer was presented it produced a dramatic rise in bar pressing during extinction. Again we see that a stimulus that has been paired with food can have a pronounced effect upon the performance of an instrumental task, appearing to motivate such performance, even though the cue to food signifies nothing in the base-line task. It signifies food only in the situation in which it was established. Nonetheless there is transfer, and we may presume that it is the classical conditioning of a reaction such as salivation or r_G in the one situation that mediates the increment in performance on the base-line task.

In a similarly conceived experiment, Morse and Skinner (1958) trained pigeons to peck a key for food; then off the base line colored lights were

---

[2] Animals are usually tested during extinction of the base-line response because, first, this ensures that the cue is never paired with reinforcement on the base-line task and, second, bigger effects are found in extinction (Bolles & Grossen, 1970). When the previously learned response is a free operant, for example, bar pressing, the cue is quite literally a probe; it is simply intruded into the situation for a few seconds or minutes to see what its effect on the rate of the base-line response will be. Hence such recent expressions as "probing the base line." Estes' procedure, like the direct-placement procedure described earlier, establishes the Pavlovian relationship between the CS and food independently of base-line behavior, that is, "off the base line." Comparable conditioning could, of course, also be done "on the base line," simultaneously with the basic reinforcement schedule.

displayed on the key. One color signified free food which could be obtained without pecking the key, whereas another color signified no food. Then the birds were returned to the base-line task and pecking was extinguished, but during extinction the different key lights were introduced as probes. Morse and Skinner found that the key color that had been associated with food helped to maintain pecking, whereas the key color associated with no food suppressed pecking and facilitated extinction.

Trapold has reported a number of experiments showing further the interaction (he calls it transfer of control) between Pavlovian training and instrumental performance. In a typical experiment (Trapold, 1966), he brought bar pressing under discriminative control so that in the presence of one stimulus, S^D, responding was reinforced, whereas in the presence of an alternative stimulus, S^Δ, responding was extinguished. After the discrimination was established, it was reversed for all animals. For the controls it was simply reversed; for the experimental animals a series of Pavlovian trials was interposed between the original discrimination learning and the reversal training in which the S^D became a signal for no food and the S^Δ became a signal for free food. During these Pavlovian trials the reversed association of the cues with their consequences occurred independently of the animal's behavior and off the base line. Discrimination reversal proceeded much more rapidly for the experimental animals that had the reversal experience off the base line than it did for the controls. In another experiment Trapold, Carlson, and Myers (1965) examined the temporal control involved in the fixed-interval scallop. Rats were first trained noncontingently with 300 free food presentations, on a fixed two-minute schedule. Control animals received 300 noncontingent free food pellets on a variable two-minute schedule. At this point all animals (which had earlier learned to press the bar for continuous reinforcement) were trained on an FI-2 reinforcement schedule. It was discovered that the animals that had been given free food at a two-minute interval off the base line developed the fixed-interval scallop much more quickly than the controls did. It could be supposed that during the noncontingent, or Pavlovian, sessions the amount of time elapsed from the last reinforcement began to serve as an S^D and as an incentive motivator, which then generated bar pressing when the animals were shifted to the base-line task.

Most of the studies just discussed have been described by their authors operationally; they emphasize the novel procedures and minimize the theoretical interpretation. Specifically, an r_G motivational interpretation is rarely offered. There is, however, another very large body of research that draws very heavily upon conventional r_G theory and lends considerable credence to it. This research is Amsel's work on frustration. It is not our purpose to survey all the research on frustration or even to draw any conclusions about what it portends for the concept of incentive motivation. But Amsel's (1962) theory must be mentioned because it constitutes an important extension of the r_G concept. Amsel's basic premise is that, whenever r_G has been elicited by cues in the situation and then reinforcement fails to occur, there will be an emotional reaction (presumably something akin to anger) and that this emotional state serves a motivational function very much as fear or the appetitive r_G is assumed to do. Amsel thus has a pair of parallel motivational agencies, one, the conventional r_G, which is the conditionable part of the consummatory response, and a new one that is the conditionable part of the anger or frustration response (which is symbolized r_F). This r_F is hypothesized to produce withdrawal and the inhibition of behavior in much the same way that r_G produces approach and the facilitation of behavior. In a discrimination task, according to Amsel (1962), r_G becomes conditioned to the positive S^D, whereas r_F becomes conditioned to S^Δ. Discrimination learning can be mediated by either or both mechanisms.

These complimentary mechanisms permit us to do a lot of explanatory tricks. Consider, for example, animals trained with intermittent reinforcement. On nonreinforced trials r_F must become conditioned to situational cues. But there must also be a number of occasions on which reinforcement follows nonreinforcement. On these occasions the animal is reinforced for responding, even though r_F tends to inhibit responding. After this had occurred a number of times (Amsel, 1962, describes evidence indicating that it must occur on the order of sixty times), then r_F will no longer be a negative factor; it will become part of the total S^D configuration in the presence of which the animal is reinforced. At this point the animal will continue to run, press the bar, or whatever, even though it is frustrated at the time it does so. Finally, if the animal learns to respond when it is frustrated, then it should not be disrupted by extinction. If an animal has been trained on continuous reinforcement, sudden frustration should produce rapid inhibition of responding; but if an animal has been reinforced for persisting in the presence of r_F, extinction presents no new inhibiting factor, and the animal should continue to respond. In short, Amsel has an explanation for the partial-reinforcement extinction effect, a phenomenon whose explanation had caused a great deal of embarrassment to earlier theorists. The Hullians had been quite unable to cope with it. Skinnerians had coped with it only by assuming that it was an empirical law of such generality that it did not have to be derived from more basic principles. Amsel has supplied a derivation.

Let us consider one further implication of Amsel's frustration theory. It is known from a variety of experiments, starting with the famous one by Crespi (1942), that rats run more quickly, press the bar more frequently, and in general perform better if they receive a large amount of reinforcement than if they receive a small amount. Intuition suggests that this superiority on the base-line task should carry over into extinction, so that the animal that has received a larger amount of reinforcement should be more resistant to extinction. But Amsel (1962) argues that, quite the contrary, there should be a reversal in much the same way—but for a different reason—that there is a reversal following partial reinforcement. He argues that with more reinforcement there is more conditioning of r_G or conditioning of a more vigorous r_G and that when frustration occurs there should be a correspondingly stronger r_F leading to greater inhibition of the learned response. In other words, a larger amount of reinforcement should lead to more rapid extinction when food is withheld because of the greater frustration that it entails. Furthermore, this reversal should occur following continuous but not intermittent reinforcement training. Two large, well-controlled studies show that this is indeed the case (Hulse, 1958; Wagner, 1961).

Amsel's frustration theory is not without its own problems. There appear to be severe constraints upon the generality of some of the phenomena that Amsel has analyzed. For example, the anomalous amount-of-reinforcement effect in extinction appears to occur only after extended training (Theios & Brelsford, 1964) and only when animals are tested while severely deprived (Marx, 1967). Amsel's interpretation of the partial-reinforcement effect has been sharply criticized on both theoretical and empirical grounds by Capaldi (1970), among others. Nonetheless Amsel's work on frustration has considerably strengthened and extended the secondary-learning system originally proposed by Hull and Spence, and it has contributed substantially to the general acceptance of the idea that instrumental behavior is in part controlled and in part motivated by classically conditioned mediating responses such as r_G and r_F.

The Logical and Empirical Status of r_G

Some theorists, for example, Spence and his students, discuss r_G, r_F, and other classically conditioned mediators as if they were real responses. Other theorists, including Skinner, Estes, and Trapold, make no specific reference to any classically conditioned response; they talk about pairing a stimulus with food and describe their experiments simply in these operational terms. This latter strategy (or personal style) is operational and descriptive; it is also conservative and safe. But consider the enormous advantage that would result if it were possible to observe r_G directly. If we could monitor r_G, perhaps by measuring salivation from moment to moment in the hungry rat, we would be able to test empirically the whole secondary learning system. Furthermore, if it could be shown that the r_G for hunger really was salivation, we could then apply the entire body of research produced by Pavlov and his followers to the explanation of incentive motivation. We would then be in an excellent position to verify and expand upon a number of implications of the secondary learning system which remain at this point largely conjectural.

It should therefore not be surprising that a number of investigators have attempted to search for the real r_G, to find whether it is in the mouth, in the stomach, or in the unfathomable depths of the central nervous system. Some of this research has monitored salivation simultaneously with the motivation of instrumental behavior; some of it has looked for the loss of motivational effects following the administration of drugs that eliminate salivation. None of this research has been very encouraging. It does not support the conclusion that the hungry animal's r_G is located in the mouth. Some of the evidence suggests this, but it is far from conclusive. A similar study of thirsty rats was reported by Miller and DeBold (1965). They measured minute tongue movements of thirsty animals on the assumption that incipient tongue movements might be a conditionable part of the consummatory response. Again the results were provocative and lent some support to the idea that r_G had really been located in the thirsty rat, but the evidence was far from conclusive and has not been confirmed by subsequent research.

So the locus of r_G remains uncertain; indeed, it remains uncertain whether r_G has any reality status at all. In their important review of this question, Rescorla and Solomon (1967) conclude that there is little justification for believing in the reality of r_G. It is, at best, a convenient fiction. It is a fiction because the concerted search for it by a number of very able investigators over a number of years has failed to reveal it; it is convenient because, if we assume that somewhere there is a classically conditioned response, we can then attribute to it all the known properties of classically conditioned responses. But perhaps this convenience is illusory: What do we really know about classical conditioning? Rescorla and Solomon conclude that it is only the Pavlovian *procedure* that matters. If we run a number of Pavlovian trials in which events are programmed independently of the animal's behavior, this experience can have a marked effect on subsequent instrumental behavior. Whatever it is that happens in the Pavlovian part of the experiment, it is the noncontingent presentation of cues and consequences, either on or off the base line, that matters and not whether some mediating response becomes attached to the cue. To put it another way, the paradigm retains its value even though the theory of what is conditioned cannot be confirmed.

Classically Conditioned Fear

The secondary learning system is often applied to aversive behavior as well as to appetitive behavior, and many of the same techniques are applicable. Indeed, the first study of classical-instrumental interaction was the famous conditioned-suppression experiment of Estes and Skinner (1941). Animals were first trained to press a bar for food on an FI four-minute schedule; when this behavior had been stabilized, there was superimposed upon the base-line task a series of tones of three minutes duration that were invariably followed by shock. Initially the tone alone produced no suppression or interference with the base-line task, but after about eight pairings of tone and shock the tone produced virtually total suppression of bar pressing. The argument is that there was classical conditioning of a fear reaction to the tone (established in this instance on the base line) and that this emotional behavior effectively interfered with and thus suppressed bar pressing. This general procedure, which has been called the "conditioned suppression" and the "conditioned emotional reaction" (CER) procedure, has become a very popular and powerful method for investigating fear conditioning. Its great virtue is that the effects on behavior are usually profound and easily measured, and fear can be conditioned in very few Pavlovian pairings.

A related procedure is that originally described by Mowrer and Solomon (1954), which we may call "conditioned punishment." Mowrer and Solomon first trained animals on bar pressing with food reinforcement and then presented off the base line a series of tones and shocks, the purpose of which was again to classically condition fear to the tone.[3] After the tone had been associated with shock a few times it was introduced, not as a probe, but as a consequence of the instrumental response. Now whenever the animal pressed the bar, it produced the tone briefly. Bar pressing was markedly suppressed, or punished, presumably by the fear that it produced. Thus, we see two effects of fear conditioning. One is to suppress ongoing behavior when the CS is introduced as a probe, and the second is to punish ongoing behavior when the CS is made contingent upon it.

There is still a third way in which fear is assumed to affect instrumental behavior, and that is in the avoidance-learning situation. When the secondary learning system was first described in Chapter 6, we noted that Mowrer and Miller had contributed greatly to its popularity by suggesting

---

[3] The main purpose of this experiment, as we noted earlier, was to show that fear is classically conditioned. The experiment is cited again here to illustrate Mowrer and Solomon's novel method of assessing the conditioning of fear.

that fear could serve as a learned source of drive. The argument is that fear becomes classically conditioned to the CS (the warning stimulus) in the avoidance situation and that this fear serves two functions. One is to motivate avoidance behavior, and the second is to set up the possibility that subsequent fear reduction will reinforce the avoidance response. This view of avoidance behavior was first spelled out in an important theoretical paper by Mowrer (1939) and then tested in a series of ingenious studies, of which we shall describe just one. Mowrer and Lamoreaux (1942) noted that if fear becomes classically conditioned to the CS, then termination of the CS should serve as an effective source of reinforcement for avoidance behavior because it should be accompanied by a rapid reduction in fear and a concomitant reduction in drive. Mowrer and Lamoreaux ran three groups of rats in a shuttle-box avoidance task. The groups differed in the relationship between the avoidance response and termination of the CS. One group received a very short CS in a trace-conditioning paradigm in which the CS came on momentarily and went off some seconds before shock was scheduled to occur. An avoidance response could avoid the scheduled shock but could not affect the brief CS. A second group received a very long CS, which persisted after the shock was scheduled to occur, and even if the animal made an avoidance response the CS persisted for some seconds afterward, so that for this group too the CS was not terminated by the response. The third group received a CS that was programmed to terminate whenever the animal made an avoidance response. To paraphrase Goldilocks and the three bears, the first group showed poor learning because the CS was too short, the second group showed poor learning because the CS was too long, and the third group did well because the CS was just right. Mowrer concluded that the reduction in fear that occurs with the termination of the CS constitutes the prime source of reinforcement for the avoidance response. The slight learning shown in the other two groups was attributed to another mechanism, which Mowrer called parasitic reinforcement, not involving fear reduction. This study, together with further results reported by Mowrer, lent tremendous plausibility to the argument that avoidance behavior is mediated by a classically conditioned fear reaction. The picture we had was that the fear motivates avoidance behavior at the onset of the CS and reinforces avoidance behavior when it is reduced at the termination of the CS. In the context of motivation, fear is usually called an "acquired drive," but its characteristics are very much like those of incentive motivation. Fear is assumed to be a classically conditioned emotional response, which is sometimes symbolized r_E, and it serves the same kind of motivational role that r_G and r_F do. It is an important, indeed a necessary, part of the secondary-learning and motivating system, for within that system it is no more possible to explain avoidance without r_E than it is to explain latent learning or the Crespi effect without r_G. The avoidance-learning experiment illustrates the same kind of interaction between a hypothetical classically conditioned response and an instrumental response that we have been discussing.

In the avoidance-learning experiment classical conditioning occurs more or less on the base line because the CS is associated with shock on trials on which the avoidance response does not occur. But fear conditioning can also be accomplished off the base line, when we seek to separate the Pavlovian aspect and the instrumental aspect of learning. This separation can be achieved by means of what has become known as the "acquired-drive experiment." Miller (1948) put rats in a white compartment, shocked them there, and required them to run through a door into an adjoining black compartment to escape the shock. After a series of such escape-training trials, Miller argued, fear should be elicited by apparatus cues, specifically the cues arising from the white shock compartment.[4] After the escape behavior had been established and fear had supposedly been conditioned, the door between the two compartments was closed, and the animals were required to learn a new response: manually turning a small wheel to open the door to the adjoining black compartment. Many of Miller's animals showed no learning; their reaction to fear was to freeze or to crouch in the white compartment. But about half the group did learn the required response. Miller argued that the acquisition of the new response was reinforced by the fear reduction that it made possible. Then he argued further that both the new wheel-turning response and the inappropriate response (freezing) were motivated by fear elicited by cues in the white compartment. This situation is thus somewhat different in procedure but essentially the same in concept as the conventional avoidance-learning experiment. The chief difference is that fear is learned off the base line before the animal is put on the base-line task.

Another ingenious approach to establishing Pavlovian fear off the base line was reported by Solomon and Turner (1962). These investigators first trained dogs on an avoidance task; the training was then interrupted and the dogs were subjected to a series of Pavlovian trials in which a tone was paired with shock. This experience was given off the base line while the dogs were deeply curarized. (The purpose of the curarization was to prevent any effect on the instrumental base-line behavior from being mediated by some inadvertently learned skeletal response during the Pavlovian session.)

---

[4] Most theorists have followed Mowrer in assuming that this fear is classically conditioned, but at that time Miller, as we have noted earlier, did not subscribe to this view. Nonetheless, the results of his experiment can be interpreted as another instance of Pavlovian-instrumental interaction.

Later, when the effects of the drug had worn off, the dogs were returned to the base-line avoidance task and the customary CS was replaced by the stimulus that had been a cue for shock in the Pavlovian session. It produced just as much and perhaps a bit more avoidance performance than the CS with which the animals had been trained. The interpretation was that, while the dogs were curarized, fear had been classically conditioned to the tone and that this new source of fear then served to motivate the well-learned avoidance response.

There was another important innovation in Solomon and Turner's experiment. During the Pavlovian session, the dogs not only received a stimulus associated with shock; they also received from time to time an additional stimulus that was not associated with shock. The experimenters were attempting to bring the fear reaction under discriminative control so that it would be elicited by the one stimulus and not by the other. When the animals were returned to the base-line task and the negative stimulus was introduced in place of the CS, the result was a decrement in avoidance performance: either no responding or rapid extinction. According to Pavlovian principles, the negative stimulus should have become a conditioned inhibitor. It should have inhibited whatever fear might be already present, for example, fear elicited by apparatus cues. This general view of the excitation and inhibition of a Pavlovian fear reaction was greatly extended and considerably strengthened by a series of studies reported by Rescorla and LoLordo (1965). The basic concept was the same as in Solomon and Turner's experiment. Dogs were first trained on an avoidance task and then given interspersed sessions in which the dogs were not curarized but were confined to one part of the shuttle-box apparatus and there subjected to a series of tones and shocks arranged so that one tone always predicted shock and the other tone always predicted a period of time free of shock. Rescorla and LoLordo found that when the S+ for shock was introduced as a probe on the avoidance base line it produced a marked acceleration of avoidance behavior, and that when the S− for shock was introduced as a probe it produced a marked inhibition of avoidance. One of the elegant features of this study was that Rescorla and LoLordo used a variety of Pavlovian inhibition procedures such as conditioned inhibition and differential inhibition for establishing the S−, and in each case the Pavlovian techniques for producing inhibition led to a loss in performance on the base-line avoidance task. Rescorla and LoLordo thus provided strong support for the argument that avoidance behavior in their situation is motivated by a classically conditioned fear reaction that seems to obey many of the general principles of Pavlovian conditioning. The argument for a conditioning interpretation of the secondary learning system looked rather convincing at this point.

The Logical and Empirical Status of r_E

We have seen that the attempts to localize, identify, and objectify the appetitive r_G have not been altogether successful. Is the situation any better in the case of the fear reaction? There is an enormous literature dealing with the conditioning of heart rate and other reactions which in some combination are commonly assumed to constitute fear. Again, it would be an enormous advantage in the interpretation of instrumental behavior and in the understanding of its motivation if we could apply what is known about heart-rate conditioning, for example, to the problem. If we could monitor the fear that is assumed to motivate avoidance behavior independently of the avoidance behavior itself, we could verify the entire theoretical structure and provide direct confirmation of the theoretical aspects of the secondary learning system. Unfortunately, this reasonable program has been fraught with difficulties. There is no more complicated part of the learning literature than that which deals with the classical conditioning of heart rate. Some of the difficulty can be attributed to the complexity of the mechanisms controlling the circulatory system. The main function of increased heart rate, whether it occurs in response to the US or to the CS, is to make possible some violent defensive reaction, like fighting or running away, by increasing the blood supply to the muscles that are involved in violent action. But the blood supply to the muscles can be increased in a variety of ways: by speeding up the heart (increased heart rate), by increasing the stroke (the amount of blood pumped out in any one heart contraction), and by constricting the blood vessels in the core of the body and dilating the blood vessels in the periphery. At the same time, blood pressure is increased by any overall constriction of arterial vessels. All these responses are neurally controlled and should therefore be conditionable. The problem is that any one change in the circulatory system is likely to trigger compensatory changes in the other mechanisms that tend to restore the overall balance. For example, if for some reason heart rate is suddenly increased, compensatory mechanisms will be stimulated to lower blood pressure and reduce the stroke, both of which tend to reduce heart rate. Thus, in a conditioning experiment, although one response of the total circulatory system may be affected in one direction, compensatory mechanisms will tend to counteract it. There is one clear methodological implication: It is necessary to monitor a number of different cardiac responses such as pressure, stroke, and rate to discover how the total system is responding in any given situation. If we fail to find heart-rate conditioning in a Pavlovian experiment, it may simply be because stroke or pressure is the response that is being changed, and this change may be accompanied by an increase, a compensatory decrease, or no change at all in heart rate. A further complication is that different species of animals have quite different circulatory mechanisms and even within a species there may be great individual differences in the ways in which the circulatory system responds during a Pavlovian experiment. Even when we think we know all about the circulatory system of our animal, we may be surprised to find that conditioned reactions can change as a function of the US, the CS, and the CS-US relationship.

Students of heart-rate conditioning have been forced to conclude that, although heart rate and other indexes of autonomic functioning are readily conditionable, there does not appear to be any one response or any simple combination of responses that can be equated with fear—if by "fear" we mean that which motivates avoidance behavior and suppresses appetitive behavior. In their review of the problem Rescorla and Solomon (1967) concluded, as they did in the case of r_G, that the hypothetical motivating fear response, let us call it r_E, appears to be a convenient fiction. It is a fiction because a number of very capable researchers have failed to find it and convenient because it seems to have many of the functional properties shown by classically conditioned responses. But again Rescorla and Solomon have concluded that it is the procedure that matters. It is clear that establishing a relationship between a cue and a consequence, such as a tone and shock or a tone and the absence of shock, in a Pavlovian manner permits the cue to have a dramatic effect upon instrumental behavior. It is clear, according to Rescorla and Solomon, that the Pavlovian procedure is effective whether or not any particular observable response is conditioned.

Perhaps it is not very important whether r_G and r_E are identifiable responses. Certainly most of the time the hypothetical fear reaction, r_E, like the incentive motivator r_G, is treated as a hypothetical construct and inferred from its effects on behavior. If these mediating reactions should ultimately prove to be central events, occurring in the central nervous system, then they may still be hypothesized to have the functional properties of classically conditioned changes in heart rate and salivation. But this argument is no good. The fact is that these functional properties are no longer very clear—that is why the problem arises. Furthermore, the whole point of the Pavlovian interpretation of the secondary learning system seems to have been forgotten. The promised virtue of the Pavlovian interpretation was that the mediating motivators had the prospects of being directly observable, so that the laws of Pavlovian conditioning could be verified for them and so that they could be measured independently of the behaviors that they were supposed to motivate. If r_G and r_E are merely constructs, then this great advantage is lost. There is the further problem that if incentive motivation (r_G) is learned by Pavlovian conditioning and if salivation is always learned by Pavlovian conditioning, then how can r_G not be correlated with salivation?

Having come to the brink of concluding that salivation is not a classically conditioned response, it is clear that we must stop to consider how classical conditioning should be conceptualized. It is a good thing to conclude with Rescorla and Solomon that it is the Pavlovian procedures that are important because they have dramatic effects upon subsequent instrumental behavior. But it would be a far better thing to know why. Classical conditioning has to be more than just a procedure—but what more?

Interpretations of Classical Conditioning

It is most often taken for granted that learning necessarily consists of attaching a response to a stimulus or of strengthening an already existing S-R connection. Granting this assumption for the moment, we may ask: What is the nature of the learned response (CR) in the Pavlovian situation? We have already seen that the CR may not be a replica of the UR. The animal does not necessarily react in the same way to the CS as it does to the US. Confronted with this apparent anomaly, a number of writers have suggested that the CR serves a preparatory function. It prepares the animal to cope in some way with the upcoming US. In some instances, as in eye-blink conditioning, which is usually established by means of puffs of air to the eyeball, the CR looks very much like the reflexive eye blink to the air puff, and it can be argued that closing the eye defends it in exactly the same way against the threatened air puff as against the real air puff. In this example, then, the CR should resemble the UR, and it does (more or less). The nictitating membrane, the third eyelid that some animals have, evidently serves functions other than protecting the eye because it does not close enough to give the eye much protection; but in spite of this curious feature the CR of the nictitating membrane again resembles the UR. We may wonder: If this CR is not a preparatory response, is it a legitimate replica? Is it a case of stimulus substitution of the sort that was suggested by earlier learning theorists as the model for all classical conditioning?

Salivation can also be said to be a preparatory response. The usual US in a salivary-conditioning experiment is a relatively hard-to-consume dry food powder. By salivating the animal is better able to ingest and digest it. So, although the CR looks like the UR in this case, we cannot be sure whether it is a replica of the UR or a preparatory response. The fact that salivation can also be conditioned with dilute acid as the US does not clarify the issue.

There is another curious conditioning phenomenon that suggests something of the complexity of the body's adjustment mechanisms and again raises the question of whether the CR is preparatory in nature. Woods, Makous, and Hutton (1969) reported that when an insulin injection is used as a US (insulin drives down the blood glucose level) and any one of a number of salient stimuli is used as the CS, it is possible to obtain a conditioned blood-sugar reaction. After a number of CS-US pairings, the CS alone produces a replica of the insulin reaction, a decrease in blood glucose level. But another investigator, Siegel (1972), who has also found conditioning using very similar experimental procedures, reports that the CR consists of a rise in blood glucose level. Siegel suggests that the rise in blood sugar is a preparatory response, occurring in anticipation of the effect of insulin. Whatever the underlying mechanisms producing the difference between Woods' and Siegel's results, it can be concluded that the CR may resemble the UR, it may be a preparatory reaction of the same or somewhat different form, or it may even be something altogether different.

The unpredictability of the CR relative to the UR suggests that what is learned in a Pavlovian situation is not a response at all. Perhaps something else, perhaps something about the S-S* (CS-US) relationship itself, is learned. The point was nicely made in an early paper by Zener (1937). Zener studied Pavlovian salivary conditioning in a dog, but in contrast to Pavlov's strictly controlled experiments Zener let his animal move around freely in the experimental space, and he observed all of its behavior. Zener found salivary conditioning, but he also found the dog displaying a great deal of other behavior such as moving around restlessly during the intertrial interval, going over to the food-delivery mechanism when the CS came on, wagging its tail, and barking at the CS. In short, Zener's dog showed every indication of anticipating or expecting food.

Perhaps, then, what is learned in a Pavlovian experiment is not a particular response to the CS but an expectancy of the US. If the experimenter only observes salivation or if he takes the trouble Pavlov did to restrain his animal and to train it to hold still, then he is only going to see the salivary response. But in the unrestrained dog it is clear that what is learned is something much more cognitive, something more like a perceptual recognition of the relationship between S and S*.

So we see that one of the most basic assumptions about the nature of the conditioning process is open to question. Even more remarkable is that in the last few years serious questions about the basic nature of the conditioning procedure have been raised. Nothing is sacred, it seems, in the world of the learning theorist. From the time of Pavlov it has been assumed that, whatever conditioning is, it occurs when the CS and US are closely contiguous. The essential ingredient of the conditioning procedure is the pairing of CS and US. But let us consider two phenomena that indicate that pairing *per se* has little to do with conditioning. Both these phenomena have attracted a good deal of interest in recent years because both promise to alter drastically the prevailing view of what Pavlovian conditioning is all about.

Rescorla (1968) trained rats to press a bar for food; then he gave them fear conditioning off the base line and then returned them to the base-line task to see if the CS would suppress base-line responding. Rescorla's study included a number of groups, but the main point can be illustrated by describing three groups that differed in the treatment received during the Pavlovian phase of the experiment. Each group received a series of CSs and a number of shocks scattered randomly through the CSs but arranged so that the probability of shock in any given CS was .40. Each group thus received the same mean number of CSs, USs, and CS-US pairings; the groups differed only in the events that were scheduled to occur between CS presentations. For one group the probability of shock in the absence of the CS was also .40, for another group this probability was reduced to .20, and for the third group it was only .10. To summarize, during the Pavlovian, off-the-base-line part of the experiment the three groups received the same number and the same probability of shocks during the CS intervals but different probabilities of shock during the non-CS intervals. When tested on the base-line task, the CS was found to produce severe suppression in the .40–.10 group, less suppression in the .40–.20 group, and virtually no suppression in the .40–.40 group. It appears that a good deal of fear had been conditioned to the CS by the Pavlovian treatment in group .40–.10 but that virtually no fear had been conditioned to the CS in group .40–.40. In spite of the fact that there were the same number of CS-US pairings, in spite of the fact that group .40–.40 received more total shocks and that a great deal of fear must have been conditioned to the total experimental situation, there was evidently no fear conditioned to the CS.

It appears, then, that fear becomes conditioned to a CS not when it is paired with shock but, to state it in simple language, when the CS predicts shock. For group .40–.10 the CS predicted shock because it was four times more likely in the presence of the CS than in its absence, but for group .40–.40 the CS did not predict shock, and so no fear was conditioned to it. To state the point in Rescorla's own more formal language, fear conditioning requires that there be a "contingency" between CS and US. "Contingency" is defined here in terms of relative probabilities. If the probability of shock is greater in the presence of the CS than in the absence of the CS, then fear will be conditioned to it, and this fear can then be manifest in the suppression of appetitive behavior or the facilitation of avoidance behavior. It is this contingency between the CS and the US and not the contiguous pairing of stimulus events that governs whether or not the Pavlovian procedure will be effective.

Recall the experiment by Rescorla and LoLordo (1965), described earlier, in which one tone had been explicitly unpaired with shock. During the Pavlovian sessions an S— or safety signal had been established by ensuring that, although a number of shocks occurred, none of them followed the tone. Recall that when this S— was then probed on base-line avoidance behavior, it produced a decrement in performance, indicating that the tone had come to act as a Pavlovian conditioned inhibitor. In this instance, Rescorla argues, the contingency relationship is simply reversed; in establishing the safety signal the Pavlovian contingencies were arranged so that the probability of shock in the presence of the CS was *less* than in the absence of the CS. Under these conditions the CS becomes a conditioned inhibitor. To put it in more simple language, if a stimulus specifically predicts no shock (in a situation in which shocks do occur), then that stimulus will become an inhibitor and will inhibit fear that might otherwise be present.

There is one further implication of Rescorla's analysis of the contingency relationship. What would we predict if the probability of shock were the same in both the presence and the absence of the CS? The CS should emerge neutral, an S^o, neither a Pavlovian excitor nor a Pavlovian inhibitor. That is precisely the way in which the experimental conditions were arranged for group .40–.40 in the experiment just described, and in accordance with this prediction S^o had no effect on base-line performance. Rescorla (1972) has described a number of experiments (mostly from his own research) that provide striking support for his new interpretation of Pavlovian conditioning. The results seem to be in very close agreement with his contingency theory. In general, fear seems to be conditioned to cues that predict shock, the inhibition of fear to cues that predict freedom from shock, and nothing much at all to cues that bear no predictive relation to shock, even when, as in Rescorla's 1968 study, the cue is frequently paired with shock.

The old idea that conditioning results from the pairing of CS and US has run into trouble in another respect: the phenomena of overshadowing and blocking. Pavlov (1927) noted that, if conditioning were carried out with a compound CS consisting of, say, a dim light and a loud noise, the CR might depend entirely upon the stronger component of the CS. When tested separately, the light might elicit no CR, whereas the noise would elicit just as strong a CR as the original compound CS with which the dog was trained. In effect, the stronger stimulus would "overshadow" the weaker one, so that no conditioning would occur to the latter, even though it was paired with food and even though it would be an effective CS if used alone from the outset of conditioning. Pavlov's overshadowing phenomenon, originally discovered in connection with salivary conditioning, has now been extensively studied by Kamin using fear-conditioning procedures. In addition, Kamin (1969) has discovered a new but related phenomenon, which he calls blocking. In a typical blocking experiment, a light is paired with a shock eight times (sufficient to produce a strong fear reaction, as indicated by suppression of bar pressing for food when the light is introduced as a probe). Then for one group the light and tone are paired an additional eight times with shock. Then when the light is introduced as a probe on the base line it continues to suppress, but when the tone is introduced as a probe no suppression is found. A control group that first receives pairings of just the light with shock and then pairings of just the tone with shock shows suppression when either the light or the tone is probed on the base line. The results from the control group indicate that the prior conditioning with the light does not prevent the tone from also becoming an effective CS, but the results of the other group show that when the light and the tone are presented together, conditioning to the tone is "blocked" by the prior conditioning to the light. (Of course, in all such studies the roles of the light and tone are interchanged to balance out any intrinsic differences among the test stimuli.)

The phenomena of overshadowing and blocking indicate again that simply pairing a stimulus with shock is not sufficient to condition fear to it and suggest a number of new ways of looking at conditioning. One way is to view it as the learning of the predictive relationship between S and S*. S provides information about S*, or, to use the phraseology first introduced by Pavlov, the CS "signals" the US. Consider the following interesting phenomenon also reported by Kamin (1969). If in the critical phase of the blocking experiment, that is, at the point where the light and tone are both paired with the shock, a new S* is introduced, or if it is altered (for example, increased in intensity), then blocking does not occur. A recent report by Gray and Appignanesi (1973) suggests that simply accompanying the shock with a relatively innocuous stimulus, one that itself would not support conditioning, also relieves the blocking effect. In other words, it looks as though, if the light plus the tone predicts an S* that is different in almost any way from that predicted by the light alone, then conditioning to the tone will occur. If the light already predicts shock, then the tone is redundant. It provides no new information about what is going to happen, and perhaps for that reason no conditioning occurs. Thus, one possible new interpretation of conditioning is that it is a procedure that permits the animal to process new information about environmental events.

An alternative view of conditioning, which has an even stronger cognitive flavor, attributes blocking to hypothetical attentional processes of the animal. When the light has been paired with shock a number of times, the animal's attention is directed entirely to the light and the tone is not perceived. Since it is not perceived, no conditioning to it can occur.[5] Still an-

[5] Let us recall that Pavlov had emphasized the importance of the original response to the CS. He suggested that there must be some orienting or investigatory reflex to the CS if conditioning is to occur. Perhaps this is just a behavioristic way of saying that the animal must pay attention to the CS.

other approach to the phenomenon of blocking is that suggested by Rescorla and Wagner (1972). They propose a semiquantitative model of conditioning from which can be derived many of the facts of overshadowing, as well as a variety of the contingency effects previously reported by Rescorla. Basically, their model defines V as the strength of conditioning, and ΔV_a as the increase in strength of conditioning to stimulus a on a given trial. Their model states that this increment, $\Delta V_a = C\ (\lambda - V_{ax})$. Here C is a constant that depends upon the specific properties of the CS and the US, λ is the possible strength of conditioning obtainable with the given US, and V_{ax} is the strength of conditioning that already exists for stimulus a together with any other stimuli X that may be present. This equation combined with parallel equations for other stimuli present in the situation carries a number of implications. One is that conditioning to a particular stimulus, such as the tone in the blocking experiment, will be minimal if there is already a strong conditioned reaction to other stimuli in the situation such as the light.

Rescorla and Wagner's model is an ingenious and powerful device for describing the results of many kinds of conditioning experiments, particularly those in which there is more than one CS and those in which background stimuli are an important part of the total situation (as they seem to be in fear-conditioning experiments). But the model is purely descriptive. It does not tell us anything about the underlying learning process. It is still a matter of each man for himself when it comes to explaining what happens in a Pavlovian experiment. Perhaps the Pavlovian procedure simply permits an animal to learn an expectancy for shock; much of the recent data is consistent with such an interpretation. Perhaps conditioning is based upon some kind of reinforcement mechanism; however, reinforcement as a learning process is itself in considerable doubt at the moment, as we shall see shortly. Perhaps some new contiguity theory will be put forward soon to restore order and to give us a new coherent picture of the conditioning process. But as it stands now, it is far from clear how learning occurs within the classical-conditioning paradigm, and it is even far from clear how the basic paradigm itself should be conceptualized.

Interpretations of Operant Conditioning

Thorndike painted a simple picture in which certain consequences of responding have automatic strengthening effects on any preceding S-R connection. Hull simply elaborated this idea and made it the basic postulate underlying his primary-learning system. The great mass of evidence accumulated over the last twenty years has, however, indicated that the primary-learning system is relatively ineffective and provides a rather inadequate account of the performance, much less the learning, that occurs even in simple instrumental-learning situations. We have seen that there is very little agreement, even among those who have defended Hull's system, on what reinforcement consists of; perhaps it is drive reduction, perhaps drive induction. Even if behavior is controlled by contingent reinforcement, it must also depend to a great extent upon the secondary-learning system, upon incentive motivation, learned fears, and secondary reinforcers. Mowrer (1960) quickly became so disenchanted with the entire primary-learning system that he abandoned it completely and attributed the strengthening of behavior entirely to the increase of incentive motivation that is assumed to occur when reinforcement is given. It is not that food progressively strengthens the running habit; it is that stimuli associated with food increasingly motivate approach behavior. The learning that occurs within the reinforcement paradigm is, therefore, not the building of an S-R connection but the establishment of classically conditioned motivators, mediating responses that control the instrumental response associatively and motivationally. In short, what remains of the Hullian school of thought appears to have little faith in the reinforcement paradigm as a description of the learning process.

Psychologists of the Skinnerian persuasion continue to emphasize the importance of reinforcement in the control of behavior, but they too have drifted away from reinforcement as a learning mechanism. Initially (Skinner, 1938) it was believed that reinforcement produces learning. But in the last twenty years or so it has become paradigmatic that reinforcement is nothing more than a procedure for controlling behavior, and the question of learning is left in abeyance. Those who are primarily interested in controlling behavior and making it highly predictable, particularly if they are interested in the predictability of asymptotic behavior, must almost necessarily ignore the question of learning. Learning means transitional changes, instability, and momentary unpredictability. If the Skinnerian runs enough sessions, all these problems disappear—along with the learning data.

Apart from these ideological confines, many operant conditioners over the years have indicated a faith in certain practical principles that look like laws of learning. It has been noted, for example, that reinforcement is more effective if it follows quickly after the response. Such a principle looks as if it is derived from an implicit belief in a reinforcement mechanism. But in the last few years even this implication of an underlying learning process has been lost, and even the practical principle of contiguity has begun to fall by the wayside. Herrnstein (1969) proposed that in the case of avoidance behavior the event that controls it (and at this point it hardly makes sense to call it a reinforcement contingency) is the reduction in the rate of shocks the behavior produces. Herrnstein and Hineline (1966) found that under appropriate conditions avoidance behavior could be maintained when responding simply decreased the probability of randomly programmed shocks. There is no localized or identifiable consequence of the response, nothing like Mowrer's fear reduction or even CS termination that maintains the behavior; it is simply maintained by the reduction in the number of shocks per minute.

Herrnstein (1970) has extended the general argument to the case of appetitive behavior. He proposes, for example, that in a choice situation in which an animal has two responses that can be made or two kinds of stimuli to respond to, behavior is distributed in proportion to the payoff proportions. For example, if the rat in a choice situation receives twice as many food pellets for responding to one stimulus as it does to another, it will respond twice as often to that stimulus. Again, it hardly seems appropriate to refer to the food pellet as a reinforcer because the discrete event of receiving a food pellet in itself is no longer related to the behavior; it is the relative frequency with which food is received over a period of time with which the animal's behavior is correlated. Baum (1973) has put the argument in even stronger language. He says that contiguity between the response and the reinforcer is immaterial; it is the correlation between behavior and its consequences over time that matters. According to Baum, reinforcement is a contingent program of events, rather than a discrete event.[6] Our views of the basic operant paradigm are changing. It is still true that the skillful use of contingent reinforcement is the best technique we have for controlling operant behavior; so the old paradigm retains considerable merit, particularly in the practical world of everyday affairs. But we need to understand why it works, when it works, and why it so often fails to work. In Chapter 9 we focus upon this troublesome matter.

In summary, it is clear that many learning situations contain procedural elements that characterize both of the basic paradigms. For example, the typical operant situation provides the opportunity for both reinforcement learning and classical conditioning to occur. It is widely assumed that both kinds of learning do occur and that they are reflected in different aspects of behavior. Reinforcement learning is assumed to determine what the response is, and classical conditioning is assumed to determine how strongly motivated it is. Although the two basic paradigms can still be seen as distinctly different procedures, there are divergent views about just what the critical features of these procedures are. There is even less consensus about what the underlying learning process is in either case.

[6] This view of the reinforcement relationship bears an interesting resemblance to Rescorla's (1968) view of classical conditioning. In both cases learning is considered to be based upon the patterning of events over time rather than upon discrete events isolated in time. In both cases the learning appears to consist of an appreciation of the pattern rather than an automatic strengthening of a response.

References for Further Reading

The evolution of thinking about two-factor theory can be traced through the important papers of Mowrer (1947), Logan (1959), Rescorla and Solomon (1967), Trapold and Overmier (1972), and Bindra (1974). The conditioning of heart rate, which has been tacitly assumed to be equivalent to the conditioning of fear, boasts a massive and complicated literature. The interested reader might well start with Schneiderman's (1970) cogent introduction to it.

CHAPTER
9

THE STRUCTURE
OF LEARNING

Whatever differences there may have been among them, all our theorists have shared a common optimistic attitude toward the uniformity and universality of nature's laws: the attitude that if we can only once discover nature's secret we shall have a general explanation of all her phenomena. Whatever the laws of learning may be, once we have found them they will explain all learning in all animals. It was no doubt this faith in the uniformity of nature and in the universality of the laws of learning that justified to Pavlov his building a general theory of learning by studying only one response system in one species of animal. What Pavlov discovered about salivation in the dog was supposed to reveal principles that would be uniformly applicable to all learning. This optimistic faith in the uniformity of nature was by no means unique to Pavlov; it is shared by virtually all learning theorists. Consider the following quotation:

> In studying (operant) behavior we must make certain preliminary decisions. We begin by choosing an organism—one which we hope will be representative but which is first merely convenient. We must also choose a bit of behavior—not for any intrinsic or dramatic interest it may have, but because it is easily observed . . . can be readily recorded, and . . . may be repeated many times without fatigue. Thirdly we must select or construct an experimental space which can be well controlled. (Skinner, 1957b, p. 344)

This quotation indicates that at that time Skinner had a profound faith in the universality of the principles controlling behavior. But what is this strange concept of a "representative" animal? Whom does the pigeon represent? Does it stand for you or me, the rat, the flatworm, or even other birds? What is this strange notion that we can come to a better understanding of animal behavior by looking at a response which is of no importance but is easily observed and can occur at a high rate? And what is this strange obligation to seek an understanding of behavior by looking at it only in situations such as the Skinner box?

The present chapter will show that the assumption of uniformity can no longer be defended and that our principles of learning no longer have a claim to universality. We will see that learning depends in very important ways upon the kind of animal that is being considered, the kind of behavior that is required of it, and the kind of situation in which the behavior occurs. Learning has a structure that must be discerned through an analysis of cases where learning occurs very rapidly and other cases where learning occurs either slowly or not at all.[1] Let us consider first an instance in which learning occurs with great rapidity under seemingly impossible conditions.

The Garcia Effect

Many psychologists were awakened to the fact that learning is much more likely to occur under some conditions than under others by the remarkable work of John Garcia. In one of the first and perhaps the most remarkable of these experiments, Garcia and Koelling (1966) trained rats to drink bright, noisy water. This feat was accomplished by attaching an

---

[1] Recent writers, perhaps struck mostly by some dramatic failures of learning, have popularized the phrase "constraints on learning" in referring to the nonuniformity of the laws of learning. But this phrase tells only half the story, for there are also "facilitations of learning." It is not that learning is limited; it is the applicability of our present laws of learning, and perhaps the laws themselves, that are limited.

electrode to the spout of the drinking tube so that whenever the rat's tongue touched it the appropriate electrical circuitry produced flashing lights and a raucous noise. For one group of animals drinking bright, noisy water was followed shortly by electric shock to the feet: Drinking bright, noisy water was punished by shock. When offered bright, noisy water the next day, these animals showed an aversion to it and would drink little of it. A second group of animals also drank bright, noisy water, but the consequence of doing so was different. This group was made ill (either by being X-irradiated or by being injected with a toxic substance). When this group was offered bright, noisy water again, they showed no aversion to it and drank as much as they had initially. A third group of animals was offered water without the lights and noises but with the distinctive taste of saccharin, and immediately following the consumption of the saccharin solution these animals were given foot shock. In contrast to the first group, however, they showed no evidence of a learned aversion on the test day; their drinking of the tasty water was not reduced. The fourth group was also given the novel taste of saccharin water and were then made ill. When these animals were tested the following day, they showed a strong aversion to the saccharin solution. These results are summarized in Figure 9.1.

		Consequences	
		illness	shock
Cues	taste	avoid	—
	audio-visual	—	avoid

Fig. 9.1 *Results of the bright, noisy water experiment showing how avoidance learning was found only with certain combinations of cues and consequences. (From Garcia & Koelling,* Psychonomic Sciences, *1966, 4, 123–124.)*

Notice how elegantly the study was counterbalanced. It cannot be argued, for example, that one group failed to learn an aversion because illness is an ineffective consequence, for another group did learn with this consequence. Nor can it be argued that foot shock is not an effective punisher, because it was effective for another group. Similarly, it cannot be argued that one group failed to learn because bright, noisy water is a poor cue, for it was a good cue for another group. Every element was counterbalanced. How are we to explain the asymmetrical results produced by the four groups? Garcia and Koelling's interpretation was simply that some things are more learnable than others. Whether or not learning occurred in a particular group was a function of the relationship between the cue properties of the water and the consequence. Indeed, the title of their paper was "Relation of Cue to Consequence in Avoidance Learning." If the relationship is suitable, for example, if both cue and consequence are external events such as light and sound followed by shock, then learning is readily obtained. If the relationship involves only the digestive system—the taste of water followed by illness—again, learning is readily found. But the attempt to train an association that runs across these two systems was not productive. In short, Garcia and Koelling showed that the effectiveness of a learning procedure depends dramatically upon there being some intrinsic relationship between the cue and the consequence. The remarkable facility with which rats (and a number of other animals) learn about the relationship between the taste of a particular food substance and a subsequent illness we shall call the "Garcia effect."[2]

There are some remarkable features of food-aversion learning. One is that, in contrast to the learning found in most situations, it occurs with remarkable rapidity. Three or four pairings of a cue and consequence are sometimes used, but the effect can be readily shown after a single pairing. Another unusual feature of the Garcia effect is that it is possible to introduce a delay of many hours between the consumption of food and the subsequent illness and still produce an aversion to the food. Shorter delays generally lead to greater aversions, but aversions have been shown with delays as long as eight hours. Unpublished results that are similar to delay gradients reported by other investigators are shown in Figure 9.2. Thus, food-aversion learning occurs under conditions that cannot produce learning, according to traditional theories; there are not enough trials and the delays are much too long. Punishment can be effective after a single trial but not when it is delayed more than a few seconds. What makes food-aversion learning possible is that the rat has a peculiar facility for just this kind of learning. Indeed, it can be argued that such learning is essential for an animal that occupies the ecological niche in which the rat is so successful. The rat is an opportunistic forager and a generalized eater, and if it is to survive eating a great variety of foods it must have a learning mechanism to protect it against those that are poisonous. We might almost expect the rat and other animals in similar ecological niches to have evolved the ability to learn under such conditions.

---

[2] The fact that rats will learn not to eat food that has been associated with illness had already been demonstrated by Garcia in earlier studies of the aversive effects of X-radiation. It had been previously noted by Rzoska (1953) in his studies of rat eradication that, while the introduction of poisonous food might kill most of a rat colony, survivors of the initial poisoning would refuse to eat the poisoned food again. But the phenomenon had not been considered from the point of view of learning theory, and it is because Garcia first saw the theoretical importance of the phenomenon that we can properly call it the Garcia effect.

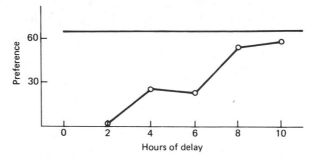

Fig. 9.2   The percentage of saccharin consumed in a choice test between water and saccharin as a function of the delay between the previous drinking of saccharin and being made sick. Nonpoisoned control rats preferred saccharin 2 to 1 over water. (Unpublished data of A. L. Riley.)

The Garcia effect has considerable generality. It can be demonstrated using a variety of toxic agents: different kinds of poison, radiation-induced illness, and perhaps any kind of bodily disturbance. It can be demonstrated with a variety of test foods, but there are some limitations. One is that some flavors appear to be much more readily associated with illness than others, a phenomenon that has been called "salience," suggesting that some flavors are inherently more discriminable than others. Kalat (1974) has determined, however, that these differences are not due to the intrinsic quality of the stimulation but reflect the animal's familiarity with the test flavor or flavors similar to it. A second limitation is that virtually all investigators find that the Garcia effect occurs much more readily in connection with novel flavors than with familiar ones. Indeed, with highly familiar substances like water the effect is virtually impossible to demonstrate.

So far in our discussion of the Garcia effect there has been an implication that learning either occurs or does not; the bright, noisy water study was described as if that were so. But it should be emphasized that there is always a continuity of effects. The aversion is not either learned or not learned; it is really learned to a greater or lesser degree. Effects are always graded. Consider, for example, the temporal gradient shown in Figure 9.2. The shorter the time interval between ingestion and illness, the stronger the learned aversion. It is also known that the greater the illness, the stronger the resulting aversion. The greater the number of pairings of the cue and the consequence, the greater the aversion. Even with cues of high familiarity or of low salience it is still possible to show aversion learning if the time intervals are short, the trials many, and the illness serious. In general, we have to think of the learning in quantitative terms; some learning can be demonstrated under a great variety of conditions, but remarkably efficient learning occurs only under optimum conditions. It even seems likely that rats could learn to avoid bright, noisy water if doing so were followed by illness if training were extended, and other experimental parameters were optimized. There is no reason to suppose that the rat is incapable of such learning, but it is evidently not easy. The main point of the bright, noisy water experiment is not that learning is impossible under some conditions but that it is enormously facilitated if the situation is arranged to take advantage of the rat's natural predisposition to learn the relationship between certain cues and certain consequences.

This continuity of effects is nicely illustrated by recent work done at the University of Washington by Anthony Riley. Riley found that under certain conditions rats will learn to avoid drinking in a particular place if such consumption is associated with illness. First, rats were trained to drink water from a bottle in a fixed location. Then the bottle was put in a new location, and drinking was followed by poisoning. If the animals were then given a one-bottle test, that is, if the water bottle was simply inserted in the new location on the day following illness, there was no reduction in the amount drunk. But given a two-bottle test, that is, the choice of drinking at either the new or the old location, the rats showed strong avoidance of the new location that had been associated with illness. This aversion appeared to be facilitated if the new place was "marked" with a new taste, like saccharin, but taste had to be held constant at the time of testing. If the animals were offered a choice between saccharin and water, they would always avoid the saccharin, regardless of where it was located. But, if both test bottles contained water, then strong aversion to the place associated with poison was found. It appears that the rat has a hierarchy of cue utilization. It will first avoid a taste if there has been a distinctive taste associated with poisoning. But in the absence of a distinctive taste cue it will avoid a place that has been associated with poisoning. There is the further interesting complication that a distinctive taste helps to mark, set off, or call attention to a distinctive place, and by this means facilitates place learning.

Similar studies by Garcia and others have shown that the rat does not readily learn to avoid foods that have been associated with distinctive odors paired with poisoning, but again this failure does not reflect all-or-none learning; using procedures like those in the place-learning experiment, Riley has been able to show clear avoidance of odors associated with illness. Again certain methodological precautions have to be taken; if there are taste differences, the rat will avoid the less familiar taste whether or not it has been associated with poisoning. But when taste is held constant an aversion to odors can be readily demonstrated.

In other animals the hierarchy of cue utilization may be quite different. Wilcoxon, Dragoin, and Kral (1971) gave blue, salty water to rats and to quail. After they had been made ill both species of animals were offered a choice between blue water and salty water. The rats avoided the salty water, which is consistent with their dependence upon taste cues, whereas the quail avoided the blue water, which is consistent with the general proposition that birds are visual eaters. Earlier, Capretta (1961) had shown that chickens would not learn to avoid a taste that had been associated with illness but would learn to avoid food of a given color that had been associated with illness.[3]

How are we to explain the Garcia effect? How are we to explain the remarkably rapid learning that occurs when certain kinds of cues and certain kinds of consequences are used? Logically, both basic paradigms are applicable. The Garcia effect can be considered an instance of punishment learning: There is a stimulus, the taste of the food; there is a response, drinking; and the connection between them is weakened by the negative consequences, the illness, that follows some time later. Garcia himself and most investigators working with the phenomenon do not accept this paradigm, and a serious question about its validity has been raised by a study of Domjan and Wilson (1972). These investigators used a variety of techniques for exposing rats to a taste cue in the absence of any consumption. In one experiment rats were curarized so that they could not drink or swallow the test substance; it was simply flowed across their tongues. Then they were poisoned. Later, when the animals recovered from the curare and illness, they showed a greater aversion to the flavor of the test fluid than did control animals that had been curarized but not poisoned. Thus it appears that the Garcia effect does not require the occurrence of the consummatory response.

The other basic paradigm, classical conditioning, seems more appropriate. According to the traditional interpretation of conditioning, the CS is the taste or other sensory quality of the food, and when it is paired with illness (the US) some part of the reaction to illness becomes conditioned to it. It is not clear what either the unconditioned or the conditioned reaction to illness might be, but modern interpretations of conditioning need not be concerned with this problem since they view conditioning as a procedure in which the animal learns something about the relationship between CS and US. The response is merely symptomatic of learning, rather than the essential thing learned. Garcia has noted that the rat's response to the test food after conditioning is a kind of disgust or rejection reaction; it reacts to

[3] The difference in cue utilization should not be attributed just to the fact that the rat has an acute sense of smell and poor vision whereas birds have keen vision and a questionable olfactory sense. Braveman (1974) has shown that, when the guinea pig, an animal not noted for its keen eyesight or its reliance upon the visual modality, was tested in an experiment like Wilcoxon's, it showed an aversion both to the color of food and to its taste. Thus, species differences in the Garcia effect probably reflect some hierarchy of cue utilization rather than different degrees of development of their sensory systems *per se.*

a food that may have been highly preferred originally as though it now tastes bad. This observation is consistent with the idea that the rat learns to expect the US when it encounters the CS. But we still need to conceptualize the learning mechanism.

Let us consider three possible learning processes that might produce the Garcia effect. One view is that an S-S association is formed (Revusky, 1971). Although the rat is predisposed to form certain kinds of associations, such as between tastes and illness, during the time between ingestion and illness the taste cue is gradually lost, either because of forgetting or because of interference. According to Revusky, what makes learned food aversions possible after such long delays is that there is relatively little interference from competing taste stimuli during the delay interval so that it is possible to remember the cue that has to be remembered if the association is to be formed. This view is inconsistent with the finding that birds, which rely upon visual cues, also show conditioned aversion learning with long intervals, even though there must be a mass of intervening visual stimulation during the delay interval. Revusky appears merely to have restated the problem of why other kinds of stimuli do not interfere with the association of the relevant cue with its ultimate consequence.

Kalat and Rozin (1973) have suggested a different mechanism. Their proposal is that the animal is initially somewhat suspicious upon encountering novel things. The rat shows neophobia particularly to new food substances, but over a period of time its suspicion is dispelled as it learns that the food is safe and may even have beneficial consequences such as quenching thirst or providing calories. Kalat and Rozin tested their proposal against the more conventional associative-learning hypothesis by providing rats with different opportunities to learn about the safety of the test food. One group, let us call it group 4, was fed a novel substance and then four hours later was made ill. Group $\frac{1}{2}$ was fed the same food and made ill $\frac{1}{2}$-hour later. The critical group 4–$\frac{1}{2}$ was offered food twice, once four hours before poisoning and again $\frac{1}{2}$ hour before poisoning. According to the forgetting or loss-of-association theory, group $\frac{1}{2}$ and group 4–$\frac{1}{2}$ should both have shown strong food aversions because they each had an equally short half-hour interval between the last presentation of food and illness. But the results of the experiment were quite different. Group 4–$\frac{1}{2}$ showed essentially the same aversion as group 4 because, it was argued, both groups had approximately the same amount of time, $3\frac{1}{2}$ hours versus 4 hours, to learn that the food was safe. According to Kalat and Rozin, the temporal gradient (see Figure 9.2) does not reflect a forgetting of the taste, but complementary or opposing learning about the safety of the new food. This hypothesis explains why the novelty of the test food is so vitally important and why some flavors appear to be more salient in that they more readily lead to acquired aversions than others. Kalat and Rozin's interpretation of the Garcia effect is somewhat reminiscent of Krechevsky's concept of hypothesis testing (Chapter 5). Upon encountering a novel food the rat appears to hypothesize that the food may be bad, and so it eats a little and waits; it tests the hypothesis. After a time, if everything is okay, the food then becomes more acceptable, and the original hypothesis is replaced by a new one that the food is good.

There is, however, a fundamental difficulty both with the more conventional associative view of Revusky and with Kalat and Rozin's interpretation of the Garcia effect. This problem is simply why does the association involve specifically the taste of the recently consumed novel food? It seems to be more a matter of memory and retrieval than of input and association. Posing the question as a problem of memory, why does the animal remember what it ate at the time it becomes sick? Why, when it becomes ill, does the rat remember specifically the taste of the novel food, and why does the bird or the guinea pig remember specifically the sight of the food? Why are these particular contents of memory retrieved and not some irrelevant event that occurred before or afterward? It is easy enough for us to see other events as irrelevant, but how does the rat do so? Perhaps all that can be said at this point is that the animal's memory is organized to do so. As Garcia and Koelling originally proposed, perhaps these kinds of cues and these kinds of consequences are organized into a closed system within which learning occurs very easily.

It is becoming clear that the proper understanding of learning requires us to know something about an animal's ecological niche; we must know how it solves its problems. It is no longer possible to assume that all problems are solved by means of learning. Even in animals as capable of learning as the rat, we see that the materials that enter into learning, the kinds of stimuli and the kinds of consequences that become related, have an intricate structure of their own that we must expect to vary with the species of animal. Learning has its own structure. And if a particular animal can learn a particular thing it is because it is genetically endowed to do so. Perhaps that is all we can take for granted at this point.

In the remainder of this chapter we shall consider briefly a number of instances of failure to learn under conditions in which the traditional learning theorist would surely have expected learning and a number of contrary instances in which animals learn under conditions that have traditionally been regarded as making learning impossible.

Constraints on Learning What to Eat

If it is possible to produce an aversion to a food by associating it with illness, then it may also be possible to produce an increased preference for a food by associating its taste with an improvement in an animal's condition. One difficulty in obtaining such an effect, however, is that there are not many states of ill health from which an animal can recover rapidly. The recovery from an illness is typically much slower than its onset. Thiamine deficiency is an exception, in that a massive dose of the vitamin can overcome a severe deficiency within an hour or so. Zahorik and Maier (1969) fed thiamine-deficient rats saccharin and followed this procedure with a large vitamin injection; they did find an increased preference for saccharin.

We might expect the same type of increased preference for a food that provides caloric value to a hungry rat. Such a mechanism, a "positive Garcia effect," would lead to animals having a convenient preference for foods of high caloric density. But so far such an effect has not been reported. A pair of studies recently conducted at the University of Washington suggests one reason why a positive Garcia effect may be difficult to find. In one experiment, Weisinger, Parker, and Skorupski (1974) gave two groups of rats insulin injections sufficient to put them into a coma. For one of these groups the novel food associated with insulin shock was salty water; these animals subsequently showed an aversion to the saline solution. But the second group of animals, tested with saccharin, failed to show an aversion to it. In two other groups gastric distress was produced by formalin injections. Again the animals were tested either with a saccharin solution, which did produce a conditioned aversion, or a salty solution, which failed to produce a learned aversion. Weisinger and his colleagues appear to have discovered a constraint upon the possible relationships between the cue and the consequence that can be learned. Their explanation is that insulin not only produces a distressing comatose state; it also produces a need for sugar and a specific appetite for sugar. Formalin, on the other hand, produces a salt imbalance such that the animal needs and will seek out salt solutions. What the experiment appears to show, then, is that if the toxic agent produces a specific kind of need state and if the animal has an "innate recognition mechanism" for dealing with that need, then this innate recognition mechanism will override any aversion that might otherwise be learned. After having gone into insulin shock, the animal develops an increased preference for sweets that overrides any possible learning to avoid the sweet flavor. In effect, the animal's innate recognition mechanism replaces the learning mechanism in the solution of this particular problem. It is as if the animal made ill by insulin cannot attribute its illness to the prior consumption of a sweet substance and as if an animal made ill by formalin cannot attribute its illness to the prior consumption of a salt solution.

To return to the question of why it is so difficult to obtain increased preference for foods associated with caloric benefit, perhaps the rat has an innate recognition of high-calorie foods like fats and sweets and because of this innate recognition mechanism there is no need for a learning mechanism to solve the problem. To test this hypothesis indirectly Parker, Failor, and Weidman (1973) produced in rats an "artificial" need state for which there could not have evolved an innate recognition mechanism, the distress produced by morphine withdrawal. Rats were first regularly injected with morphine until they became physiologically dependent. Morphine was then withdrawn until the animals became ill. Then, just before being given a maintenance dose of morphine, the animals were fed a saccharin solution. Compared with controls, these animals quickly developed a preference for saccharin. One implication of this research is that the rat has two kinds of systems for solving its general nutritional problems. First, it has innate recognition mechanisms such that a certain need produces an appetite for the needed substance. Then, to take care of the multitude of cases where the conditions of need, particularly illness, lead to no innate recognition, there is the learning mechanism. If this analysis is correct, then we have a further structuring of what an animal can learn about the relation between particular foods and the consequences of ingesting them. Garcia showed that it is the relationship between particular cues and particular consequences that makes such learning possible, and what continued research on the Garcia effect seems to show is that some further, rather specific requirements must also be met before such learning occurs.

Hogan (1973) posed the question of how chickens learn to recognize food. A young chick approximately three days old pecks at anything on the ground: food, inedible objects, shadows, anything. But as the chick grows older, it becomes much more selective in its pecking and pecks primarily at edible objects. Some sand and gravel are still taken in and are useful in ensuring that the gizzard functions properly, but as the chick matures it mostly pecks at food objects such as seeds and insects. Does this change in behavior reflect learning of what to eat? That was the question to which Hogan addressed himself. He confronted young chicks with equal piles of sand and seeds whose stimulus properties were such that the chicks pecked approximately equally often at sand and food, that is, there was no initial preference. Then he presented one group of chicks with just sand. Approximately an hour later, when offered the same choice between food and sand, they still showed no preference. Another group was presented with only seeds. About an hour later, when offered the choice, these chicks showed a strong preference for seeds over sand. Given sand, the birds thus seem to learn nothing about it, but, given seeds, they seem to learn that they are food. The most interesting group was given only sand and then fed a high-calorie meal through a tube directly into the stomach. When tested an hour later, these chicks showed a strong preference for the sand. It appears that the chicks show a preference on the subsequent test for whatever it was they ate, provided that they have derived some nutritional benefit during the interim.

One of the most interesting findings reported by Hogan is that a delay of about an hour between the initial exposure and the subsequent test is necessary if the preference is to develop. Here, then, we have an unusual form of learning, which occurs only when the consequence is considerably delayed after the cue is presented. From a nutritional point of view, of course, the necessity of such a delay is reasonable. But from the point of view of traditional learning theory, we find an anomalous inverted delay gradient such that, the longer the delay, up to a point, the better the learning. Hogan has found that there are innate recognition mechanisms in addition to the learning mechanism just described. For example, if a chick is offered a highly palatable mealworm, it shows a strong and immediate preference for mealworms over either seeds or sand. It appears that the chick must learn about the nutritional benefits of seeds but that it recognizes, probably from the taste, the value of mealworms.

Constraints on Cue Utilization

An interesting case where we might have expected learning yet find none was reported some years ago by Schneirla (1933). Schneirla had found ants capable of learning in various situations, so he tested them on a maze problem. The starting point was placed at the ants' nest, and food was placed in the goal box. When the ants left the nest to forage for food, they would wander through the maze, but Schneirla found that they showed little or no learning of the maze pattern; there was no reliable decrease in errors. Does this negative finding mean that ants cannot learn mazes? Not at all. Schneirla found that if the maze was turned around so that the ants had to run through it to carry food back to the nest, they quickly learned it. The ants' ability to solve the maze pattern depended upon their motivation; they could learn how to get to the nest but not how to get to the food.

It could be said, of course, that ants are simple-minded animals; certainly there would be more generalized learning ability among vertebrates. Better perhaps, but not infallible. Kramer (1957) was working with starlings that he kept captive in a large enclosure. They roosted in the center of the enclosure, and he trained them to go off each morning to a particular part of the enclosure, for example, the eastern side of it, to obtain food. The starlings quickly learned the problem. But Kramer, who was primarily concerned with navigation in animals, evidently became concerned with whether or not his birds were really navigating. The sun was in the east in the morning, so perhaps they were merely flying toward it (and the birds trained to go to other parts of the enclosure might be flying at some fixed angle to the sun). The critical test, of course, was to move the sun. Kramer did this by testing the birds in the afternoon. The results showed that the birds were not approaching or orienting with regard to the sun but were in fact flying to the eastern part of the enclosure. Kramer then attempted to train his birds to approach or orient with regard to the sun by feeding them in the east in the morning and the west in the afternoon. He found that the starlings had great difficulty learning this simple problem. Here we have the irony of an experimenter using the most splendid stimulus in the solar system and finding his animals apparently unable to learn simply to approach it. In a series of further experiments Kramer demonstrated that the starlings not only noticed the sun's location but were actually using this information in conjunction with their own biological clocks to navigate in the appropriate direction. It was as if the birds made a calculation involving the location of the sun and the known time of day and then used this information to navigate quite accurately in a given compass direction. But the much simpler task of simply approaching the sun wherever it happened to be was not so easy to learn.

It could be said that birds are simple-minded animals; surely better cue utilization would be shown by mammals. However, Konorski (1967) has described a series of studies with dogs that show serious constraints on learning in man's best friend. One experiment required the dog to go forward and approach food upon receiving a given signal and not to approach food in the presence of an alternative signal. The two signals were auditory stimuli that differed in quality; one was a tone, and the other was a buzzer. The dogs had no difficulty learning this so-called go–no go discrimination. But then Konorski used the same two cues to signal which arm of a T maze would contain food. One signal indicated food would be on the right, and the other indicated it would be on the left. He reported that the dogs could not solve this problem. It might be argued that the T-maze problem was inherently more difficult than the go–no go problem. But this was shown not to be the case in two further experiments. In one, the cues for the T-maze task were two tones, one placed directly above and the other placed directly below the dog, each tone signifying on which side of the T maze the food would be located in a given trial. Now the T-maze problem was solved with little trouble. But when the same spatially differentiated cues were used in the go–no go discrimination, this task became unsolvable. We are forced to the conclusion that spatially localized cues are effective in the solution of spatial problems but not for the go–no go discrimination, whereas auditory signals of different qualities are effective for a go–no go discrimination but not for simple spatial learning.

The skeptic could say that even the dog is not so smart, and when it comes to the proper utilization of sensory information, there can be no question of the human's ability. But this confusion, too, is unjustified. Recall that Watson had conditioned fear in little Albert using a terrible noise as the US and a white rat as the CS. A careful replication of this study was reported by Bregman (1934). She was able to obtain the same kind of fear conditioning with an animal as the CS, but when she used an inanimate object such as a block or a bottle as the CS she found no fear conditioning. The infants were reported to be unhappy about the conditioning experiment, but the tremendous conditioning of fear reported by Watson and Rayner and widely accepted as a model for all fear conditioning was found to be restricted in the young human subject to animate things. Even a wooden animal will not do (Jones, 1924).

We may suspect that little Albert was very much like Kalat's rat in that, on his first encounter with a strange animal, he was suspicious of it. Perhaps humans are neophobic about certain classes of events, but if everything turns out all right they learn that they are safe. But let there be some disturbance, and fear will be quickly learned. We may suspect, too, that in the absence of this initial suspicion it may be quite difficult to condition fear. Seligman (1972) has made a similar analysis of phobias in adults. It turns out that virtually all the millions of people suffering from phobias share just a few specific fears, restricted to certain narrow classes of events. Phobias nearly always pertain to animals, snakes being the most common, and certain situations, being closed in or falling off high places being the most common. None of these millions of people has a phobia about coke bottles, door knobs, ash trays, or any of the other multitude of inanimate things that crowd our everyday world. Seligman therefore calls into question the notion that phobias develop as a result of classical fear conditioning, as had been said by Mowrer (1939) and accepted by most other writers. Another reason for skepticism is that the people who have phobias about snakes or high places have never experienced an appropriate US; that is, they have not been bitten by snakes or fallen off high places. The fear of such events is incipient, or latent. It is probably triggered as much as anything by cultural factors. There is thus every reason to believe that even in the all-learning human, who can learn to go to or from, who can use the sun either to approach or to navigate with, who can use all kinds of audio signals for all kinds of purposes, there are biological considerations that govern how likely he is to learn about certain classes of stimuli.

All the examples that we have discussed so far illustrate constraints upon or special facilitations of learning about the relationships between cues and consequences. To the extent that these specific relationships give structure to what is learned, they impose a constraint upon the generality of the Pavlovian paradigm. But there is another large class of constraints in learning that has to do with the ability of a particular animal to be controlled by particular reinforcement contingencies. In the remainder of this chapter, we shall look at some of these constraints and special facilitations.

Constraints on Response Acquisition

Keller and Marion Breland made a business of training unusual forms of animal behavior for commercial purposes. They made their living shaping unusual behaviors in unusual animals that might be desired by an advertising agency or for the movies. The Brelands used well-established operant techniques, often involving considerable shaping to obtain the desired response and often involving the chaining of simple behaviors into complex sequences. The standard operant techniques were generally successful but not always. In a paper entitled "The Misbehavior of Organisms" (Breland & Breland, 1961) they describe troubles they had fulfilling a contract that called for a pig to put pseudomonies (wooden disks) into a piggy bank. The pig was intelligent, friendly, and it loved to eat. The trouble began when the Brelands required the pig to drop a coin in the slot to obtain food. Everything went awry; the pig began tossing the coin in the air, snuffling and snorting, rooting on the ground, tossing and rooting, and so on instead of dropping the coin in the bank. The misbehavior was so serious that further training was abandoned. The Brelands decided to use a raccoon. Raccoons are extremely dextrous, highly intelligent, and just as cute putting money in the bank as pigs are. There was no problem on a continuous-reinforcement schedule, but as soon as a two-to-one ratio was required the raccoon's behavior deteriorated. It would take the two coins and instead of depositing them in the slot would dip them in and out and rub them together, as raccoons do when they are washing their food. This behavior was so persistent that the project had to be given up.

The Brelands describe another disaster that occurred when they attempted to train a chicken to play baseball. The game was arranged on a sort of pinball machine. The idea was that the ball would roll toward home plate, and the chicken would pull a chain to swing a little metal bat; if the ball was hit out through the outfield, a bell would ring, and the chicken could run off toward first base to get its food. It was a fairly simple matter of chaining, and everything went well; the chicken was pulling the chain and running to first base, and everything was in order until the ball was introduced into the game; then—chaos. Whenever the chicken hit the ball, instead of going off to first base to collect its food it would attempt to field the ball itself, pecking furiously at it, flapping and chasing the ball all around the diamond. The baseball game had to be abandoned.

What is the explanation of these dramatic failures of learning and all this misbehavior? Notice that some segments of the desired behavior were readily obtained but that at some point the reinforced behavior collapsed and was replaced by each animal's own specific food-getting behavior. Each animal had a token that represented food and could be exchanged for food, but because the token did represent food each of the animals began to act toward it as if it were food. The pig rooted around with its food token, the raccoon dipped and rubbed it, and the chicken pecked it. In each case the animal's species-specific food-getting behavior intervened and interfered with the behavior that the Brelands were attempting to instill. In some of the failures that the Brelands described, the interfering behavior become so strong that the animal was completely cut off from further reinforcement. So, whereas animals can frequently learn unusual food-getting behaviors, the innate relationships between particular behaviors and particular consequences can supersede, preventing the reinforcement contingency from controlling the animal's behavior.

Another illustration of the same type of constraint appeared in Stevenson-Hinde's study (1973) of learning in chaffinches. She found that she could train these birds to perch on a specific part of the apparatus, which was arranged to produce the recorded sounds of chaffinch songs. She also found that chaffinches would learn to peck a key to obtain food. But at the same time she had great difficulty training them to perch in a particular location to obtain food and had no success when she attempted to reinforce pecking a key with song. Evidently pecking for food is an appropriate food-getting response, and perching in a particular place is an appropriate response for producing song, but it is very difficult to interchange the parts of these two systems.

The Dutch ethologist Sevenster (1973) had similar problems in producing learning in the stickleback fish. These animals are highly aggressive fighters under appropriate conditions, and males will chase off other males in a characteristic manner. They are also highly aggressive lovers and will give characteristic courting displays to female sticklebacks. Sevenster then made the presentation of either the male to fight or the female to court contingent upon one of two different operant responses. One response was to bite at a glass rod inserted in the tank. He found that this response was rapidly learned when reinforced by presentation of the male, but it was not learned when the female was presented. The second operant required the fish to swim through a wire hoop. It was found that the stickleback would quickly learn this response when it was reinforced by the presentation of the female but not when the attempt was made to reinforce it by presenting the male. Again, there seem to be two separate systems, an aggression system and a courting system. Sevenster analyzed the consummatory behaviors for each system and concluded that the constraints on learning could be characterized in the following way. If the operant response is a part of, closely resembles, or is compatible with some part of the consummatory reaction, then it is learned. Otherwise it is not. Biting the rod is compatible with aggression, so it is learned as an operant, but in courting aggressive responses must be inhibited, and so biting is not learned. The courting response involves swimming toward the female in a characteristic zigzag manner, so it is easy to go through the hoop; attacking the male, however, requires a different kind of approach, so the hoop response is not learned.

In all these failures of learning we can see that the animal was required to perform an operant that was incompatible with the consummatory response. What can we learn about learning from situations in which the operant is highly compatible with the consummatory response? One of the most interesting and most widely investigated situations of this type is the so-called autoshaping experiment. In Chapter 7 we mentioned briefly the customary procedure for shaping bar pressing in rats. Essentially the same techniques are used to establish key pecking in pigeons. Briefly, the animal is first magazine-trained; then from time to time the plastic key is illuminated, and the experimenter gradually shapes orienting, approaching, tentative pecks, and finally outright pecks at the illuminated key, using the sound of the feeding magazine and food to obtain the desired key-peck response. The entire process can be carried out in an hour or two if the experimenter is careful and does not reinforce inappropriate behavior. In 1968 Brown and Jenkins reported a technique that tremendously facilitates the entire process. What they did was simply give animals free food, that is, food presented without regard to the birds' behavior, every fifteen seconds, and they illuminated the key just before food was presented. In the same amount of time that tedious hand shaping ordinarily requires, their pigeons were busily pecking the key and obtaining food. During the session the birds had shaped themselves or had become "autoshaped."

There are a number of possible interpretations of autoshaping. Within the Skinnerian framework, it may be supposed that pecking the illuminated key has a very high operant rate, so that there is a high chance that the reinforcement contingency will make contact with the behavior. Within the Hullian framework, there is an additional factor: Because the illumination of the key is repeatedly associated with food, it must become an incentive motivator, further raising the animal's motivational level and further increasing the operant level of key pecking. But such interpretations would appear to be excluded in an autoshaping study reported by Williams and Williams (1969). They repeated the basic procedure used by Brown and Jenkins, with one important change: The animals received free food every fifteen seconds, and presentation was regularly preceded by illumination of the key, but whenever a key peck occurred it prevented the delivery of food. Thus, whatever incentive motivation or other factors were initially producing the behavior, the reinforcement contingency was an omission-training schedule that worked against key pecking. The more the bird pecked, the less food it received. Nonetheless, Williams and Williams reported obtaining substantial amounts of key pecking; in some birds the response became so strong that virtually all food reinforcement was eliminated. The Williams' phenomenon, which they labeled "negative automaintenance," appears similar to the behavior of the Brelands' animals: A species-specific food-getting behavior becomes so strong that it totally overrides the reinforcement contingency.

We have become accustomed to thinking of the key-peck response as an operant and as an arbitrary, convenient, easily measured response whose strength can be controlled by its consequences. But we can see, in the autoshaping procedure generally and in the negative automaintenance procedure particularly, that the strength of the response is not controlled by its consequences. It is evidently controlled by the signaling properties of the illuminated key.

Further doubt about the validity of the conventional operant interpretation of key pecking has been raised by Moore (1973). Before describing Moore's results, we should note that the consummatory response in the pigeon is unique in one respect: The pigeon does not drink as most birds do, by filling its bill, tossing its head back, and letting the water run down its throat; it drinks by giving a series of bill movements that is evidently equivalent to licking in mammals. The bill makes a series of rather gentle, comparatively slow, and relatively prolonged movements. The eating response, on the other hand, consists of a single sharp, very fast, and rather forceful stroke of the beak. There are other parts of the total pattern: for example, the eating response is executed with the eyes shut and the beak opened to seize food just at the moment of contact. Moore autoshaped pigeons under conditions in which one key color signaled food and another key color signaled water. His birds were both hungry and thirsty and were given free food and water intermittently in association with the appropriately colored key. High-speed photographs of the birds' autoshaped responses show that the pigeons were, in effect, eating the food key and drinking the water key.[4] Moore's (1973) interpretation of these results is that the key-peck response is not really an operant at all but is a classically conditioned consummatory response. In his experiments, a particular key color becomes a discriminative CS, which is paired with a particular US, and the appropriate consummatory response simply becomes classically conditioned to it.

Moore's interpretation can be applied to a number of the other phenomena that have been previously described. For example, the misbehavior

[4] The same finding about the different topographies of pecking for food and pecking for water under normal conditions of reinforcement had been briefly noted earlier by Wolin (1968), but the phenomenon did not attract any attention until Moore rediscovered it in the autoshaping situation.

of the Brelands' animals can also be attributed to the fact that consummatory or food-getting behaviors become conditioned to the food tokens because the latter are CSs for food. Moore's peculiarly conservative view of conditioning as involving attachment of a replica of the UR to the CS can be modernized along the lines indicated in Chapter 8, without reducing the force of Moore's argument or detracting from the importance of his data. We may think of the illuminated key as a CS in the more modern sense that it predicts food (or water) or provides information about when it will be forthcoming. The key has the additional property of being a highly localized discrete object that lends itself admirably to being pecked. The same point can be made about the different food tokens or food predictors that so disrupted the behavior of the Brelands' animals: In each case the animal was able to direct its species-specific food-getting behavior toward the token. A recent study by LoLordo, MacMillan, and Riley (1974) indicates that the more localized the food predictor is and the better it predicts food, the more likely the pigeon is to peck it. In short, it appears as if the autoshaping phenomenon requires, first, that the key or whatever be a predictor of food and, second, that it have stimulus properties such that the animal can direct food-getting behavior at it.

The whole series of experiments that we have described indicates that there are a number of situations in which operant-conditioning procedures are ineffective in controlling operant behavior. Many of these situations appear to share a common characteristic: They require the animal to make a response that is different in form from the relevant consummatory response. Then the autoshaping phenomenon indicates that there are other situations in which, again, operant-conditioning procedures are ineffective in controlling operant behavior, and these situations appear to have the characteristic that the required operant is too much like the relevant consummatory response. We must begin to wonder, just what is the domain of responses that are subject to operant control? Is the operant paradigm only properly applicable to animals and to motivational systems in which there is some flexibility of the consummatory and food-getting behaviors?

Peter Covey, working at the Seattle zoo, has made some interesting observations about the flexibility of consummatory behavior. A problem at the zoo was that the nighthawk (*Chordeiles minor*) would not eat food from a dish. Normally the nighthawk picks up insects by flying around with its mouth open. In order to feed the animal in the zoo, it was necessary to wave a piece of prepared food over its head until its mouth opened and then quickly pop it in. This procedure was laborious and uncertain, but nothing else would induce the captive bird to eat. Covey's approach consisted of gradually lowering the angle of the food and gradually waving it less. After a few weeks the nighthawk would feed at a downward angle and from a stationary piece of food. Eventually, it would take some food from a dish on the ground, but the bird did not eat enough this way, so the original problem had not been solved. The next step was to present morsels of food, not in the shape of a ball, as they had been up to this point, but in a rolled-out shape about the size of a cricket. Eventually Covey was able to get the bird to eat its entirely daily ration from cricket-sized pieces of food in a dish, a kind of consummatory behavior that is never seen in the wild nighthawk.

Here, then, we appear to have an instance in which a shaping procedure, used in conjunction with contingent reinforcement, was effective in changing a behavior. But there are other possible interpretations. There is the basic question that has so dramatically split the once-unified Hullian theorists: How much of the change in behavior can be attributed to the response-reinforcement contingency *per se*, and how much of it should be attributed to learning about the altered S-S relations that occur during training? During the course of training was the response really being modified by reinforcement, or was the perception of food being modified? Did the learning consist of new responses, or did it consist primarily of the establishment of new food tokens or symbols? However the question is answered in this particular instance, it is clear that much of what passes for operant conditioning consists of changes in the perception of the stimuli that control the animal's behavior. In the Skinner box the original effect of illuminating the key is only to produce some orienting behavior or investigatory reflex. But eventually the key appears to become virtually synonymous with food, so that, as we have seen in Moore's research, the pigeon will literally eat it.

Avoidance Behavior

Avoidance learning has always been a great challenge to the reinforcement theorist. One of the peculiarities of the avoidance procedure is that when the avoidance response occurs there may be no explicit event that can be pointed to as the reinforcer for the response. By definition, the avoidance response prevents shock from occurring, at least with most avoidance procedures, so we cannot point to the shock as a potential source of reinforcement. On the other hand, it is not satisfactory to cite the nonoccurrence of shock as a reinforcer because logically there is a host of things that do not occur, and the behaviorist is hard put to say why not being shocked should be relevant in the avoidance situation, whereas, say, not being stepped on is irrelevant. The problem is eased somewhat if a warning stimulus, or CS, is introduced before a scheduled shock, particularly if it is arranged so that the avoidance response terminates it. Recall that Mowrer and Lamoreaux (1942) found that CS termination facilitated learning. Under these conditions the termination of the CS can be and usually is cited as a source of reinforcement (the reduction in fear that is conditioned to the CS can also be, and usually is, cited by those of the Hullian persuasion).

But this explanation does not entirely solve the problem because Mowrer and Lamoreaux also found some learning when either a trace-conditioning procedure or a prolonged-CS procedure was used. The theorist is therefore obliged to hypothesize the existence of some internal and unobservable CS whose termination is reinforcing. The explanation of avoidance behavior then depends on a number of hypothetical internal events, including a classically conditioned fear, which is supposed to motivate the response and provide stimulus control for it, and some other stimulus event to serve as a source of reinforcement.

Another approach to the problem of what reinforces avoidance behavior is to raise the pragmatic question: What are the experimental conditions that control it? What are the contingencies that produce avoidance learning? Kamin (1956) appears to have been the first to approach the problem in this way. His experiment included four groups of rats, all of which were required to run from one side to another in a shuttle box. For one group the response had the usual effect of terminating the CS and allowing them to avoid the shock. In the second group the response (it can no longer be called an avoidance response) neither terminated the CS nor avoided scheduled shocks. The interesting groups were the two that were permitted to have one or the other contingency: One group could avoid shock but not terminate the CS, whereas the other could terminate the CS but could not avoid shock. Kamin's results showed that animals with both contingencies learned quickly and performed well. The group with neither contingency performed very badly and evidenced little learning. The groups with just one contingency showed intermediate and approximately equivalent performance. It could be concluded therefore that there are two effective contingencies: one the avoidance of shock and the other termination of the CS. The conventional view was exonerated; CS termination did make a contribution. The other troublesome factor, the avoidance of shock, could be handled by supposing that reinforcement is not dependent upon avoidance itself but that competing behavior that fails to avoid is punished by unavoided shocks.

Bolles, Stokes, and Younger (1966) replicated Kamin's experiment (incorporating additional groups to determine if the possibility of escaping from shock, if it came on, also contributed to the acquisition of avoidance behavior). We found that all three contingencies made approximately equal contributions to the overall acquisition of avoidance. It appeared therefore that shuttle-box avoidance depended upon three important contingencies: the avoidance of shock (or freedom from punishment), termination of the CS, and escape from shock on nonavoidance trials. Everything appeared to be in order, then, except for one further problem: We replicated this entire design using a different avoidance-learning situation. In the second experiment rats were required to run in a wheel. Again the different contingencies were either allowed or not allowed for different groups, so that their individual contributions to running-wheel avoidance could be determined. The results indicated that escape from shock made very little contribution, and termination of the CS made very little contribution; the all-important factor in this experiment was the avoidance contingency. At this point it began to appear that an analysis of avoidance behavior, in terms of the experimental contingencies that control it, might not have any general answer because the relative effectiveness of the different contingencies depends upon what the avoidance response is.

Subsequent research at the University of Washington has confirmed this conclusion. In the one-way situation (which is like the shuttle box except that the animal is returned to the same side of the apparatus between trials, so that the running response is always executed in the same direction rather than back and forth) the acquisition of avoidance appears to be wholly uninfluenced either by CS termination (Bolles & Grossen, 1969) or by the escape contingency (Bolles, Grossen & Hargrave, 1969). More recent and still unpublished results from our laboratory indicate that learning of bar-press avoidance is actually impaired when rats are given the escape contingency and that neither the CS-termination contingency nor the avoidance of shock appears to have any consistent effect. Although rats are generally poor at learning bar-press avoidance, some do learn and those that learn do not seem to be benefited by any of the experimental contingencies that we so carefully arrange to produce learning. In short, our investigation of avoidance learning in a variety of different situations requiring different responses from the animal indicates that there is no consistent pattern of experimental contingencies responsible for the learning. A further problem in such an analysis of contingencies has been noted by Bolles, Moot, and Grossen (1971): The contingencies that appear to be important in maintaining avoidance behavior and preventing its extinction are not necessarily the same as those that are responsible for producing the initial learning. Whole new patterns of contingencies turn out to be important in extinction, at least in the shuttle box, which is the only situation that has been extensively studied. The pattern of controlling contingencies just does not seem to be coherent enough to have much explanatory power.

The most obvious and impressive thing about avoidance learning in different situations is that in some situations the avoidance response is acquired in just a few trials, whereas in other situations learning appears barely possible and in many instances really is impossible. To put it frankly, the average rat does not learn to press a bar to avoid shock. A few animals learn, but they typically perform inconsistently, and giving them extended training does not always help. Over the years a variety of tricks have been discovered that provide some relief (for example, minimizing the amount of shock improves performance somewhat) but none of these tricks can be counted on to give good bar-press avoidance. It remains a very difficult problem for the rat. By contrast, most rats learn to perform rather well in the shuttle box. A group may avoid on 80 percent of the trials after 100 or 200 training trials. Running in a wheel is learned even faster, typically taking only forty trials, and performance typically reaches an asymptote close to 100 percent. Then there are situations such as one-way avoidance task and situations in which the animal jumps out of the shock box—in these situations some learning can be shown after a single trial, and the whole group may perform at 100 percent after a dozen trials. In other words, there is an extremely wide spectrum of ease in learning different avoidance responses. The rat will evidence some learning in some situations after a single trial and may show no indication of learning in another situation after 1000 trials.

It is a serious indictment of our conventional theories of learning that they provide no hint that the choice of response is so important. The most casual observation of rats in difference avoidance-learning situations reveals that what response is required of the animal is a tremendously important parameter. It is vastly more important than the analysis of contingencies, the manipulation of other experimental conditions, the prior experience of the animals, or various kind of physiological interventions that might be made. Clearly, then, the determination of what the avoidance response shall be is not just a matter of convenience; it is the all-important consideration.

An attempt to explain these vast differences in ease of learning was proposed in a paper entitled "Species-Specific Defense Reactions and Avoidance Learning" (Bolles, 1970). The argument is that, just as animals have species-specific behaviors for obtaining food, mating, and solving other biological problems, so they must have innate defensive behaviors. Such behaviors must be innately organized because nature provides little opportunity for the animal to learn to avoid predators and other natural hazards. A small and relatively defenseless animal like the rat cannot afford to learn to avoid these hazards; it must have innate defensive behaviors that keep it out of trouble. The same argument applies, of course, to other animals. The mouse is "a wee timorous beastie" because there is no other way that it could have survived. Birds have the marvelous defensive behavior of flying away, and it is not surprising that Bedford and Anger (1968) had little difficulty training pigeons to fly from one perch to another to avoid shock in a sort of avian analog of the shuttle box. At the same time, it has been found to be almost impossible to train pigeons to peck a key to avoid shock. The importance of the species-specific defense reaction (SSDR) suggests a new hypothesis about avoidance learning. In its most objective form the

SSDR hypothesis states merely that animals have characteristic defensive behaviors and that avoidance learning in the laboratory is possible only if the response that we require of our animal is an SSDR or is at least highly compatible with the animal's SSDR repertoire. What does the rat do when it fails to learn the response that we require of it? It misbehaves. The frightened rat, much like the Brelands' hungry animals, displays its own species-specific behavior; it freezes.

We will continue the analysis of avoidance behavior, emphasizing the SSDR concept, in Chapter 10. Here we must sum up to see if we can draw some general conclusions about the structure of learning. It should be apparent that the operant behaviors that have been most widely studied in the laboratory, key pecking for food by the pigeon and running in a shuttle box or pressing a bar or traversing a maze by the rat, are not just typical and convenient behaviors. They are behaviors that these particular animals are especially adept at learning, and they learn them at least as much because these behaviors are part of their natural means of solving particular problems as because they are reinforced.

We have surveyed a variety of learning situations in which the behavior does not seem to follow the generally accepted rules of the basic paradigms. We have noted two kinds of constraints: constraints on the Pavlovian paradigm, in which only certain S-S* relations can be readily learned, and constraints on the reinforcement paradigm, in which only certain R-S* relationships can be readily learned. Often, of course, these paradigms do work, and we must be thankful for that. But we must also wonder why they work when they do. Some writers (for example, Seligman, 1970), have suggested that there are no general rules of learning; Seligman proposes that because of its genetic endowment, a particular species of animal may be "prepared" to learn one association and quite "unprepared" to learn another. But what we have seen of the structure of learning suggests an even more profound problem with the basic paradigms. It suggests that the idea of a learned association may not be useful. We have to take a new look at learning, keeping in mind our new discovery that learning seems to depend upon an interaction between an animal's genetic constitution and some fundamental property of the learning procedure that, apparently, we have not yet fully grasped.

References for Further Reading

The early experiments on the Garcia effect have been reviewed by Revusky and Garcia (1970), but a lot has happened since then. Rozin and Kalat (1971) present a valuable analysis of the Garcia effect and related food-preference phenomena from a somewhat different point of view. Various constraints on learning are described in two recent collections of papers: Seligman and Hager (1972) present a number of the original studies, including some of Garcia's work, while Hinde and Stevenson-Hinde (1973) present a number of more recent studies and more extended analyses. Much of the research mentioned in this chapter can be found in these two books. In addition, Shettleworth (1972) has made a detailed analysis of the structure of learning in different species of animals. An introduction to the avoidance-learning literature can be found in Bolles (1975).

CHAPTER
10

PREDICTIVE ·
CUES

In this last chapter an attempt will be made to synthesize the various parts and pieces of the total learning puzzle. It may have seemed in earlier chapters that we were close to putting some major parts of the puzzle in the right places, but in each case we found serious problems. There were problems with the early formulations of Thorndike and Watson and with the more contemporary formulations of Hull and Skinner. There are problems with the current tendency to view procedures for producing learning as more important than the theoretical underlying processes. Although in some respects this approach is a clear advance over some earlier theoretical statements, it is not entirely satisfactory because sometimes the procedures work and sometimes they do not. The learning theorist must almost necessarily be an optimist. He must be guided by the hope that, if only he can manage a clearer view of what is going on, everything will make sense, and he will know why the basic learning paradigms are only sometimes effective.

In the last few years a new approach has engendered considerable optimism. It is a cognitive interpretation of behavior that makes use of terms such as expectancy and emphasizes the perceptual determinants of behavior. Although many of the basic concepts are derived historically from the work of Edward Tolman, a great deal of this new thinking is derived from contemporary research. The theoretical synthesis that we are now about to undertake is not really associated with any one theorist or any one body of research. The present author subscribes to it and has made some contributions to its formulation, but I cannot lay claim to it as my own because a number of other psychologists also subscribe to it and have contributed to it. Perhaps it reflects the spirit of the times, just as Watson's frankly mechanistic approach reflected the thinking of his era and Hull's deductive approach reflected the common background of thought during the 1940s. At any rate, psychology appears ready for a new kind of cognitive learning theory. In this last chapter I will present my own view of how this new cognitive psychology is taking shape. I will take the further liberty of beginning the presentation by describing some more of my own research on avoidance learning.

Avoidance Behavior

One of the most troublesome problems for contemporary views of learning is, as we saw in Chapter 9, that some avoidance responses are very rapidly acquired whereas others are acquired only slowly, if at all. We will consider here two experiments, one that produced a failure of learning and one that produced extremely rapid learning. We shall try to discover a common principle uniting these apparently disparate results; such a principle would be clearly much more powerful than the conventional idea that avoidance behavior is acquired when it is properly reinforced. For the first instance, let us consider two groups that constituted part of a larger study (Bolles, 1969) in which rats were trained in a running wheel. One group was required simply to run in the wheel a quarter-turn or more. This response avoided shock, terminated the CS, and escaped the shock following a failure to avoid it. Thus, this was a straightforward avoidance-learning situation in which the animal had the advantage of all the customary reinforcement contingencies, and we know from previous work that they should easily learn the running response. Figure 10.1 shows that this group did acquire the response rapidly and in a few trials was approaching 100 percent performance.

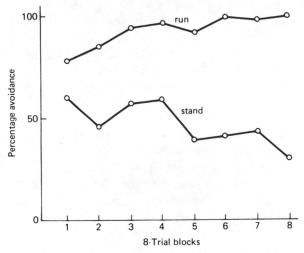

Fig. 10.1 *Rats learn to run to avoid shock, but they do not learn to stand on their hind legs. (From Bolles, Avoidance and escape learning, Journal of Comparative and Physiological Psychology, 1969, 68, 355–358. Copyright 1969 by the American Psychological Association. Reprinted by permission.)*

For the second group all the contingencies were in effect, but the response requirement was changed. These animals were required to stand on their hind legs to avoid shock, terminate the CS, and escape shock. This group showed no learning (see Figure 10.1). Indeed, when training was extended beyond that shown in the figure, the response gradually disappeared. It might be argued that running in the wheel is a more natural response than standing up, that standing up has a low operant rate in this apparatus, that standing up is not an "available" response in the frightened rat. But we notice that on the first few trials both responses had essentially the same high incidence, both occurring on about half the initial trials. The failure to learn by the "stand" group thus cannot be dismissed as a failure of the response to occur; it must be a failure of reinforcement, a genuine failure of the behavior to be controlled by its consequences or a failure of learning. Now in its original form the SSDR hypothesis (Bolles, 1970) stated that there are innate defensive behaviors that may either compete with or facilitate a learned avoidance reaction. This idea gave us some purchase on differential rates of avoidance learning but no way to handle a failure of learning. We could explain why running away (an SSDR) is quickly learned, as in one-way avoidance, and why freezing (another SSDR for the rat) governs what happens in bar-press avoidance, but we could not account for a response, like standing up, that occurs but is not learned.

Apparently it is not the topography of the response, that is, what muscles are contracted, that matters; otherwise learning in the wheel, the shuttle box, and the one-way situation would not be so different. The important consideration seems to be the functional property of the behavior, what it accomplishes, and specifically whether it permits the animal to get away. Consider again the animals that were required to stand up in the wheel. Let us imagine that there was a small window about eight inches above the floor of the wheel and that if the animal stood up it could reach the window, pull itself up, and scramble out of the apparatus. Can there be any question that the animal would have learned to do this? Anyone who has attempted to train rats to avoid in the Skinner box and who has not taken the precaution to fasten the lid of the box securely can testify to the ingenuity and persistence with which the rat will try to escape from the box after it has once succeeded in doing so. The point is that standing up would undoubtedly have been rapidly acquired if this response had been successful in getting out of the apparatus.

The point is nicely illustrated by unpublished results obtained in our laboratory by Perry Duncan. Rats were put in a box about twenty inches square. They were required simply to run a distance of about six inches; they could run back and forth, around in circles, or in any manner. Any movement, as long as it involved the animal's moving a body length or more, would terminate the CS, avoid the shock, and do everything that an avoidance response normally accomplishes—except, of course, that it would not permit the animal to leave the situation. In spite of the fact that the response had a very high operant rate, occurring on more than half of all the trials, Duncan found no increase in response strength with continued training. Indeed, as in the animals required to stand in the previous experiment, running gradually disappeared with continued training. All that was necessary to produce learning in this situation was to put a strip of tape across the center of the box, dividing it perceptually into two compartments. The rat is evidently able to solve such a problem, and it evidently does so on the basis of discriminating the two halves of the box and learning the rather complex abstraction of running from one side to the other. But the much simpler task of making the flight movement is not learned.

The reinforcement paradigm fails us here; so let us introduce a more cognitive concept. The solution of an avoidance problem seems to depend upon how the animal perceives the situation. If the situation is perceived as escapable, then the rat will flee from it. If the situation is perceived as involving two compartments, like the shuttle box, then the rat will go from one compartment to the other in a kind of limited flight. If the situation is perceived as inescapable, if the rat can perceive no way for even limited flight, then this perception is manifest in freezing. Because the rat's basic repertoire of defensive behaviors consists of flight and freezing, it will flee if it can perceive a way out, and it will freeze if it cannot. Two features of this analysis make it cognitive; one is that it emphasizes the perception-like factors governing behavior, and the second is that it emphasizes that it is these factors, rather than behavior *per se*, that are learned in the situation. The change in behavior is merely an index, a symptom, or a manifestation of what is learned.

There is still one last way out for the traditional S-R associationist. It could be argued that even though the frightened rat has a limited repertoire of defensive behaviors, learning can still be assumed to be based upon the strength of S-R associations if we include the operation of a punishment mechanism. The argument is basically that if the rat can only flee or freeze, then the real impact of avoidance training is the punishment that it provides for inappropriate behavior. If we require the animal to run in the shuttle box, then it is necessary only to punish freezing, and this is accomplished by programming the avoidance of shock to be contingent upon running. Over a series of trials freezing will be weakened by the punishment that it receives, and so running will emerge as the stronger response.[1] One way to test this hypothesis is to try to establish freezing as an avoidance response by punishing attempts at flight. The final avoidance-learning experiment to be described here (Bolles & Riley, 1973) was an attempt to do this. The results from four groups will be described. For one group brief shocks were scheduled to occur every five seconds as long as the animal remained in motion. As soon as the animal began to freeze the series of shocks was terminated, and no more shocks were received until fifteen seconds after freezing had been discontinued. If freezing was resumed during this fifteen-second interval shock was again avoided. Thus, by continued freezing, or at least by not being active for more than fifteen seconds at a time, the rat could avoid all shock. We may call this group the "contingent-avoidance group" because the avoidance of shock was contingent upon freezing. In the second group, which we may call the "contingent-punishment group," freezing was punished by a series of brief shocks every five seconds if it persisted longer than fifteen seconds. Thus, these animals could avoid all shocks by being constantly active or at least by engaging in some activity every fifteen seconds. One complication in the procedure was that the contingent-punishment group first received five minutes of avoidance training before being shifted to the punishment contingency. The learning curves for these first two groups are shown in Figure 10.2.

Note the extremely rapid acquisition of freezing by both groups in the

---

[1] This solution to the avoidance-learning problem had been suggested some years ago by Sidman (1953) and by Kamin (1956) but had not appeared very plausible because it put a large burden upon the punishment mechanisms. It was revived later (Bolles, 1970) because the idea of a limited SSDR repertoire and a small number of alternative responses made it seem somewhat more plausible.

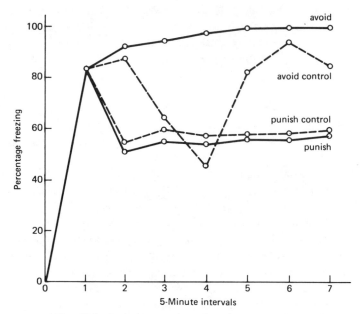

Fig. 10.2 *Percentage of freezing in rats avoiding shock by freezing, being punished for freezing, or control rats receiving shock at the same rate but independently of their behavior. Note how freezing seems to extinguish in the avoidance control group but is reinstated when the next shock is received. (From Bolles & Riley,* Freezing as an avoidance response, *Learning and Motivation, 1973, 4, 268–275. By permission of Academic Press.)*

first five minutes, the continued rise toward 100 percent avoidance in the avoidance group, and the rapid drop in freezing in the punishment group. It would appear from these results that freezing can be readily acquired as an avoidance response and that it is also weakened by punishment. If we define an operant as a response that can be controlled by its programmed consequences, then freezing is clearly an operant. There is, however, one odd feature of these data: Although avoidance training produced about 97 percent avoidance, punishment training under these conditions reduced freezing only to about 56 percent. It could be argued that freezing is only partly an operant and that it is also like a respondent in that it is elicited at a fairly high level by shock. To test this possibility Riley and Bolles ran two additional groups of animals under noncontingent conditions. One group, a noncontingent-avoidance group, received shocks at the same average time interval as the contingent-avoidance group, that is, every 900 seconds; the second control group, designated "noncontingent-punishment group," received shocks scheduled randomly in time, averaging one every 43 seconds, to match the shock density of the contingent-punishment group. The performances of these animals are also shown in Figure 10.2.

Here we discover a curious thing. The punishment contingency appears to have no effect; exactly the same suppression of freezing was found when we simply shocked animals randomly in time as when we explicitly punished freezing. There still appears to be a small but genuine avoidance effect, but it too appears to be an artifact. Consider the following observation. Under the conditions that we used, that is, with the particular shock intensity, the particular apparatus, and so on, we found that shock invariably produced a variety of violent reactions. It always broke up freezing. Then, in about ten seconds, on the average, the rats would begin to resume freezing, and the probability of freezing would increase toward 100 percent. A minute or two after the previous shock the probability of freezing always rose to 100 percent and stayed at that level for a number of minutes (see Figure 10.3). As the animals gradually began to move about and the probability of freezing gradually decreased, the durations of movement became longer, so that after fifteen minutes (900 seconds, on the average) a consecutive period of fifteen seconds of movement occurred, defining the avoidance contingency. At this point the contingent-avoidance animals received another shock. What was really happening to animals given avoidance training was that, following a shock, they would move for about ten seconds, would then freeze for a number of minutes, and would break off freezing for a moment, accumulating a few more seconds of nonfreezing time. As soon as fifteen seconds of movement had occurred the animals would be recycled back to the start of the freezing function (Figure 10.3). In other words, the apparent learning curve under the avoidance condition was a result of the fact that early in training a number of shocks were received which produced an appreciable amount of movement, but as shock density

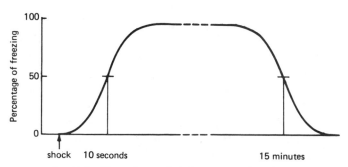

Fig. 10.3 How the probability of freezing in the experimental situation is assumed to change with time following the last shock.

was reduced to one every fifteen minutes, the animals froze more (97 percent of the time), just as the freezing function dictates. The entire "learning curve" was dictated by the tendency for shock to disrupt freezing for a few seconds and then to produce a prolonged period of freezing. When the animals were shocked noncontingently every fifteen minutes, less total freezing was found, not because of the absence of the avoidance contingency, but because of a statistical artifact. The fifteen minutes of freezing found under the contingent condition represent an average. It includes animals that, in an analysis like that of Figure 10.3, persisted in freezing for longer than fifteen minutes and others that resumed movement in less than fifteen minutes. These differences were averaged out under the contingent condition because each animal was allowed to accumulate only fifteen seconds of movement time. But under the noncontingent condition these individual differences do not average out. The animals that are slow to resume movement can contribute nothing but freezing to the group average, but animals that are quick to resume movement can reduce the group average appreciably. A statistical analysis of the variance among animals shows that this artifact accounts almost exactly for the difference between groups.

Other aspects of the data suggest an absence of learning, in the generally accepted sense of the word. The performance of the punished animals dropped immediately as soon as the punishment conditions were introduced, so that there was no "learning curve" under the contingent-punishment condition. As soon as the punishment contingency was introduced the rate of freezing dropped immediately to the new level appropriate to the rate at which shock was being received, which was dictated entirely by the rising portion of the freezing function diagrammed in Figure 10.3. A final indication that there was no learning in any group is that the time following the last shock at which the animals resumed freezing averaged approximately 10 seconds for all groups. That is, animals that were punished for freezing resumed freezing just as quickly as animals that avoided shock by freezing. The programmed consequences of freezing had no effect whatever upon the latency of animals' resumption of freezing. Bolles and Riley therefore concluded that in spite of the fact that freezing can be controlled, at least to some extent, by making shock either contingent on the occurrence or the nonoccurrence of freezing, this control cannot be said to be produced by the experimental contingencies *per se*, because it can be completely accounted for in terms of the function shown in Figure 10.3. Freezing was elicited, and it was elicited differently under avoidance and punishment conditions; this difference accounts for the different results so completely that there is no reason to suppose that any animal's behavior was being affected either by punishment or by any other programmed consequence of its behavior.

We have the paradox of what appears to be very effective avoidance learning, yet the behavior can be completely described in terms of the conditions that elicit it. In a sense, Figure 10.3 describes the entire experiment and tells us everything we might want to know about freezing. Let us consider, then, the nature of this all-important freezing function. The absence of freezing in the first few seconds following shock is simple enough to explain: It was caused by unconditioned reactions to shock. The animal was leaping about, squealing, and running. All these responses are what we ordinarily think of as elicited, or respondent, behavior. The interesting question is why we obtained prolonged bouts of freezing lasting fifteen minutes on the average. Are they due to a persistent emotional reaction? Are they caused by a high level of arousal? Further unpublished research from our laboratory indicates that none of these possibilities accounts for the effect, except in small part. If an animal is removed from the situation a few seconds after it is shocked and placed in a different box, very little freezing is found. It is clear, then, that this freezing occurs simply because the animal remains in the situation in which it was shocked. The simplest way to describe it, and perhaps the only way to describe it, is to say that the rat continues to freeze in the shock situation for several minutes because it expects shock there. When the rat is placed in a neutral situation where there has been no shock, there is no expectation of shock, there is very little residual emotional reactivity, and there is very little freezing.

We may conclude from this rather involved analysis that the rats' freezing behavior in the shock situation is dictated almost entirely by the characteristics of the situation. If the situation is perceived as inescapable, which of course it is, the rat will freeze and will continue to do so, on the average, for fifteen minutes. We suggest that at that point the expectation of shock weakens and is replaced by the expectation of safety. Freezing stops, and normal patterns of activity resume. There is one further conclusion that we can draw from this study: If we think of the animal as having just two classes of behavior, freezing and activity, then the fact that the one class, freezing, is not an operant implies that the other class is also not an operant. If the rat could learn to run to avoid, then that learning would have been manifest in less freezing when freezing was punished. By the same token, if it were possible to weaken running by punishment, then we should have seen a gradual learned increase in freezing. Our tentative overall conclusion from recent avoidance-learning studies in our laboratory is that changes in behavior that occur in an avoidance-learning experiment are caused entirely by the animal's altered perception of the situation, specifically its altered perception of what is dangerous and what is safe. There seems to be no reinforcement mechanism and no punishment mechanism operative in the avoidance-learning situation. We therefore suggest that the animal behaves as it does entirely because it expects shock here and it expects safety there. Because of these expectancies it gives us SSDRs: flight from dangerous locations, approach toward safe locations, and freezing when no safety is perceived.

The Revival of Cognitive Psychology

This account of avoidance behavior draws heavily upon Tolman's old expectancy theory. It may seem ironic that, after his system was largely passed over during the 1950s and 1960s, it should be rejuvenated during the 1970s, but that is what seems to be happening. Many psychologists who are not too committed to either the Skinnerian or the neo-Hullian framework are now turning to a much more cognitive point of view. There are undoubtedly a number of reasons for this current trend, but one is that Tolman's original expectancy theory was never discredited; it was simply outstripped in popularity by alternative points of view that seemed, for a time, more attractive. Partly because they were so attractive and generated so much research and theoretical activity, we have begun to see the limitations and defects of these points of view. A second reason for turning to cognitive models of animal learning is the great success that this type of approach has enjoyed in the field of human learning. Although many of the early learning theories were initially based on animal studies and then generalized to the human case, the tables seem to be turned, and in some respects current animal-learning theorists seem to be following the lead of psychologists studying human learning. Another reason for the trend toward cognitive interpretations of animal behavior is that the strength of the positions that have been dominant over the last few years has been seriously undermined by the work of Rescorla, Kamin, and others in classical conditioning and the work of Garcia and others in operant conditioning. It is no longer possible to conceive of the basic paradigms in the same manner that was possible just a few years ago. Classical conditioning now looks quite different, and recent studies of operant conditioning have revealed that it has a peculiar structure that depends, among other things, upon the species of animal being studied. It is no longer possible to accept the old view of classical conditioning, and it is no longer possible to accept reinforcement as the universal basis for operant learning. In short, we are in desperate need of some kind of conceptual reorganization, and the cognitive approach suggests itself as relatively fresh and unconfining and at the same time relatively familiar.

Modern cognitive psychology obviously owes a great deal to Tolman's earlier work. Many of the ideas and much of the language were originally his. The idea that learning consists of the acquisition of information about the environment, rather than the attachment of particular responses to particular stimuli, is certainly owing to Tolman. He defended it at a time when almost no one else did.[2] But modern cognitive psychology is not just a revival of Tolman's position, and it is surely not a step backward over the last forty years. Let us note some of the important advances that have been made during these years. There is the obvious fact that we know enormously more about animal learning and motivation than we did then. There is the further advantage that we have a much more sophisticated technology. We have better equipment, better experimental designs, and better experimental traditions and methodologies. There have also been some important conceptual advances. It seems undeniable that much of Tolman's insight into animal behavior was derived by analogy from his understanding of the human mind. Tolman probably saw animal learning as a rough facsimile of the acquisition of knowledge by man. Contemporary cognitive psychology is based much more upon the analogy of the computer. The heuristic model is not the mind of man but the computer. We refer not to knowledge, ideas, and perceptions so much as to input and assimilation, as well as to the storage and retrieval of information. We talk about the processing of information rather than about what the subject knows.

But perhaps the greatest advantage that we enjoy today in developing a cognitive theory is that we now know how to operationalize our cognitive concepts into experimental procedures. We have a number of extremely useful experimental procedures and paradigms that are well worth retaining once we translate them into informational terms. For example, we may conceive of a classical-conditioning experiment as a situation in which we as experimenters introduce a certain lawfulness or orderliness into the animal's world. One event S* always follows a prior event S. With this procedure we are conveying, or attempting to convey, to the animal some information about its world. If the animal's behavior changes, we may say that it has assimilated this information, at least in part.

The cognitive psychologist certainly does not have to be a mentalist, though he may be one if he is so inclined. He may speculate about the awareness or the perceptions of the animal, as I have done here to emphasize a point, or he may use a more easily operationalized language, the "as if" language of Tolman, in which critical terms such as expectancy are given operational definitions. But he also has the option of using a strictly objective language; he may describe the information embedded in or conveyed by his experimental situation and merely record how the animal's behavior changes when this information is presented. For example, he may

---

[2] Tolman was not entirely alone in this; the Gestalt psychologists were actively pressing the same point. But although the Gestaltists had considerable impact on psychology generally, they had relatively little influence on the mainstream of learning theory.

describe a Pavlovian experiment as one in which a particular stimulus, S+, predicts S*, and another stimulus, S—, predicts no S*. This language is cognitive, but it is language about the procedure, not about psychological processes. The modern cognitive psychologist thus really has two kinds of language, a theoretical language containing hypothetical constructs like expectancy and words of less certain status like perception, as well as a procedural language containing terms like prediction, information, and memory that can be applied to operant-conditioning and classical-conditioning experiments. He can use an information-processing language to describe these experiments.

We may note that different theoretical positions, as typified by the early theorists discussed in this book, not only have different conceptions of the nature of the learning process; they must also necessarily have different conceptions of the learning procedures. For example, for Hull reinforcing a rat in a Skinner box meant producing the learning of new responses. For Skinner it means controlling the animal's rate of responding, something quite different. For Tolman it meant satisfying an animal's demand or confirming its expectancy, something different again. So the new cognitive psychology not only gives us a partly new and partly old idea of what the learning process consists of; it also gives us what may be much more important, a new look at our familiar experimental procedures. Having once seriously thought about classical conditioning as a procedure for making an S predict an S*, it is different; we can no longer see it as just a procedure for connecting a CR to a CS.

Not all modern cognitive psychologists think alike, of course. There is a healthy diversity of opinion on many issues. We all pay homage to Tolman and are grateful for his historical contribution, but he is not our leader or our spokesman. We scatter our efforts in different directions, emphasize different kinds of concepts, work on different kinds of problems, and, of course, we have different ideas about just what cognitive psychology is. Rather than attempting to survey this diffuse and unstructured diversity, the remainder of this chapter will develop an objective information-processing language in which the key term is *predictive cue*. This is my own term for conceptualizing what I believe is the most important procedural aspect of many learning situations. In the rest of this chapter we will survey briefly a variety of different learning situations to show how they can be interpreted in terms of predictive cues.

Predictive Cues

It has already been noted at several points in preceding discussions that the classical conditioning situation is one in which a fixed S-S* relationship is imposed upon the animal. In a Pavlovian experiment everything else is held as constant as possible so that, ideally, S and S* are the only events conveying any information to the animal. The S is then a predictive cue for S*. Pavlov said it first: The S "signals" S*. The recent work of Rescorla described in Chapter 8 indicates that what the animal learns in a conditioning experiment can be aptly described as the predictive relationship between S and S*. Rescorla has also shown that, if the predictive relation is reversed so that S* is more probable in the absence of S than in its presence, then we obtain inhibitory conditioning. The inhibition of a response that would otherwise occur can be found with either fear (Rescorla) or salivation (Pavlov). Again we clearly have a predictive relationship between S and S*; it is simply reversed. S predicts no shock or no food. It is convenient to designate the predictor of S* by the symbol S+ and a cue that predicts the absence of S* by S−. The establishment of conditioned inhibition therefore can be regarded simply as an experimental procedure in which S− predicts the absence of S*, whereas the context or some other S+ predicts the occurrence of S*. Discrimination training can be regarded as a procedure in which two kinds of predictive relations involving both an S+ and an S− are imposed on the animal more or less simultaneously.

There is one complication: The S is always presented against some background of stimuli; there has to be an apparatus, and there have to be prevailing stimulus conditions, and they too are part of the total informational package. As Pavlov observed, even when a dog has been well trained to salivate to a bell in the laboratory, it is not likely to salivate to the bell out on the street. It is a well-known observation from fear-conditioning studies that a rat that shows suppression to a tone predicting shock in the Skinner box may show little suppression when the tone is presented in a different experimental situation. Unfortunately, we know relatively little about the extent to which a cue conveys information apart from the experimental episode in which the cue is embedded, but it is possible to conceive of a variety of experiments to answer this question. To what extent does the context itself become a predictor? To what extent do different kinds of contexts have different predictive values? Is it possible, for example, that a rat will more readily learn to avoid a place where shock has been experienced than it will learn to react in some other way to a light or a tone that provides a contextual cue? We know from a variety of research on the Garcia effect that rats are more likely to avoid food with a distinctive taste that has been associated with illness than they are to avoid food with a distinctive odor or food in a distinctive location. We know further that other species of animals may show different hierarchies of cue utilization.

When behavior changes during a conditioning experiment, we assume that the change reflects the learning of the predictive relationship. We assume that the predictive relationship itself becomes internally represented as an expectancy. The basic theoretical question then becomes why the animal behaves in a particular way when a particular S* is predicted. Why did Pavlov's dog salivate when the bell was sounded? There are two possible answers to this question. One requires falling back on the procedural or operational aspect of the predictive cue: The bell is a predictor of food. This answer is operational, but it is not entirely satisfactory because it bypasses the question of learning. The bell is a predictor of food whether or not the dog has learned anything about the relationship. The animal usually has to undergo a number of trials before the CR occurs. So the cognitive psychologist must give a second answer, which is that the dog salivates because it expects food. Note that this answer is ultimately a tautology, but then so is any answer to the question of what is learned. The cognitive answer is no more tautological than the conventional answer that the dog salivates because the salivary response has become conditioned to the CS. The one answer is just as basic and just as explanatory as the other; it is simply a different answer based upon a different conception of how the results of learning experiments are to be explained.

The predictive-cue analysis of instrumental or operant learning is a little more complex because more kinds of information are conveyed by the different possible procedures. Typically, however, the operant situation contains an S^D, a stimulus in the presence of which responding is reinforced. This stimulus becomes a predictive cue for the reinforcer, the S*. The predictive relationship is, however, conditional in that S is a predictor only if the animal responds. By the same token, the animal's own behavior becomes a predictor of S*, but again there is the condition that S^D must also be present. Thus the basic S-R-S* operant paradigm contains a pair of conditional predictive relationships.

Consider a simple learning experiment in which a rat must run in an alley to obtain food. On the initial trials the cues present in the start area are not predictors of food, but after perhaps just a few trials, particularly if the animal moves through the apparatus with some speed, they become predictors, and the animal begins to expect food. This expectancy may produce salivation, a general state of excitement, and behavior such as locomotion. Then as the animal runs more rapidly, cues in the start box become increasingly better predictors of food. Ultimately the animal will be running at a high rate of speed.

It should be apparent that the phenomenon that Skinnerians call stimulus control is a predictive relationship in which the predictor of food may be such a subtle and esoteric cue as the lapse of time since the last reinforcement, the lapse of time since the last response, or the number of responses since the last reinforcement—or it may be a very simple and easily discriminated thing like the color of the key. But, whatever the controlling conditions may be, they are necessarily predictive cues.

Predictive cues perform the same kind of function r_G and r_E did in Hull's secondary learning system. We have been presenting an analogy or a translation of what Hull, Spence, and other theorists in that tradition called incentive motivation. We noted in Chapter 8 that in the hands of some theorists incentive motivation was an extremely powerful explanatory mechanism. For example, Mowrer (1960) has suggested that, given sufficient incentive motivation, a response did not have to have its own habit; a reinforcement mechanism was unnecessary. Mowrer's argument can be translated into the present framework if we propose that predictive cues constitute a sufficient explanation of an animal's behavior; a reinforcement mechanism is unnecessary. For many of his readers, however, Mowrer's incentive-motivation theory had an unpleasant feel of incompleteness about it, and perhaps so does this simple account of predictive cues. Some additional mechanisms can be introduced to fill it out.

One possible mechanism simply recognizes that animals do not respond diffusely and at random to predictive cues but respond to them in particular ways. For example, as the animal looks down the alley, it can see portions of the apparatus that are better or more proximate predictors of food than the cues where it is. We may assume that when there are good predictors and poor predictors, the rat will prefer the good ones and that, when there are proximate predictors and distal predictors, the rat will approach the proximate ones. We thus have a mechanism that ensures that the animal will run down the alley, rather than just salivating or engaging in diffuse excited activity. The importance of this kind of mechanism has been emphasized by Bindra (1974). According to Bindra's cognitive interpretation of behavior, the stimuli lying just ahead of the rat in the alley are particularly good predictors of food; stimuli arising in the goal box are still better; those arising from the food cup are the best. So there is a gradient of predictiveness that produces a gradient of approach behavior. The same argument can be applied to the Skinner box. The box as a whole is a contextual cue, a diffuse and distal predictor of food. The discriminative stimulus is a better predictor. The conjunction of these cues with the stimuli arising from the bar itself is a still better predictor. Therefore the animal approaches the lever and manipulates it.

There is the further consideration that once the bar becomes a predictor of food, there is not a great deal the rat can do with it besides manipulate it. (It is probably not just a coincidence that the posture and the paw movements involved in bar pressing are topographically similar to those accompanying the consummatory response.) So the occurrence of operant bar presses is explained partly by the peculiar stimulus properties of the bar itself and partly by the fact that the bar is a predictor of food. Bindra (1974) proposes that in other situations, in which there are other objects to manipulate and different paths to navigate, these two mechanisms—the predictiveness of the cue and its special response-eliciting properties—can often be counted on to zero the animal in on the appropriate response.

There is a third possible mechanism. The operant situation is conventionally defined in terms of a response contingency and not by the stimulus properties of the situation. Perhaps the animal learns specifically that running in the alley produces food and that pressing the bar in the Skinner box produces food. Perhaps the animal learns a specific expectancy of a form that matches the defining contingency. Perhaps rats are capable of learning not only expectancies of the S-S* form but also expectancies of the R-S* form. Such expectancies were hypothesized by Tolman (he called them "means-end expectancies"), and they have been adopted by such recent writers as Irwin (1971) and Seligman and Johnston (1973). This general conception provides a simple and straightforward translation of the operant paradigm into the cognitive model. But let us remember that the operant paradigm suffers from the problem that a reinforcement contingency is sometimes effective and sometimes not. There are, as we have seen, constraints on learning. The existence of such constraints means that there must be limits upon the kinds of information that an animal can process and utilize. Can the rat really learn to expect that its behavior will have certain consequences? And, if it can, then why do we find constraints on learning? Why did the Brelands' animals misbehave? If the rat can learn that shock will not occur if it makes a certain response, as Seligman and Johnston propose, then why does the rat perform so poorly in a variety of different avoidance-learning situations?

At the present time there are no answers to any of these questions, and there is clearly no consensus among contemporary cognitive theorists. Elsewhere (Bolles, 1972) I have proposed a compromise position that involves two assumptions. The first is that S-S* expectancies are learned relatively quickly and that they are generally rather accurate representations of S-S* contingencies in the environment. The second assumption is that R-S* expectancies are learned too, but this learning is slower, more uncertain, and much more highly constrained by the animal's innate response tendencies. It also seems possible that a rat might be able to learn the relationship between bar pressing and food and can learn the corresponding expectancy, but that it cannot ordinarily learn the relationship between bar pressing and shock avoidance. Perhaps other animals are capable of such learning but the poor bar-press avoidance performance of the rat suggests that such information is either not processed at all or for some reason cannot be retrieved at the appropriate time.

There is still a fourth possible mechanism that might operate to help control operant behavior. It is conceivable that all learning is of the S-S* type but that one of the important predictive cues is the immediate stimulus consequences of the animal's behavior—perhaps the proprioceptive feedback from responding. For example, it may be that the "feel" of pressing the bar is the best predictor of food. Then, when the rat has learned the appropriate expectancy, that the feel of pressing the lever precedes food, this expectancy produces the appropriate behavior through some type of retrieval mechanism. Back at the very beginning of American psychology William James (1890) observed that the proper execution of a skilled performance requires the individual to learn what the correct performance feels like. A tennis player placing a volley has to know what the necessary stroke feels like; if it feels right, then it probably will be right. Once that "feel" is learned, the response takes care of itself. Perhaps such a mechanism works for the rat, at least in some instances.

It should be apparent that the cognitive theorist has a variety of mechanisms to explain what happens when learning occurs with the operant paradigm. He has a variety of alternative models, some of which are based exclusively upon the notion of predictive cues and some of which require additional mechanisms.

The basic issue for the cognitive theorist is what kinds of information can be processed by a particular animal? We know that a predictive cue conveys not only that S* will occur but also that a relatively specific S* will occur. Crespi's experiment, discussed earlier, shows that the rat not only expects food but also expects a particular amount of food. Such studies, as well as Tinklepaugh's (1928) classic experiment indicate that an animal may expect a particular quality of food. There is a variety of evidence (summarized by Capaldi, 1970) to indicate that, with proper training, rats can come to expect particular sequences of reinforced and nonreinforced trials. In the present section, however, we shall focus upon just one dimension of information processing: whether behavior is governed just by predictive cues or if it is also controlled at least partly by the information conveyed by the response-reinforcement contingency. Can animals acquire something like an R-S* expectancy? We can expect no general answer to this question; we must anticipate different answers for different species of animals. There can be no question that humans can learn specific relationships between their behavior and the consequences of their behavior (for example, Estes, 1969). With dogs there is the interesting phenomenon of learned helplessness. Seligman and Maier (1967) have shown that after dogs are given a series of inescapable shocks they perform very poorly on even the simplest aversive-learning tasks. The results from a number of such experiments suggest that during the preliminary inescapable-shock phase of the experiment the dog learns that there is no relationship between its behavior and the consequences. It learns that it is helpless, and the "attitude" of helplessness transfers to the test situation to prevent any learning. The other side of the coin is that, in the absence of this prior traumatic experience, the dog must have something like a hypothesis about the solvability of the problem. Presumably it would also be possible to train dogs to give them "learned confidence."

The rat seems to have a marginal ability. It appears able to process information about the consequences of its behavior in some situations but not in others. Rats appear much more able to learn how their behavior relates to food than how their behavior relates to a traumatic S* like shock. So we must suppose that, in addition to the existence of species specificities, there are also motivational specificities in the extent to which the response contingency contributes to behavior. The rat may simply be able to process more different kinds of information about how to obtain food than it can about how to avoid shock.

In animals below the rat in information-processing ability, there seem to be obvious and serious restraints upon the kind of R-S* information that can be handled. Perhaps that is why the pigeon shows such a limited repertoire of learnable responses, even though it has tremendous ability to learn sensory discriminations. Perhaps that is why the pigeon is so easily duped in the autoshaping experiment. Autoshaping, and more specifically the phenomenon of negative automaintenance, illustrate clear failures of pigeons to process R-S* information. The latter procedure pits the response-producing effect of an S-S* expectancy against what should be the response-inhibiting effect of a negative R-S* expectancy. In the case of the pigeon, the S-S* factor predominates almost totally, though recent evidence from Schwartz and Williams (1972) indicates that the response contingency can have subtle but measurable effects on the pigeon's behavior. There is also a variety of evidence showing that other animals may not be subject to autoshaping. Gamzu and Schwam (1974) found little of it in the monkey; at the University of Washington we find little of it in rats, and Jenkins (personal communication) finds little autoshaping in dogs. One possible explanation of these species differences is that in the bird there is a highly stereotyped response that is used both for obtaining food and for eating it, whereas mammals have a variety of food-getting behaviors that are distinctly different from their consummatory responses. But a simpler interpretation is that different animals have markedly different capacities for processing and using R-S* information.

If an animal cannot use R-S* information in a particular situation, then the R-S* contingency can have no direct control over its behavior. But it may still be possible for the reinforcement contingency to exert a powerful indirect effect because the reinforcement schedule can establish predictive cues that control the behavior through S-S* mechanisms. That is precisely what happens, I believe, with the rat in a variety of situations where S* is electric shock. Recall the earlier discussion of the Bolles and Riley experiment on freezing where it was found that the reinforcement procedure was very effective in producing high levels of freezing but that the data showed that this behavior was due entirely to S-S* mechanisms. That experiment also showed no weakening of behavior that could be attributed to the direct effect of the punishment contingency. It has now become apparent that the rat is peculiarly insensitive to R-S* contingencies in the punishment situation. Let us look briefly at some relevant research.

A Cognitive Interpretation of Punishment

Consider the following experiment reported by Azrin (1956). Azrin first trained pigeons to peck a key for food on a VI 3-minute schedule. Superimposed on this base-line task was a discriminative punishment procedure. The food key was illuminated by either blue or orange light during alternate two-minute periods. The blue condition was always safe; shocks were never presented while the key was blue. But when the key was orange shocks were programmed according to one of four sets of experimental conditions. Under one condition shock was contingent upon a key peck after a fixed time in the presence of the orange light; that is, the first response occurring after the light had been on for one minute was punished. This condition was the so-called fixed-contingent condition. There was also a fixed noncontingent condition in which the animal was shocked one minute after the onset of the orange light whether or not it had pecked the key. In the variable-contingent condition, the animal was punished for the first key peck at some randomly selected time (averaging one minute) after the onset of the orange light. Finally, under the variable-noncontingent condition, the birds were shocked independently of their behavior at unpredictable times, which also averaged one minute after the beginning of the orange light. Under each condition shock was thus set up, on the average, once during each orange key illumination.

The different experimental conditions are a little difficult to keep in mind, and they were evidently a little difficult for the birds to discriminate too; Azrin reported that it required extensive training to reach asymptotic behavior. But once the behavior had stabilized, it showed a very interesting pattern. The results are diagrammed in Figure 10.4. Each experimental condition produced its own pattern of suppression. Notice that behavior occurred at the high rate characteristic of a VI-3 schedule in the presence of the safe blue light. But notice that suppression occurred at different points during the orange light as a function of the different experimental conditions. The results can be described objectively in a number of ways, but all such descriptions are rather complicated. The simplest way to interpret and summarize the results is simply to say that base-line responding was sup-

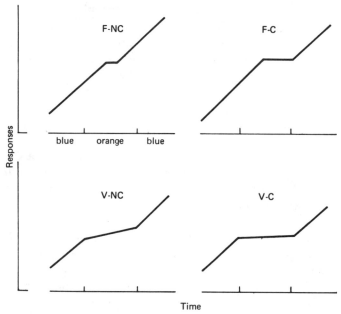

Fig. 10.4   *Composite cumulative records of pigeons*
pecking for food while receiving shock either con-
tingently (C) or noncontingently (NC) scheduled
either at a fixed time (F) or at varied times (V) into
the orange light. (From Azrin, The Journal of Psychology, *1956,* 42, *3–21 by permission of* The Journal
Press.)

pressed whenever the animal was in jeopardy of being shocked. For example, suppression was found only at the scheduled fixed time for shock in the fixed-noncontingent animals; at all other times the animal was safe, and responding on the base-line task occurred at a high and constant rate. There were a variety of different cues that served to signal danger and safety under the different conditions: the lapse of time, the color of the key, and the dependence of shock upon the animal's own behavior. That is the main point here. The two conditions that involved a response contingency produced results showing that the birds were responsive to it. But notice that this kind of control was established only after quite extensive training. We can conclude that, when pigeons are punished, they very quickly learn about the dangerous predictive cues in the situation and only very slowly learn the specific dangers attendant upon responding.

This conclusion is also supported by recent, still unpublished results from our own laboratory. We used a technique originally described by Church, Wooten, and Matthews (1970), in which animals work on a bar-press base-line task and every few minutes a cue comes on for a few minutes to signal that bar pressing might be punished. Punishment was scheduled on a VI 2-minute schedule, so that this danger cue was comparable to the orange key light in Azrin's experiment. As Figure 10.5 indicates, within a few sessions the cue produced marked suppression (measured as the proportion of total responses occurring in the presence of the cue). In other words, a cue associated with punishment quickly suppressed behavior. The basic question then is whether these animals discriminated the punishment contingency *per se* and withheld responses for that reason or whether their behavior was simply suppressed by the cue because the cue predicted shock. To get at this question group 2 was run, for which the cue signaled punishment, as it had for group 1, but additional, noncontingent shocks were programmed during the noncue periods, that is, between cue presentations, at the same rate that they were received during the cue. Under such conditions the cue provides no information about the occurrence of shock because shock is arranged to be as probable in the absence of the cue as in its presence. The only information that the cue conveyed in this instance was that the punishment contingency was in effect. As Figure 10.5 indicates, this information

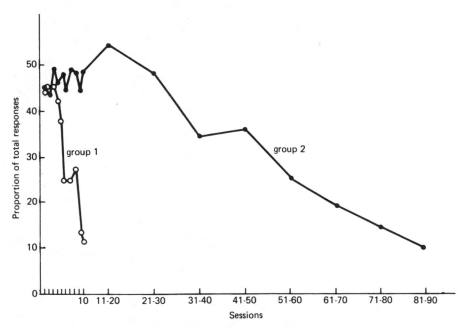

Fig. 10.5 Proportion of total responding in the presence of a cue signaling for both groups that responding might be punished. The difference between the groups was that noncontingent shocks also occurred in the absence of the cue for group 2.

was evidently not used at all during the first thirty training sessions but was eventually reflected in a change in behavior. The initial results are comparable to those reported by Rescorla (1968) showing that if a cue signals no increase in the probability of S*, then it has little effect upon behavior. What these results show, in addition, is that the specific information about the response contingency is only very gradually assimilated. After ninety training sessions the discrimination of the contingency was still not complete. We are therefore led to the conclusion that in those cases where punishment has an immediate suppressive effect upon behavior, it can be attributed entirely to S-S* learning and that, as in the two experiments just described, it is only when extensive training is given that the rat or the pigeon gradually begins to assimilate and use information about the response contingency.

A Cognitive Interpretation
of Secondary Reinforcement

There is one more phenomenon to clear up, one more cognitive bridge to cross. Secondary reinforcement is a concept that has long enjoyed considerable acceptance among reinforcement theorists. Indeed, it is a necessary part of their explanatory systems because so often in so many kinds of situations human behavior is controlled by events like social approval, praise, obtaining the right answer, and money, which are obviously not primary reinforcers. Because a concept like secondary, or conditioned, reinforcement was necessary for the explanation of human behavior, it was natural enough to look for comparable secondary reinforcement effects in the animal laboratory. The problem arose because, the more carefully the phenomenon was sought, the more elusive it seemed to be. There has never been much trouble in maintaining previously established behavior with conditioned, or secondary, reinforcers. The use of the term "reinforcement" seems justified by this criterion, but when the tougher criterion of establishing new learning with secondary reinforcement was employed, the results were typically negative. Most reviewers of the secondary reinforcement phenomenon have reluctantly come to the conclusion that new learning with secondary reinforcement has yet to be demonstrated—and perhaps cannot be convincingly demonstrated. There have been some scattered positive reports here and there, but the bulk of the experimental literature indicates that new learning is at best very difficult to obtain.

Those who would invoke secondary reinforcement to explain learning that cannot otherwise be explained have been further embarrassed by their

inability to put forth a convincing interpretation of how secondary reinforcers are established. Hull and his followers assumed that secondary
reinforcers are established by the Pavlovian operation of pairing an initially
neutral cue with reinforcement. Thus, the box in which the rat eats becomes
a reinforcer in its own right and should then be able to reinforce the learning
of new behavior even when food is withheld. The difficulty is that when
food is withheld the animal quickly detects the worsening of experimental
conditions and refuses to run. At any rate, after having examined recent
developments in the interpretation of classical conditioning, we must be
skeptical about whether pairing *per se* is the appropriate procedure for
establishing secondary reinforcers. Perhaps it is the predictive value of the
cue that is important rather than being paired with the reinforcer.

We saw in Chapter 7 that as early as 1936 Skinner had started the tradition among operant conditioners of treating the secondary reinforcer for one
response as an S^D for another response. The click in the Skinner box or the
color of the goal box in the runway situation is a secondary reinforcer
because it has stimulus control over some subsequent behavior. But again,
in view of our analysis of classical conditioning, we must wonder whether
stimulus control is itself anything but the predictiveness of the cue. What
indeed is a controlling stimulus if it is not a predictor of some upcoming S^*?

The hypothesis that a secondary reinforcer is fundamentally a source of
information about primary reinforcement was tested by Egger and Miller
(1962). They trained groups of rats to press a bar for food. This response was
then extinguished under a variety of different conditions. Pressing the bar
produced no food but did produce a stimulus S_2 that had been associated
with food during training. For one group S_2 had been consistently presented
before food but had been redundant or uninformative because it had been
consistently preceded by another stimulus S_1, which was also consistently
associated with food. For a second group, there were again two stimuli, but
this time S_2 was a good predictor of food, even though it was preceded by
S_1 because S_1 had frequently been presented without food. In short, for the
first group S_2 was a reliable but uninformative predictor of food, and for
the second group S_2 was both reliable and informative. When Egger and
Miller tested for the ability of the different cues S_1 and S_2 to maintain bar
pressing during extinction, they found that S_1 maintained the response
better for the first group, for which it was informative, but that S_2 better
supported bar pressing for the second group, for which it was informative. A variety of controls and the results from another study (Egger &
Miller, 1963) gave additional support to the general proposition that
the effectiveness of a secondary reinforcer in maintaining behavior depends upon the degree to which it is a predictor of primary reinforcement.
This view of secondary reinforcement also explains the failure of so many
prior secondary-reinforcement studies to yield positive results. One reason

why it is difficult to produce learning of a new response based on secondary reinforcement alone, that is, a cue unsupported by primary reinforcement, is that in this situation the secondary reinforcer is no longer a predictor of S*, and the animal very quickly makes the discrimination between the training situation in which the cue predicts S* and the test situation in which it does not. It appears, then, that what controls the animal's behavior is not the reinforcing property of the cue *per se* but rather the value of the information about S*.

There are some troubles and difficulties with this information hypothesis of secondary reinforcement; they can be cleared up only by further investigation, but in principle the predictive-cue concept appears as profitable and instructive when applied to secondary reinforcement as it is when applied to other learning phenomena. It raises the interesting question, however, of whether a new concept of reinforcement may be salvaged from what remains of the old concept. If we think of S* as an event that is of value to the animal, one for which it will work or for which it has a demand, then S* is, for all practical purposes, a reinforcer. What Egger and Miller seem to have shown is that, just as S* is of value to the animal, so is information about S*. Just as the animal will work for S* and use predictive cues to obtain S*, so it will work for these predictive cues.

Prospects for the Future

One potential virtue of an historical approach, such as we have taken to animal learning, is that, by properly aligning ourselves with the flow of past developments, we may be able to see into the future and obtain some perception of the developments that are about to occur. One trend should be apparent from the flow of events that we have traced in the present chapter. It should be apparent that there has been a recent acceleration of activity in cognitive psychology and in the application of cognitive principles to the problems of animal learning. In part, this new emphasis reflects the vitality of cognitive concepts in other areas of psychology, especially in developmental and human learning. But its reception in animal learning is undoubtedly conditioned upon a prior dissatisfaction with the heritage of the mechanistic philosophy, which has continued to govern much of our thinking even though it has not been officially sanctioned by learning theorists for a number of years. There was also undoubtedly a general dissatisfaction with a purely empirical approach such as the inductive method advocated by Skinner and his followers. Many psychologists enjoy the intellectual activity of theorizing, and cognitive psychology provides a kind of new intellectual toy to play with. It will undoubtedly take a number of years to work out its implications, and even if cognitive psychology never becomes more than a toy, it will take some time for us to tire of playing with it. It seems safe to conclude that the current trend of growing interest in cognitive psychology is going to continue at least through the 1970s.

In Chapter 9 we emphasized another current trend, the attempt to relate learning theory to certain broad principles of the biological sciences, particularly the principles of evolution. Specifically, we have begun to appreciate the fact that an animal's behavior is as much a reflection of evolutionary selection pressures as are its form, coloration, and other physical characteristics. An animal's sensory capacities and its motor capacities are obviously dependent upon its ecological niche, but it has not been so obvious—although it is becoming more so—that the ability to learn and the kinds of motivational systems that characterize a particular animal are also dependent upon how the animal has evolved under particular ecological pressures. Breland and Breland (1961) report that, whereas the dog or the rat may tend to become more active when it is deprived of food, an animal like the cow clearly does not. And the common cat, as it turns out, is a very poor subject in a Skinner box; one reason is that, instead of working for food and then going over to the food hopper, the cat becomes increasingly inclined to sit in front of the food source and wait. It does not seem to follow the laws of behavior that have been developed over the years to explain learning in laboratory animals; it simply behaves like a cat.

The discovery (or recognition) of these species-typical behavior styles suggests that the laws of learning that have gradually emerged from the animal laboratory have a rather narrow range of applicability. They apply, at best, only to the rat and the pigeon, and their application to other animals must be tested in appropriate experiments. On the other hand, we may anticipate that the study of learning in other animals will reveal other laws of learning that may well conflict with those that are already familiar. The prospects may seem discouraging. The laws that we have been attempting to produce now seem to have little generality, and the task of finding truly general laws of animal learning seems to have been just begun. But a more optimistic attitude is that the principles of learning that will ultimately be obtained will be integrated into a better and more meaningful framework than that based on the traditional assumption that it did not matter what animal we study because all animals are the same. And the task need not be so difficult either, because now that we have recognized the scope of the problem and have some broad biological principles to guide us, we may be able to find out something about learning in other animals in much less time than the seventy years or so that it has taken us to find out something about learning in the rat. In any case, if general laws of learning are ultimately found, they will have a much stronger claim to generality than the traditional laws that have been merely assumed to be general. It seems safe to conclude that the introduction of evolutionary considerations into learning theory is a development that cannot be undone—and that the current emphasis upon these considerations will continue at least for the next several years.

In Chapter 8 we noted another general trend. In recent years there has been a decline of interest in the major theoretical positions and an increased reliance upon a more procedural and more empirical approach to the phenomena of learning. Classical and operant conditioning are most commonly defined not in terms of hypothetical underlying learning processes but in terms of the experimental procedures that we impose on our animals. This trend has been very profitable in several respects. It has forced us to examine our conventional procedures more carefully, and it has forced us to determine, for example, what the critical procedural element really is in an operant learning experiment or in a Pavlovian conditioning experiment. The trend toward operationalism has been healthy, too, in that it has led to a variety of new procedures to supplement the old ones. Thus, in addition to classical conditioning and operant learning we have latent learning and transfer of control experiments, avoidance-learning experiments, and other kinds of experiments in which the conventional procedural elements are regrouped in new combinations.

Although it is true that there have been no new major comprehensive theories on the scale that Guthrie or Tolman proposed, there have been compensating theoretical developments in the last few years. For one thing, there has been a flood of minitheories, small theories designed to cope with the phenomena of food aversion, avoidance learning, or discrimination learning. These limited theories help to organize our thinking about particular learning phenomena. At the same time there has been a proliferation of different points of view. The Hullian or the Skinnerian tends to do experiments in a particular way and to regard the phenomena of learning in a particular way as dictated by his theoretical background. These traditional, theory-based points of view are valuable and have been quite productive, but now there are other points of view—cognitive, comparative, physiological, and so on—that may be adopted without a commitment to a systematic theory. We have discovered that one can do a Pavlovian experiment without believing in Pavlov's particular theory of learning. We can look at the Pavlovian procedure as one in which certain environmental information is transmitted to the animal, in which certain predictive relationships are established, or in which certain contingencies prevail. Or we can think of it as one in which the excitation and inhibition of behavior can be studied. The psychology of the 1970s is clearly going to be characterized by a rich diversity of limited, specialized theories and provocative new ways of thinking about familiar learning phenomena. These developments constitute theory and contribute theoretically just as much as the great systematic formulations do, and perhaps they will ultimately constitute a more important contribution to science.

Finally, in the last few years we have witnessed the discovery of a variety of new phenomena such as autoshaping and the Garcia effect. Avoidance learning and punishment are not new phenomena by any means, but the widespread empirical and theoretical interest in them is new. Other interesting learning phenomena will surely be discovered, and the importance of phenomena that are now known but neglected will be revealed. This diversity of situations in which learning is now being studied is another healthy development. It means that when these phenomena are understood the laws of learning that they reveal can then be embedded in a theory of greater generality. The ultimate encompassing theory will then have a broader empirical base.

In conclusion, we should emphasize that theory development proceeds on several different levels. It proceeds by the intrusion of ideas and material from such other areas as cognitive psychology and comparative psychology. It proceeds by an analysis of its own methods; the theory of learning is greatly stimulated by analysis of the procedures used to produce learning. Theory also proceeds by the empirical analysis of particular phenomena. If we really had a grasp of why behavior occurs in the way it does in the autoshaping situation or in the punishment situation, then we would be well on our way toward developing a theory that would encompass both of these phenomena as well as the more traditional phenomena that entered into learning theories. There are great challenges to anyone who would develop a new comprehensive theory of learning. The challenges are greater, the task is bigger, and the competition more able than when Watson or Guthrie advanced their theories. But I am confident that it will be done—perhaps by some enterprising reader.

References for Further Reading

A variety of contemporary approaches to the phenomena of conditioning and learning, some of them quite cognitive, can be found in the book edited by McGuigan and Lumsden (1973). Irwin (1971) shows systematically how rigorous and objective a thoroughgoing cognitive analysis of behavior can be. The topics of punishment, frustration, and secondary reinforcement, which have barely been touched on here, are discussed further, and the implications of a cognitive approach to these topics are indicated by Bolles (1975).

REFERENCES

Adelman, H. M., & Maatsch, J. L. (1955) Resistance to extinction as a function of the type of response elicited by shock. *Journal of Experimental Psychology, 50,* 61–65.

Allport, F. H. (1924) *Social psychology.* Boston: Houghton Mifflin.

Amsel, A. (1962) Frustrative non reward in partial reinforcement and discrimination learning: Some recent history and a theoretical extension. *Psychological Review, 69,* 306–308.

Azrin, N. H. (1956) Some effects of two intermittent schedules of immediate and non-immediate punishment. *Journal of Psychology, 42,* 3–21.

Baum, W. M. (1973) The correlation-based law of effect. *Journal of the Experimental Analysis of Behavior, 20,* 137–153.

Bechterev, V. M. (1913) *La psychologie objective.* Paris: Alcan.

Bedford, J., & Anger, D. (1968) Flight as an avoidance response in pigeons.

Paper presented at the meeting of the Psychonomic Society, St. Louis, 1968.

Bindra, D. (1974) A motivational view of learning: Performance and behavior modification. *Psychological Review, 81,* 199–213.

Black, A. H., & Prokasy, W. F. (Eds.) (1972) *Classical conditioning: II. Current theory and research.* New York: Appleton.

Bolles, R. C. (1969) Avoidance and escape learning: Simultaneous acquisition of different responses. *Journal of Comparative and Physiological Psychology, 68,* 355–358.

Bolles, R. C. (1970) Species-specific defense reactions and avoidance learning. *Psychological Review, 71,* 32–48.

Bolles, R. C. (1972) Reinforcement, expectancy, and learning. *Psychological Review, 79,* 394–409.

Bolles, R. C. (1975) *Theory of motivation.* 2nd ed. New York: Harper & Row.

Bolles, R. C., & Grossen, N. E. (1969) Effects of an informational stimulus on the acquisition of avoidance behavior in rats. *Journal of Comparative Physiological Psychology, 68,* 90–99.

Bolles, R. C., & Grossen, N. E. (1970) The noncontingent manipulation of incentive motivation. In J. H. Reynierse (Ed.), *Current issues in animal learning.* Lincoln: University of Nebraska Press.

Bolles, R. C., Grossen, N. E., & Hargrave, G. E. (1969) The effects of an escape contingency upon running wheel and one-way avoidance learning. *Psychonomic Science, 16,* 33–34.

Bolles, R. C., Moot, S. A., & Grossen, N. E. (1971) The extinction of shuttlebox avoidance. *Learning and Motivation, 2,* 324–333.

Bolles, R. C., & Riley, A. L. (1973) Freezing as an avoidance response: Another look at the operant-respondent distinction. *Learning and Motivation, 4,* 268–275.

Bolles, R. C., & Seelbach, S. E. (1964) Punishing and reinforcing effects of noise onset and termination for different responses. *Journal of Comparative and Physiological Psychology, 58,* 127–131.

Bolles, R. C., Stokes, L. W., & Younger, M. S. (1966) Does CS termination reinforce avoidance behavior? *Journal of Comparative and Physiological Psychology, 62,* 201–207.

Braveman, N. S. (1974) Poison-based avoidance learning with flavored or colored water guinea pigs. *Learning and Motivation, 5,* 182–194.

Bregman, E. O. (1934) An attempt to modify the emotional attitudes of infants by the conditioned response technique. *Journal of Genetic Psychology, 45,* 169–198.

Breland, K., & Breland, M. (1961) The misbehavior of organisms. *American Psychologist, 16,* 681–684.

Brown, J. S. (1961) *The motivation of behavior.* New York: McGraw-Hill.

Brown, J. S., Anderson, D. C., & Brown, C. S. (1966) Conflict as a function of food-deprivation time during approach training, avoidance training, and conflict tests. *Journal of Experimental Psychology, 72,* 390–400.

Brown, P. L., & Jenkins, H. M. (1968) Auto-shaping of the pigeon's key-peck. *Journal of the Experimental Analysis of Behavior, 11,* 1–8.

Burnham, W. H. (1924) *The normal mind.* New York: Appleton.

Capaldi, E. J. (1970). An analysis of the role of reward and reward magnitude in instrumental learning. In J. H. Reynierse (Ed.), *Current issues in animal learning.* Lincoln: University of Nebraska Press.

Capretta, P. J. (1961) An experimental modification of food preference in chickens. *Journal of Comparative Physiological Psychology, 54,* 238–242.

Cason, H. (1922) The conditioned pupillary reaction. *Journal of Experimental Psychology, 5,* 108–146.

Church, R. M., Wooten, C. L., & Matthews, T. J. (1970) Contingency between response and an aversive event in the rat. *Journal of Comparative Physiological Psychology, 72,* 476–485.

Clark, F. C. (1958) The effect of deprivation and frequency of reinforcement on variable interval responding. *Journal of the Experimental Analysis of Behavior, 1,* 221–228.

Crespi, L. P. (1942) Quantitative variation of incentive and performance in the white rat. *American Journal of Psychology, 55,* 467–517.

Cuny, H. (1966) *Ivan Pavlov: The man and his theories.* New York: Fawcett.

Denny, M. R. (1971) Relaxation theory and experiments. In F. R. Brush (Ed.), *Aversive conditioning and learning.* New York: Academic Press.

Denny, M. R., & Adelman, H. M. (1955) Elicitation theory: I. An analysis of two typical learning situations. *Psychological Review, 62,* 290–296.

DiCara, L. V., & Miller, N. E. (1968) Changes in heart rate instrumentally learned by curarized rats as avoidance responses. *Journal of Comparative and Physiological Psychology, 65,* 8–12.

Domjan, M., & Wilson, N. E. (1972) Contribution of ingestive behaviors to fast aversion learning. *Journal of Comparative and Physiological Psychology, 80,* 403–412.

Dulany, D. E. (1968) Awareness, rules, and propositional control: A confrontation with S-R behavior theory. In T. R. Dixon & D. L. Horton (Eds.), *Verbal behavior and general behavior theory.* Englewood Cliffs, N.J.: Prentice-Hall.

Egger, M. D., & Miller, N. E. (1962) Secondary reinforcement in rats as a function of information value and reliability of the stimulus. *Journal of Experimental Psychology, 64,* 97–104.

Egger, M. D., & Miller, N. E. (1963) When is a reward reinforcing? An experimental study of the information hypothesis. *Journal of Comparative Physiological Psychology, 56,* 132–137.

Elliott, M. H. (1928) The effect of change of reward on the maze performance of rats. *University of California Publications in Psychology, 4,* 19–30.

Estes, W. K. (1943) Discriminative conditioning: I. A discriminative property of conditioned anticipation. *Journal of Experimental Psychology, 32,* 150–155.

Estes, W. K. (1950) Toward a statistical theory of learning. *Psychological Review, 57,* 94–107.

Estes, W. K. (1958) Stimulus-response theory of drive. In M. R. Jones (Ed.), *Nebraska symposium on motivation.* Lincoln: University of Nebraska Press.

Estes, W. K. (1969) Reinforcement in human learning. In J. Tapp (Ed.), *Reinforcement and behavior.* New York: Academic Press.

Estes, W. K., & Skinner, B. F. (1941) Some quantitative properties of anxiety. *Journal of Experimental Psychology, 29,* 390–400.

Ferster, C. B., & Skinner, B. F. (1957) *Schedules of reinforcement.* New York: Appleton.

Findley, J. D., & Brady, J. V. (1965) Facilitation of large ratio performance by use of conditioned reinforcement. *Journal of the Experimental Analysis of Behavior, 8,* 125–129.

Fowler, H., & Miller, N. E. (1963) Facilitation and inhibition of runway performance by hind- and forepaw shock of various intensities. *Journal of Comparative and Physiological Psychology, 56,* 801–805.

Gamzu, E., & Schwam, E. (1974) Autoshaping and automaintenance of a keypress response in squirrel monkeys. *Journal of the Experimental Analysis of Behavior, 21,* 361–371.

Garcia, J., & Koelling, R. A. (1966) Relation of cue to consequence in avoidance learning. *Psychonomic Science, 4,* 123–124.

Glickman, S. E., & Schiff, B. B. (1967) A biological theory of reinforcement. *Psychological Review, 74,* 81–109.

Gray, T., & Appignanesi, A. A. (1973) Compound conditioning: Elimination of the blocking effect. *Learning and Motivation, 4,* 374–380.

Greenspoon, J. (1955) The reinforcing effect of two spoken sounds on the frequency of two responses. *American Journal of Psychology, 68,* 409–416.

Grether, W. F. (1938) Pseudo-conditioning without paired stimulation encountered in attempted backward conditioning. *Journal of Comparative Psychology, 25,* 91–96.

Grice, G. R., & Davis, J. D. (1957) Effect of irrelevant thirst motivation on a response learned with food reward. *Journal of Experimental Psychology, 53*, 347–352.

Guthrie, E. R. (1930) Conditioning as a principle of learning. *Psychological Review, 37*, 412–428.

Guthrie, E. R. (1935) *The psychology of learning.* 2nd ed., 1952. New York: Harper & Row.

Guthrie, E. R. (1938) *The psychology of human conflict.* New York: Harper & Row.

Guthrie, E. R. (1959) Association by contiguity. In S. Koch (Ed.), *Psychology: A study of a science*, vol. 2. New York: McGraw-Hill.

Guthrie, E. R., & Horton, G. P. (1946) *Cats in a puzzle box.* New York: Holt, Rinehart and Winston.

Hamel, I. A. (1919) A study and analysis of the conditioned reflex. *Psychological Monographs, 27* (118).

Hefferline, R. F., Keenan, B., & Harford, R. A. (1958) Escape and avoidance conditioning in human subjects without their observation of the response. *Science, 130*, 1338–1339.

Herrnstein, R. J. (1969) Method and theory in the study of avoidance. *Psychological Review, 76*, 49–69.

Herrnstein, R. J. (1970) On the law of effect. *Journal of the Experimental Analysis of Behavior, 13*, 243–266.

Herrnstein, R. J., & Hineline, P. N. (1966) Negative reinforcement as shock-frequency reduction. *Journal of the Experimental Analysis of Behavior, 9*, 421–430.

Hilgard, E. R., & Bower, G. H. (1974) *Theories of learning.* 4th ed. New York: Appleton.

Hilgard, E. R., & Marquis, D. G. (1940) *Conditioning and learning.* Rev. by G. A. Kimble, 1961. New York: Appleton.

Hinde, R. A., & Stevenson-Hinde, J. (Eds.) (1973) *Constraints on learning.* New York: Academic Press.

Hogan, J. A. (1973) How young chicks learn to recognize food. In R. A. Hinde and J. Stevenson-Hinde (Eds.), *Constraints on learning.* New York: Academic Press.

Holman, G. L. (1969) Intragastric reinforcement effect. *Journal of Comparative and Physiological Psychology, 69*, 432–441.

Holmes, S. J. (1911) *The evolution of animal intelligence.* New York: Holt, Rinehart and Winston.

Hovland, C. I. (1937) The generalization of conditioned responses: I. The sensory generalization of conditioned responses with varying frequencies of tone. *Journal of Genetic Psychology, 17*, 125–148.

Hull, C. L. (1920) Quantitative aspects of the evolution of concepts. *Psychological Monographs 28* (123).

Hull, C. L. (1928) *Aptitude testing.* Chicago: World.

Hull, C. L. (1929) A functional interpretation of the conditioned reflex. *Psychological Review, 36,* 498–511.

Hull, C. L. (1930) Knowledge and purpose as habit mechanisms. *Psychological Review, 37,* 511–525.

Hull, C. L. (1933) Differential habituation to internal stimuli in the albino rat. *Journal of Comparative Psychology, 16,* 255–273.

Hull, C. L. (1935) Special review: Thorndike's fundamentals of learning. *Psychological Bulletin, 32,* 807–823.

Hull, C. L. (1943) *Principles of behavior.* New York: Appleton.

Hull, C. L. (1952a) *A behavior system.* New Haven: Yale University Press.

Hull, C. L. (1952b) Autobiography. In *A history of psychology in autobiography,* vol. 4. Worcester, Mass.: Clark University Press. Reprinted, 1968, by Russell & Russell.

Hull, C. L. (1962) Idea books, ed. by R. Hays. *Perceptual and motor skills (Monograph Supplement), 9,* V15.

Hull, C. L., Hovland, C. I., Ross, R. T., Hall, M., Perkins, D. T., & Fitch, F. B. (1940) *Mathematico-deductive theory of rote learning.* New Haven: Yale University Press.

Hull, C. L., Livingston, J. R., Rouse, R. O., & Barker, A. N. (1951) True, sham and esophageal feeding as reinforcements. *Journal of Comparative and Physiological Psychology, 44,* 236–245.

Hulse, S. H., Jr. (1958) Amount and percentage of reinforcement and duration of goal confinement in conditioning and extinction. *Journal of Experimental Psychology, 56,* 48–57.

Irwin, F. W. (1971) *Intentional behavior and motivation.* New York: Lippincott.

Jacobson, E. (1932) Electrophysiology of mental activities. *American Journal of Psychology, 44,* 677–694.

James, W. (1890) *Principles of psychology.*

Jennings, H. S. (1906) *Behavior of the lower organisms.* New York: Columbia University Press. Reprinted, 1962, by Indiana University Press.

Jensen, D. D. (1962) Foreword. In H. S. Jennings, *Behavior of the lower organisms.* Bloomington: Indiana University Press.

Joncich, G. (1968) *The sane positive: A biography of Edward L. Thorndike.* Middleton, Conn.: Wesleyan University Press.

Jones, M. C. (1924) The elimination of children's fears. *Journal of Experimental Psychology, 7,* 383–390.

Kalat, J. W. (1974) Taste salience depends on novelty, not concentration, in taste-aversion learning in the rat. *Journal of Comparative and Physiological Psychology, 86,* 47–50.

Kalat, J. W., & Rozin, P. (1973) Learned safety as a mechanism in long-delay taste-aversion learning in rats. *Journal of Comparative Physiological Psychology, 83,* 198–207.

Kamin, L. J. (1956) The effects of termination of the CS and avoidance of the US on avoidance learning. *Journal of Comparative and Physiological Psychology, 49,* 420–424.

Kamin, L. J. (1969) Predictability, surprise, attention, and conditioning. In B. A. Campbell & R. M. Church (Eds.), *Punishment and aversive behavior.* New York: Appleton.

Kantor, J. R. (1947) *Problems of physiological psychology.* Bloomington, Ind.: Principia Press.

Keller, F. S., & Schoenfeld, W. N. (1950) *Principles of Psychology.* New York: Appleton.

Kendler, H. H., & Gasser, W. P. (1948) Variables in spatial learning: I. Number of reinforcements during training. *Journal of Comparative and Physiological Psychology, 41,* 178–187.

Kimble, G. A. (1961) *Hilgard and Marquis' conditioning and learning.* New York: Appleton.

Konorski, J. (1967) *Integrative activity of the brain.* Chicago: University of Chicago Press.

Koppman, J. W., & Grice, G. R. (1963) Goal-box and alley similarity in latent extinction. *Journal of Experimental Psychology, 66,* 611–612.

Kramer, G. (1957) Experiments on bird orientation and their interpretation. *Ibis, 99,* 196–227.

Krechevsky, I. (1932) "Hypotheses" in rats. *Psychological Review, 39,* 516–532.

Krechevsky, I. (1938) A study of the continuity of the problem-solving process. *Psychological Review, 45,* 107–134.

Lashley, K. S. (1916) The human salivary reflex and its use in psychology. *Psychological Review, 23,* 446–464.

Logan, F. A. (1959) The Hull-Spence approach. In S. Koch (Ed.), *Psychology: A study of a science,* vol. 2. New York: McGraw-Hill.

LoLordo, V. M., MacMillan, J. C., & Riley, A. L. (1974) The effects upon food-reinforced pecking and treadle pressing of auditory and visual signals for response-independent food. *Learning and Motivation, 5,* 24–41.

Maatsch, J. L. (1954) Reinforcement and extinction phenomena. *Psychological Review, 61,* 111–118.

MacCorquodale, K., & Meehl, P. E. (1954) Edward C. Tolman. In W. K. Estes *et al.* (Eds.), *Modern learning theory.* New York: Appleton.

Macfarlane, D. A. (1930) The role of kinesthesis in maze learning. *University of California Publications in Psychology, 4,* 277–305.

Marx, M. H. (1967) Interaction of drive and reward as a determiner of resistance to extinction. *Journal of Comparative and Physiological Psychology, 64,* 488–489.

Mateer, F. (1918) *Child behavior: A critical and experimental study of young children by the method of conditioned reflexes.* Boston: Badger.

McGuigan, F. J. (1973) Electrical measurement of covert processes in an explanation of "higher mental events." In McGuigan & R. A. Schoonover (Eds.), *The psychophysiology of thinking.* New York: Academic Press.

McGuigan, F. J., & Lumsden, D. B. (Eds.), (1973) *Contemporary approaches to conditioning and learning.* Washington, D.C.: Winston.

Meyer, M. F. (1911) *The fundamental laws of human behavior.* Boston: Badger.

Miller, N. E. (1948) Studies in fear as an acquirable drive: I. Fear as motivation and fear-reduction as reinforcement in the learning of new responses. *Journal of Experimental Psychology, 38,* 89–101.

Miller, N. E. (1951) Learnable drives and rewards. In S. S. Stevens (Ed.), *Handbook of experimental psychology.* New York: Wiley.

Miller, N. E. (1957) Experiments on motivation. *Science, 126,* 1271–1278.

Miller, N. E. (1959) Liberalization of basic S-R concepts: Extensions to conflict behavior, motivation, and social learning. In S. Koch (Ed.), *Psychology: A study of a science,* vol. 2. New York: McGraw-Hill.

Miller, N. E. (1963) Some reflections on the law of effect produce a new alternative to drive reduction. In M. R. Jones (Ed.), *Nebraska symposium on motivation.* Lincoln: University of Nebraska Press.

Miller, N. E. (1969) Learning of visceral and glandular responses. *Science, 163,* 434–445.

Miller, N. E., & Carmona, A. (1967) Modification of a visceral response, salivation in thirsty dogs, by instrumental training with water reward. *Journal of Comparative and Physiological Psychology, 63,* 1–6.

Miller, N. E., & DeBold, R. C. (1965) Classically conditioned tongue-licking and operant bar pressing recorded simultaneously in the rat. *Journal of Comparative Physiological Psychology, 59,* 109–111.

Miller, N. E., & Dollard, J. (1941) *Social learning and imitation.* New Haven: Yale University Press.

Moore, B. R. (1973) The role of directed Pavlovian reactions in simple instrumental learning in the pigeon. In R. H. Hinde & J. Stevenson-Hinde (Eds.), *Constraints on learning.* New York: Academic Press.

Morgan, C. L. (1912) *Instinct and experience.* New York: Macmillan.

Morse, W. H., & Skinner, B. F. (1958) Some factors involved in the stimulus control of behavior. *Journal of the Experimental Analysis of Behavior, 1,* 103–107.

Mowrer, O. H. (1938) Preparatory set (expectancy)—a determinant in motivation and learning. *Psychological Review, 45,* 62–91.

Mowrer, O. H. (1939) A stimulus-response analysis of anxiety and its role as a reinforcing agent. *Psychological Review, 46,* 553–564.

Mowrer, O. H. (1947) On the dual nature of learning: A reinterpretation of "conditioning" and "problem-solving." *Harvard Educational Review, 17,* 102–148.

Mowrer, O. H. (1960) *Learning theory and behavior.* New York: Wiley.

Mowrer, O. H., & Lamoreaux, R. R. (1942) Avoidance conditioning and signal duration: A study of secondary motivation and reward. *Psychological Monographs, 54* (Whole No. 269).

Mowrer, O. H., & Solomon, L. N. (1954) Contiguity versus drive-reduction in conditioned fear: The proximity and abruptness of drive-reduction. *American Journal of Psychology, 67,* 15–25.

Olds, J., & Milner, P. (1954) Positive reinforcement produced by electrical stimulation of septal area and other regions of the rat brain. *Journal of Comparative and Physiological Psychology, 47,* 419–427.

Osgood, C. E. (1950) Can Tolman's theory of learning handle avoidance training? *Psychological Review, 57,* 133–137.

Parker, L., Failor, A., & Weidman, K. (1973) Conditioned preferences in the rat with an unnatural need state: Morphine withdrawal. *Journal of Comparative and Physiological Psychology, 82,* 294–300.

Pavlov, I. P. (1906) The scientific investigation of the physical faculties or processes in the higher animals. *Science, 24,* 613–619.

Pavlov, I. P. (1927) *Conditioned reflexes.* Trans. by G. V. Annep. London: Oxford University Press.

Pavlov, I. P. (1928, 1941). *Lectures on conditioned reflexes.* 2 vols. Trans. by W. H. Gantt. New York: International Publishers.

Perin, C. T. (1942) Behavioral potentiality as a joint function of the amount of training and the degree of hunger at the time of extinction. *Journal of Experimental Psychology, 30,* 93–113.

Postman, L. (1947) The history and present status of the Law of Effect. *Psychological Bulletin, 44,* 489–563.

Postman, L. (1962) Rewards and punishments in human learning. In L. Postman (Ed.), *Psychology in the making.* New York: Knopf.

Powell, R. W. (1971) Effects of deprivation and prefeeding on variable interval responding. *Psychonomic Science, 25,* 141–142.

Prokasy, W. F. (Ed.) (1965) *Classical conditioning.* New York: Appleton.

Rachlin, H. (1970) *Introduction to modern behaviorism.* San Francisco: Freeman.

Rescorla, R. A. (1968) Probability of shock in the presence and absence of CS in fear conditioning. *Journal of Comparative and Physiological Psychology, 66,* 1–5.

Rescorla, R. A. (1972) Informational variables in Pavlovian conditioning.

In G. H. Bower (Ed.), *The psychology of learning and motivation,* vol. 6. New York: Academic Press.

Rescorla, R. A., & LoLordo, V. M. (1965) Inhibition of avoidance behavior. *Journal of Comparative and Physiological Psychology, 59,* 406–412.

Rescorla, R. A., & Solomon, R. L. (1967) Two-process learning theory: Relationships between Pavlovian conditioning and instrumental learning. *Psychological Review, 74,* 151–182.

Rescorla, R. A., & Wagner, A. R. (1972) A theory of Pavlovian conditioning: Variations in the effectiveness of reinforcement and nonreinforcement. In A. H. Black & W. F. Prokasy (Eds.), *Classical conditioning: II. Current research and theory.* New York: Appleton.

Revusky, S. H. (1971) The role of interference in association over a delay. In W. K. Honig (Ed.), *Animal memory.* New York: Academic Press.

Revusky, S., & Garcia, J. (1970) Learned associations over long delays. In G. Bower and J. A. Spence (Eds.), *The psychology of learning and motivation,* vol. 4. New York: Academic Press.

Romanes, G. J. (1882) *Animal intelligence.*

Rotter, J. B. (1954) *Social learning and clinical psychology.* Englewood Cliffs, N.J.: Prentice-Hall.

Rozin, P., & Kalat, J. W. (1971) Specific hungers and poison avoidance as adaptive specializations of learning. *Psychological Review, 68,* 459–486.

Rzoska, J. (1953) Bait shyness: A study in rat behavior. *British Journal of Animal Behavior, 1,* 128–135.

Saltz, E. (1971) *The cognitive bases of human learning.* Homewood, Ill.: Dorsey.

Schneiderman, N. (1970) Determinants of heart rate classical conditioning. In J. H. Reynierse (Ed.), *Current issues in animal learning.* Lincoln: University of Nebraska Press.

Schneirla, T. C. (1933) Motivation and efficiency in ant learning. *Journal of Comparative Psychology, 15,* 243–366.

Schwartz, B., & Williams, D. R. (1973) Two different kinds of key peck in the pigeon: Some properties of responses maintained by negative and positive response-reinforcer contingencies. *Journal of the Experimental Analysis of Behavior, 18,* 201–216.

Seligman, M. E. P. (1970) On the generality of the laws of learning. *Psychological Review, 77,* 406–418.

Seligman, M. E. P. (1972) Phobias and preparedness. In M. E. P. Seligman & J. L. Hager (Eds.), *Biological boundaries of learning.* New York: Appleton.

Seligman, M. E. P., & Hager, J. L. (Eds.) (1972) *The biological boundaries of learning.* New York: Appleton.

Seligman, M. E. P., & Johnston, J. C. (1973) A cognitive theory of avoidance learning. In F. J. McGuigan & D. B. Lumsden (Eds.), *Contemporary approaches to conditioning and learning.* Washington, D.C.: Winston.

Seligman, M. E. P., & Maier, S. F. (1967) Failure to escape traumatic shock. *Journal of Experimental Psychology, 74*, 1–9.

Sevenster, P. (1973) Incompatibility of response and reward. In R. A. Hinde & J. Stevenson-Hinde (Eds.), *Constraints on learning.* New York: Academic Press.

Seward, J. P. (1949) An experimental analysis of latent learning. *Journal of Experimental Psychology, 39*, 177–186.

Seward, J. P. (1956) Drive, incentive, and reinforcement. *Psychological Review, 63*, 195–203.

Seward, J. P., Datel, W. E., & Levy, N. (1952) Tests of two hypotheses of latent learning. *Journal of Experimental Psychology, 43*, 274–280.

Seward, J. P., & Levy, N. (1949) Sign learning as a factor in extinction. *Journal of Experimental Psychology, 39*, 660–668.

Sheffield, F. D. (1949) Hilgard's critique of Guthrie. *Psychological Review, 56*, 284–291.

Sheffield, F. D. (1966) New evidence on the drive-induction theory of reinforcement. In R. N. Haber (Ed.), *Current research in motivation.* New York: Holt, Rinehart and Winston.

Sheffield, F. D., & Roby, T. B. (1950) Reward value of a non-nutritive sweet taste. *Journal of Comparative and Physiological Psychology, 43*, 461–481.

Shettleworth, S. J. (1972) Constraints on learning. In D. S. Lehrman, R. A. Hinde & E. Shaw (Eds.), *Advances in the study of behavior,* vol. 4. New York: Academic Press.

Sidman, M. (1953) Two temporal parameters of the maintenance of avoidance behavior by the white rat. *Journal of Comparative and Physiological Psychology, 46*, 253–261.

Siegel, S. (1972) Conditioning of insulin-induced glycemia. *Journal of Comparative and Physiological Psychology, 78*, 233–241.

Siegel, S., Hearst, E., George, N., & O'Neal, E. (1968) Generalization gradients obtained from individual subjects following classical conditioning. *Journal of Experimental Psychology, 78*, 171–174.

Skinner, B. F. (1931) The concept of the reflex in the description of behavior. *Journal of Genetic Psychology, 5*, 427–458.

Skinner, B. F. (1935a) The generic nature of the concepts of stimulus and response. *Journal of Genetic Psychology, 12*, 40–65.

Skinner, B. F. (1935b) Two types of conditioned reflex and a pseudo-type. *Journal of Genetic Psychology, 12*, 66–77.

Skinner, B. F. (1936) The reinforcing effect of a differential stimulus. *Journal of Genetic Psychology, 14*, 263–278.

Skinner, B. F. (1937) Two types of conditioned reflex: A reply to Konorski and Miller. *Journal of Genetic Psychology, 16,* 272–279.

Skinner, B. F. (1938) *The behavior of organisms.* New York: Appleton.

Skinner, B. F. (1948a) "Superstition" in the pigeon. *Journal of Experimental Psychology, 38,* 168–172.

Skinner, B. F. (1948b) *Walden two.* New York: Macmillan.

Skinner, B. F. (1950) Are theories of learning necessary? *Psychological Review, 57,* 193–216.

Skinner, B. F. (1953) *Science and human behavior.* New York: Macmillan.

Skinner, B. F. (1956) A case history in scientific method. *American Psychologist, 11,* 221–233.

Skinner, B. F. (1957a) *Verbal behavior.* New York: Appleton.

Skinner, B. F. (1957b) The experimental analysis of behavior. *American Scientist, 45,* 343–371.

Skinner, B. F. (1960) Pigeons in a pelican. *American Psychologist, 15,* 28–37.

Skinner, B. F. (1961) The flight from the laboratory. In *Current trends in psychological theory.* Pittsburgh: University of Pittsburgh Press.

Skinner, B. F. (1971) *Beyond freedom and dignity.* New York: Knopf.

Skinner, B. F. (1972) *Cumulative Record.* 3rd ed. New York: Appleton.

Smith, S., & Guthrie, E. (1921) *Chapters in general psychology.* Seattle: University of Washington Press.

Solomon, R. L., & Turner, L. H. (1962) Discriminative classical conditioning in dogs paralyzed by curare can later control discriminative avoidance responses in the normal state. *Psychological Review, 69,* 202–219.

Spence, K. W. (1937) The differential response in animals to stimuli varying within a single dimension. *Psychological Review, 44,* 430–444.

Spence, K. W. (1944) The nature of theory construction in contemporary psychology. *Psychological Review, 51,* 47–68.

Spence, K. W. (1945) An experimental test of continuity and non-continuity theories of discrimination learning. *Journal of Experimental Psychology,* 253–266.

Spence, K. W. (1947) The role of secondary reinforcement in delayed reward learning. *Psychological Review, 54,* 1–8.

Spence, K. W. (1951) Theoretical interpretations of learning. In S. S. Stevens (Ed.), *Handbook of experimental psychology.* New York: Wiley.

Spence, K. W. (1954) The relation of response latency and speed to the intervening variables and N in S-R theory. *Psychological Review, 61,* 209–216.

Spence, K. W. (1956) *Behavior theory and conditioning.* New Haven: Yale University Press.

Spence, K. W. (1960) *Behavior theory and learning.* Englewood Cliffs, N.J.: Prentice-Hall.

Spencer, H. (1880) *Principles of psychology.* 2nd ed.

Spragg, S. D. S. (1940) Morphine addiction in chimpanzees. *Comparative Psychology Monographs, 15* (No. 7).

Stevenson-Hinde, J. (1973) Constraints on reinforcement. In R. A. Hinde & J. Stevenson-Hinde (Eds.), *Constraints on learning*. New York: Academic Press.

Stone, G. R. (1953) The effect of negative incentives in serial learning: VII. Theory of punishment. *Journal of Genetic Psychology, 48,* 133–161.

Theios, J., & Brelsford, J. (1964) Overlearning-extinction effect as an incentive effect. *Journal of Experimental Psychology, 67,* 463–467.

Thorndike, E. L. (1898) Animal intelligence: An experimental study of the associative processes in animals. *Psychological Review Monograph Supplement, 2* (No. 8).

Thorndike, E. L. (1911) *Animal intelligence.* New York: Macmillan.

Thorndike, E. L. (1913) *Educational psychology.* New York: Teachers College Press.

Thorndike, E. L. (1935) *The psychology of wants, interests, and attitudes.* New York: Appleton.

Thorndike, E. L. (1936) Autobiography. In C. Murchison (Ed.), *History of psychology in autobiography,* vol. 3. Worcester, Mass.: Clark University Press.

Tinklepaugh, O. L. (1928) An experimental study of representative factors in monkeys. *Journal of Comparative Psychology, 8,* 197–236.

Tolman, E. C. (1920) Instinct and purpose. *Psychological Review, 27,* 218–233.

Tolman, E. C. (1923) The nature of instinct. *Psychological Bulletin, 20,* 200–218.

Tolman, E. C. (1932) *Purposive behavior in animals and men.* New York: Century.

Tolman, E. C. (1936) Operational behaviorism and current trends in psychology. In Tolman, *Collected papers in psychology.* Berkeley: University of California Press, 1951.

Tolman, E. C. (1942) *Drives toward war.* New York: Appleton.

Tolman, E. C. (1951) *Collected papers in psychology.* Reprinted as *Behavior and psychological man.* Berkeley: University of California Press.

Tolman, E. C. (1952) Autobiography. In *A history of psychology in autobiography,* vol. 4. Worcester, Mass.: Clark University Press. Reprinted, 1968, by Russell & Russell.

Tolman, E. C. (1959) Principles of purposive behavior. In S. Koch (Ed.), *Psychology: A study of a science,* vol. 2. New York: McGraw-Hill.

Tolman, E. C., & Brunswik, E. (1935) The organism and the causal texture of the environment. *Psychological Review, 42,* 43–77.

Tolman, E. C., & Honzik, C. H. (1930a) Degrees of hunger, reward and nonreward, and maze learning in rats. *University of California Publications in Psychology, 4,* 241–256.

Tolman, E. C., & Honzik, C. H. (1930b) Introduction and removal of reward and maze performance in rats. *University of California Publications in Psychology, 4,* 257–275.

Tolman, E. C., & Honzik, C. H. (1930c) "Insight" in rats. *University of California Publications in Psychology, 4,* 215–232.

Tolman, E. C., Ritchie, B. F., & Kalish, D. (1946) Studies in spatial learning: II. Place learning versus response learning. *Journal of Experimental Psychology, 36,* 221–229.

Trapold, M. A. (1966) Reversal of an operant discrimination by noncontingent discrimination reversal training. *Psychonomic Sciences, 4,* 247–248.

Trapold, M. A., Carlson, J. G., & Myers, W. A. (1965) The effect of noncontingent fixed- and variable-interval reinforcement upon subsequent acquisition of the fixed-interval scallop. *Psychonomic Sciences, 2,* 261–262.

Trapold, M. A., & Overmier, J. B. (1972) The second learning process in instrumental learning. In A. H. Black and W. F. Prokasy (Eds.), *Classical conditioning II: Current theory and research.* New York: Appleton.

Trowill, J. A. (1967) Instrumental conditioning of the heart rate in the curarized rat. *Journal of Comparative and Physiological Psychology, 63,* 7–11.

Upton, M. (1929) The auditory sensitivity of guinea pigs. *American Journal of Psychology, 41,* 412–421.

VanDercar, D. H., & Schneiderman, N. (1967) Interstimulus interval functions in different response systems during classical discrimination conditioning of rabbits. *Psychonomic Science, 9,* 9–10.

Voeks, V. W. (1950) Formalization and clarification of a theory of learning. *Journal of Psychology, 30,* 341–363.

Voeks, V. W. (1954) Acquisition of S-R connections: A test of Hull's and Guthrie's theories. *Journal of Experimental Psychology, 47,* 137–147.

Wagner, A. R. (1961) Effects of amount and percentage of reinforcement and number of acquisition trials on conditioning and extinction. *Journal of Experimental Psychology, 62,* 234–242.

Watson, J. B. (1903) *Animal education.* Chicago: University of Chicago Press.

Watson, J. B. (1907) Kinesthetic and organic sensations: Their role in the reactions of the white rat to the maze. *Psychological Monographs, 8* (No. 33).

Watson, J. B. (1913) Psychology as the behaviorist views it. *Psychological Review, 20,* 158–177.

Watson, J. B. (1914) *Behavior: An introduction to comparative psychology.* New York: Holt, Rinehart and Winston.

Watson, J. B. (1916) The place of the conditioned reflex in psychology. *Psychological Review, 23,* 89–116.

Watson, J. B. (1917) The effect of delayed feeding upon learning. *Psychobiology, 1,* 51–59.

Watson, J. B. (1919) *Psychology from the standpoint of a behaviorist.* 2nd ed., 1924. Philadelphia: Lippincott.

Watson, J. B. (1925) *Behaviorism.* New York: Norton.

Watson, J. B. (1936) Autobiography. In C. Murchison (Ed.), *History of psychology in autobiography,* vol. 3. Worcester, Mass.: Clark University Press.

Watson, J. B., & Rayner, R. (1920) Conditioned emotional reactions. *Journal of Experimental Psychology, 3,* 1–14.

Webb, W. B. (1949) The motivational aspect of an irrelevant drive in the behavior of the white rat. *Journal of Experimental Psychology, 39,* 1–14.

Weisinger, R. S., Parker, L. F., & Skorupski, J. D. (1974) Conditioned taste aversions and specific need states in the rat. *Journal of Comparative and Physiological Psychology, 87,* 655–660.

Weiss, A. P. (1925) *A theoretical basis of human behavior.* Columbus, O.: Adams.

Wilcoxon, H. C., Dragoin, W. B., & Kral, P. A. (1971) Illness-induced aversions in rat and quail: Relative salience of visual and gustatory cues. *Science, 171,* 826–828.

Williams, D. R., & Williams, H. (1969) Auto-maintenance in the pigeon: Sustained pecking despite contingent non-reinforcement. *Journal of Experimental and Analytical Behavior, 12,* 511–520.

Williams, S. B. (1938) Resistence to extinction as a function of the number of reinforcements. *Journal of Experimental Psychology, 23,* 506–521.

Wolin, B. R. (1968) Difference in manner of pecking a key between pigeons reinforced with food and with water. In A. C. Catania (Ed.), *Contemporary research in operant behavior.* Glenview, Ill.: Scott, Foresman.

Woods, S. C., Makous, W., & Hutton, R. A. (1969) Temporal parameters of conditioned hypoglycemia. *Journal of Comparative and Physiological Psychology, 69,* 301–307.

Wyrwicka, W. (1972) *The mechanisms of conditioned behavior.* Springfield, Ill.: Thomas.

Yerkes, R. M., & Morgulis, S. (1909) The method of Pawlow in animal psychology. *Psychological Bulletin, 6,* 257–273.

Zahorik, D. M., & Maier, S. F. (1969) Appetitive conditioning with recovery from thiamine deficiency as the unconditioned stimulus. *Psychonomic Science, 17,* 309–310.

Zener, K. (1937) The significance of behavior accompanying conditioned salivary secretion for theories of the conditioned response. *American Journal of Psychology, 50,* 384–403.

INDEX

Note that page numbers given in bold face indicate where a technical term is defined.